GROWING UP IN AMERICA

The U.S. Bureau of the Census publishes information on American life in its *Current Population Reports*, including *Marital Status and Living Arrangements: March 1991* (WDC, 1992), *Money, Income of Households, Families, and Persons in the United States: 1991* (WDC, 1992), *Poverty in the United States: 1991* (WDC, 1992), *Child Support and Alimony: 1987* (WDC, 1990), *Household and Family Characteristics: 1991 (WDC, 1992), The United States Population Estimates by Age, Sex, and Race* (WDC, 1990), and *Who's Minding the Kids?* (WDC, 1990). A survey from the Bureau of the Census, Center for International Research, *Children's Well-Being: An International Comparison* (WDC, 1990) gave a global view of the condition of children.

The Children's Defense Fund is a child advocacy group that provides information on the welfare of American children. *The Health of America's Children 1992* (WDC, 1992) and *The State of America's Children 1992* (WDC, 1992) were used in the preparation of this book.

The Department of Health and Human Services (HHS) publishes a wide assortment of statistical data. The Centers for Disease Control (CDC) releases the *Morbidity and Mortality Weekly Report* (MMWR), concentrating on various aspects of death and disease, as well as *Trend and Current Status in Childhood Mortality, United States, 1990-1985 and the 1990 Youth Risk Behavior Survey*. The CDC is also the leading source of AIDS statistics with its monthly *HIV/AIDS Surveillance*. The United States Department of Agriculture prepared the report, *Expenditures on a Child by Families, 1991* (WDC, 1992).

A new longitudinal study, *A Profile of Parents of Eighth Graders* (WDC, 1992) from the National Center for Educational Statistics of the U.S. Department of Education discussed the involvement of parents of eighth graders in the educational process. The U.S. Department of Agriculture's "Expenditures on a Child by Husband-Wife Families," *Family Economics Review*, Vol. 3, No. 3, September 1990 and *Adolescent Health* (WDC, 1991) tell how much it costs to raise a child. The U.S. Department of Justice's *Crime in the United States, 1991* (WDC, 1992) covers crime in general while the special report, *Missing, Abducted, Runaway, and Thrownaway Children in America* (WDC, 1990) deals with missing children.

Information Plus would like to thank the Philip Morris Companies, Inc. for permission to use material from its *Family Survey II: Child Care* (NY, 1989), and the Warner-Lambert Company for the 1987 *American Chicle Youth Report*. Special thanks also to the Alan Guttmacher Institute of New York for use of tables from "HIV/AIDS Knowledge and Sexual Behavior Among High School Students," in *Family Planning Perspectives*. We also thank Dr. Philip Johnson and Dr. Jerald Bachman for data from *Monitoring the Future*, an annual survey of drug use among young people. Information Plus is especially appreciative to the Gallup Poll, Princeton, NJ for its continued support. The College Board kindly granted permission to use charts from its *1991 Profile of SAT and Achievement Test Takers*. The National Coalition of Hispanic Health and Human Services Organizations provided *The State of Hispanic Health* (WDC, 1992). Appreciation goes to National Council on Family Relations for its *Journal of Family Issues* (Vol. 12, No. 1, March 1991) for information regarding performance of household tasks. Jack Frymier's book, *Growing Up is Risky Business* (Bloomington, Indiana, 1992), provided information on children at risk. Also used were the *Kids Count Data Book*, a publication of the Center for the Study of Social Policy (WDC, 1992), and *Who Decides? A State-By-State Review of Abortion Rights* prepared by the National Abortion Rights Action League (NARAL, 1993).

INFORMATION PLUS
WYLIE, TEXAS 75098
©1987, 1989, 1991, 1993
ALL RIGHTS RESERVED

EDITORS:
CORNELIA B. CESSNA, B.S., M.A.
CAROL D. FOSTER, B.A., M.L.S.
NANCY R. JACOBS, B.A., M.A.

CHAPTER I

HOW MANY CHILDREN?

BIRTH INDICATORS

Historical events greatly influence the number of births. During the Great Depression of the 1930s, fewer births occurred because most people knew they could not afford large families. As a result, during the late 1980s there was a relatively small population of people in their late forties and early fifties. On the other hand, the nation recorded its highest level of births in the years following World War II (1939-1945)—a period that has come to be known as the Baby Boom (1946-1964)—when soldiers returned home from the war and began families. This period of record high births is now reflected in the large numbers of people in their early thirties through mid-forties. (See Figure 1.1.)

The "Echo Effect"

There are many lasting results of the Baby Boom. One is the "echo effect," or the increase of births since 1975 when many women born during the Baby Boom entered their childbearing years. The number of births in 1990 (4.2 million) broke the 4 million mark for the second year in a row. The Bureau of the Census reports that the increase in the numbers of births among this group does not reflect an increase in fertility rates (based roughly on how

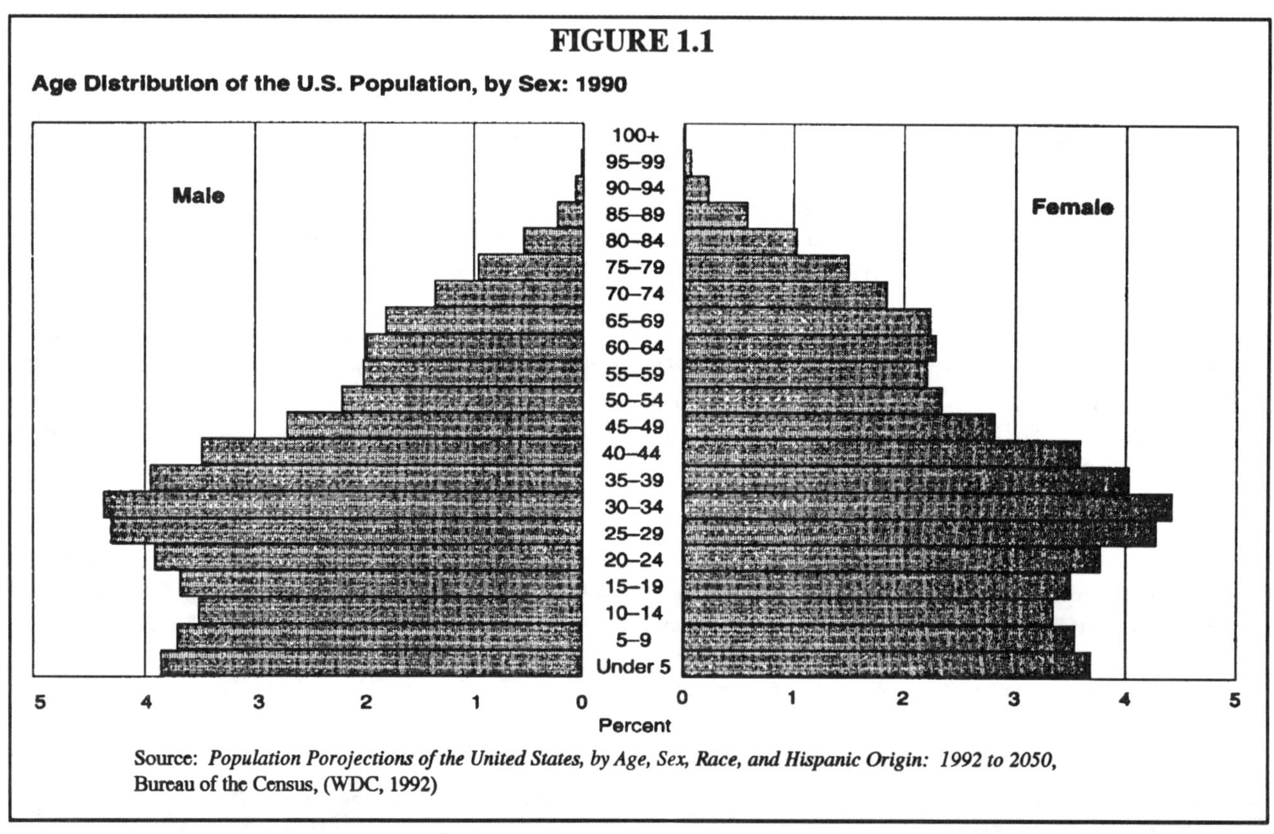

FIGURE 1.1

Source: *Population Porojections of the United States, by Age, Sex, Race, and Hispanic Origin: 1992 to 2050,* Bureau of the Census, (WDC, 1992)

TABLE 1.1

Total Population, by Age and Sex: 1980 to 1991

[In thousands, except as indicated. 1980, as of April 1, other years as of July 1. Includes Armed Forces abroad. For derivation of estimates, see text, section 1. For definition of median, see Guide to Tabular Presentation. See also *Historical Statistics, Colonial Times to 1970*, series A23-25 and A29-41]

YEAR AND SEX	Total, all ages	Under 5 years	5 to 9 years	10 to 14 years	15 to 19 years	20 to 24 years	25 to 29 years	30 to 34 years	35 to 39 years	40 to 44 years	45 to 49 years	50 to 54 years	55 to 59 years	60 to 64 years	65 to 74 years	75 years and over	5 to 13 years	14 to 17 years	18 to 24 years	16 years and over	65 years and over	Median age (yr.)
Total:																						
1980	227,061	16,348	16,700	18,242	21,226	21,529	19,629	17,629	14,010	11,688	11,095	11,711	11,615	10,088	15,581	9,969	31,159	16,249	30,289	171,711	25,549	30.0
1990	249,924	18,874	18,064	17,191	17,790	19,305	21,356	21,990	20,031	17,814	13,826	11,368	10,473	10,618	18,098	13,127	32,000	13,312	27,038	192,458	31,224	32.8
1991	252,688	19,222	18,237	17,871	17,242	19,372	20,844	22,242	20,573	18,779	14,101	11,646	10,423	10,582	18,280	13,474	32,500	13,423	26,599	194,285	31,754	33.1
Male:																						
1980	110,528	8,362	8,539	9,316	10,808	10,852	9,803	8,742	6,906	5,726	5,394	5,622	5,482	4,870	6,757	3,548	15,923	8,299	15,295	82,241	10,305	28.7
1990	122,049	9,658	9,247	8,805	9,141	9,897	10,764	10,974	9,951	8,800	6,782	5,521	5,004	4,947	7,932	4,624	16,384	6,843	13,863	92,624	12,557	31.6
1991	123,431	9,836	9,337	9,051	8,866	9,931	10,502	11,107	10,225	9,282	6,913	5,657	4,987	4,945	8,022	4,769	16,641	6,901	13,644	93,517	12,791	31.9
Female:																						
1980	116,533	7,986	8,161	8,926	10,418	10,677	9,826	8,887	7,105	5,961	5,702	6,089	6,133	5,418	8,824	6,420	15,237	7,950	14,995	89,470	15,245	31.2
1990	127,875	9,216	8,817	8,385	8,649	9,408	10,592	11,016	10,080	9,014	7,043	5,847	5,469	5,671	10,165	8,502	15,616	6,469	13,175	99,834	18,668	34.0
1991	129,257	9,386	8,900	8,620	8,376	9,440	10,341	11,135	10,349	9,498	7,188	5,989	5,436	5,637	10,258	8,705	15,859	6,522	12,955	100,748	18,962	34.3
PERCENT																						
Total:																						
1980	100.0	7.2	7.4	8.0	9.3	9.5	8.6	7.8	6.2	5.1	4.9	5.2	5.1	4.4	6.9	4.4	13.7	7.2	13.3	75.6	11.3	(X)
1990	100.0	7.6	7.2	6.9	7.1	7.7	8.5	8.8	8.0	7.1	5.5	4.5	4.2	4.2	7.2	5.3	12.8	5.3	10.8	77.0	12.5	(X)
1991	100.0	7.6	7.2	7.0	6.8	7.7	8.2	8.8	8.1	7.4	5.6	4.6	4.1	4.2	7.2	5.3	12.9	5.3	10.5	76.9	12.6	(X)
Male:																						
1980	100.0	7.6	7.7	8.4	9.8	9.8	8.9	7.9	6.2	5.2	4.9	5.1	5.0	4.2	6.1	3.2	14.4	7.5	13.8	74.4	9.3	(X)
1990	100.0	7.9	7.6	7.2	7.5	8.1	8.8	9.0	8.2	7.2	5.6	4.5	4.1	4.1	6.5	3.8	13.4	5.6	11.4	75.9	10.3	(X)
1991	100.0	8.0	7.6	7.3	7.2	8.0	8.5	9.0	8.3	7.5	5.6	4.6	4.0	4.0	6.5	3.9	13.5	5.6	11.1	75.8	10.4	(X)
Female:																						
1980	100.0	6.9	7.0	7.7	8.9	9.2	8.4	7.6	6.1	5.1	4.9	5.2	5.3	4.6	7.6	5.5	13.1	6.8	12.9	76.8	13.1	(X)
1990	100.0	7.2	6.9	6.6	6.8	7.4	8.3	8.6	7.9	7.0	5.5	4.6	4.3	4.4	7.9	6.6	12.2	5.1	10.3	78.1	14.6	(X)
1991	100.0	7.3	6.9	6.7	6.5	7.3	8.0	8.6	8.0	7.3	5.6	4.6	4.2	4.4	7.9	6.7	12.3	5.0	10.0	77.9	14.7	(X)

X Not applicable.

Source: U.S. Bureau of the Census, *Current Population Reports*, series P-25, No. 1045; and unpublished data.

many children each woman has), but rather is the result of large numbers of women in their prime childbearing years.

A good example of the echo effect is the growth in the under-5 population since 1980. In 1980, there were 16.3 million preschoolers in the U.S. By 1991, the number had risen to over 19 million. This was an 18 percent increase, whereas the population ages 6 to 24 declined since 1980. (See Table 1.1.)

Decline in School-Age Children and Young Adults

In contrast to the increase in the number of births, the rest of the population of children and young adults has decreased over the last decade. The 6-to-13-year-old population decreased by 1.0 percent between 1980 to 1990, while the high school age population, 14 to 17 years, decreased more than any other age group since 1980. The 18 percent drop from almost 16.1 million to 13.2 million high schoolers was a result of the diminishing number of births during the early 1970s. Some observers see a correlation between the decline of this age group and the legalization of abortion in

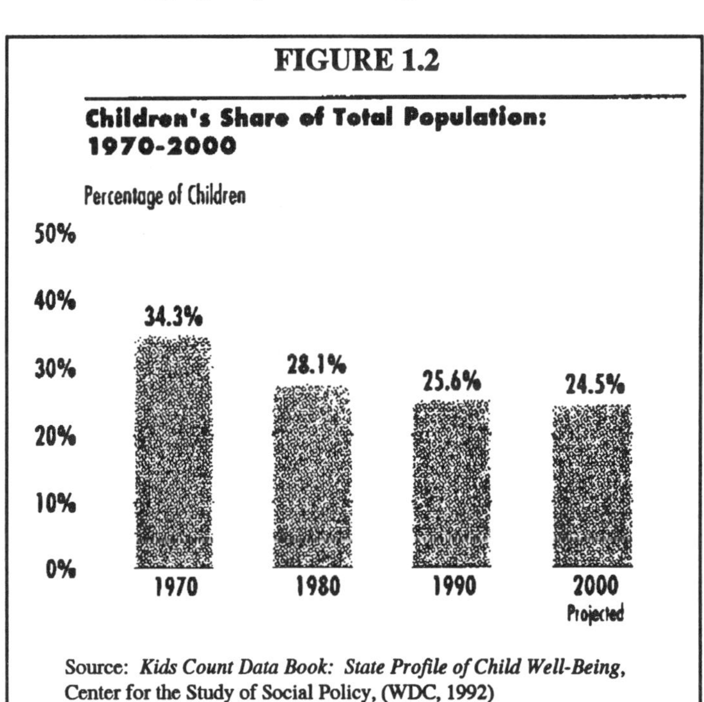

FIGURE 1.2

Children's Share of Total Population: 1970-2000

Source: *Kids Count Data Book: State Profile of Child Well-Being*, Center for the Study of Social Policy, (WDC, 1992)

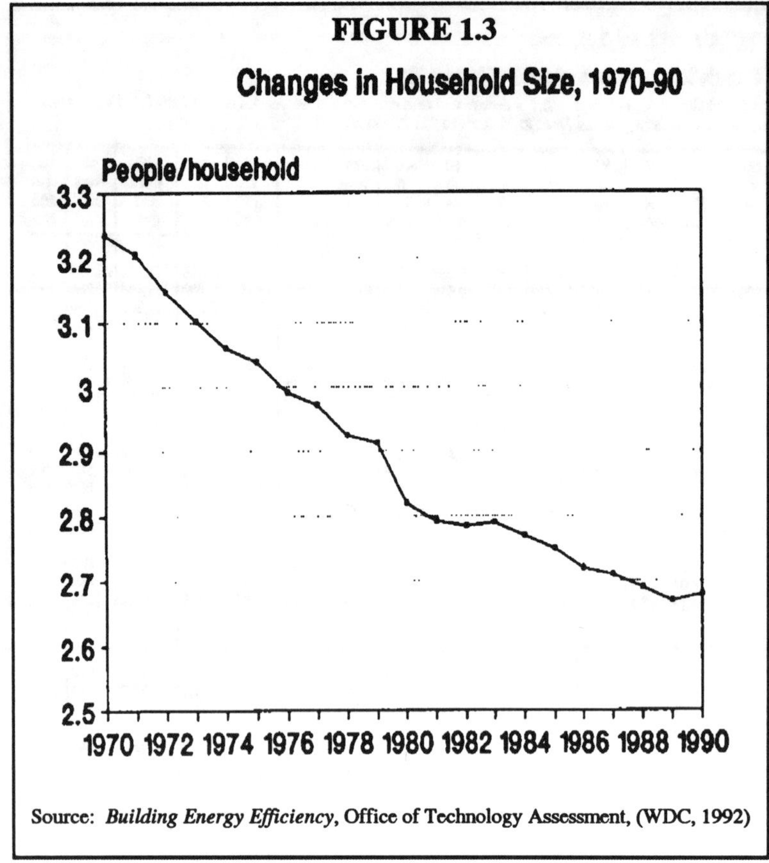

Source: *Building Energy Efficiency*, Office of Technology Assessment, (WDC, 1992)

1974. The 18- to 24-year-old population, 26.7 million, decreased by 11 percent between 1980 and 1990. Children are a shrinking proportion of the population. While children made up over one-third of the population in 1970, by 1990, they constituted about one-fourth (Figure 1.2).

Families with children made up a diminishing portion of all American households. While they were 45 percent of all households in 1970, they represented only 35 percent in 1990. Household size has declined from 3.2 persons per household to 2.63 in 1991 (Figure 1.3).

AN AGING POPULATION

The American population is aging. The median age (half are older and half are younger) of the American population rose from 30.0 years in 1980 to 32.8 years in 1991. The fastest growing age groups were the 35 to 44 year olds and those 85 years and over. This aging of America is the result of three separate trends. First, Americans are hav-ing fewer children than their parents did. Second, baby boomers are heading into middle age and out of primary child-bearing years. Third, Americans are living longer. The American attitude towards aging will have to undergo major changes in its approach to health, housing, medical care and cost, pensions, transportation, and various other aspects of American life if it hopes to meet the challenges of this rapidly expanding generation of "graying Americans."

RACIAL AND ETHNIC DIFFERENCES

The black population is younger than the white population. Over 9 percent of the black population is under the age of 5, compared to 7 percent of the white population. Hispanics have the youngest population, with 11 percent under age 5. The population of "other" races, classified by the Census Bureau into two major groups—Native American (American Indians), Eskimo, or Aleut; and Asian or Pacific Islander is similar to that of blacks. The mean age for whites is 36 years; for blacks, 30.7; for Hispanics, 28.2; and other races were the same as blacks, 30.7. (See Table 1.2.)

Almost one-quarter (24 percent) of Hispanics, 23 percent of blacks, 22 percent of other races, and less than 18 percent of whites are in the elementary and high school age population (5 to 17 years). These proportions continue through the 25 to 29 year age group, after which whites make up a larger percentage of each age group, especially among males. One explanation for the difference between white and minority men is the higher mortality (deaths) of minority men between the ages of 25 and 34, both from natural causes and homicide. Early mortality rates are especially high for black men. In addition, the birth rates among minorities have been higher in the last generation.

TABLE 1.2

Total Population Including Armed Forces Overseas—Estimates, by Age, Sex, Race and Hispanic Origin: 1980 and 1986-89

[Numbers in thousands]

Date and age	Total			Race — White			Race — Black			Race — Other races			Hispanic origin[1]		
	Total	Male	Female	Total	Male	Female	Total	Male	Female	Total	Male	Female	Total	Male	Female
JULY 1, 1989															
All ages	248 762	121 445	127 317	209 326	102 552	106 774	30 786	14 652	16 136	8 647	4 240	4 407	20 526	10 336	10 190
Under 5 years	18 752	9 598	9 155	15 050	7 716	7 335	2 890	1 469	1 421	813	414	399	2 222	1 131	1 091
Under 1 year	3 945	2 020	1 925	3 163	1 623	1 541	619	314	305	163	83	80	463	236	228
1 year	3 717	1 904	1 813	2 983	1 530	1 453	577	293	284	156	80	76	453	230	223
2 years	3 660	1 872	1 788	2 931	1 501	1 429	567	288	279	161	82	79	448	228	220
3 years	3 710	1 898	1 812	2 983	1 528	1 455	561	286	275	165	83	82	438	223	215
4 years	3 721	1 904	1 816	2 989	1 533	1 457	565	287	278	166	84	82	420	214	206
5 to 9 years	18 212	9 321	8 891	14 628	7 504	7 124	2 802	1 423	1 378	782	394	389	1 996	1 019	977
5 years	3 605	1 844	1 761	2 895	1 484	1 411	550	280	270	160	81	80	407	208	199
6 years	3 678	1 883	1 795	2 959	1 518	1 441	558	284	274	161	81	80	407	208	199
7 years	3 733	1 910	1 822	3 000	1 539	1 462	573	291	282	159	81	79	403	206	197
8 years	3 573	1 831	1 742	2 874	1 476	1 398	549	279	270	150	76	75	392	200	192
9 years	3 624	1 853	1 770	2 900	1 487	1 412	573	290	283	151	76	75	387	197	189
10 to 14 years	16 950	8 689	8 260	13 574	6 973	6 601	2 679	1 362	1 318	696	355	342	1 877	957	920
10 years	3 563	1 826	1 737	2 846	1 462	1 384	571	290	281	146	74	72	385	197	189
11 years	3 418	1 751	1 667	2 740	1 406	1 334	540	275	265	139	70	69	382	195	187
12 years	3 384	1 735	1 649	2 712	1 394	1 318	534	271	263	137	70	67	376	192	184
13 years	3 257	1 668	1 589	2 608	1 338	1 270	513	260	253	137	70	67	370	188	181
14 years	3 327	1 708	1 619	2 668	1 372	1 296	522	265	256	138	71	67	364	185	178
15 to 19 years	17 847	9 123	8 725	14 367	7 349	7 018	2 767	1 401	1 366	713	372	341	1 775	907	868
15 years	3 278	1 681	1 598	2 619	1 344	1 275	520	265	255	140	72	68	359	183	176
16 years	3 355	1 718	1 637	2 672	1 369	1 303	542	276	267	141	73	67	355	181	174
17 years	3 536	1 815	1 720	2 832	1 455	1 377	561	286	276	142	74	68	352	180	172
18 years	3 794	1 936	1 858	3 088	1 567	1 501	583	294	289	143	75	68	352	180	172
19 years	3 884	1 973	1 911	3 177	1 614	1 563	561	281	279	147	78	69	356	182	173
20 to 24 years	18 886	9 529	9 356	15 490	7 849	7 641	2 695	1 316	1 379	701	365	336	1 932	1 003	929
20 years	3 772	1 913	1 859	3 078	1 564	1 514	549	272	277	145	77	68	361	186	175
21 years	3 625	1 835	1 790	2 964	1 505	1 460	523	258	265	137	73	65	369	190	179
22 years	3 671	1 851	1 820	3 014	1 526	1 488	521	254	267	136	71	65	383	199	185
23 years	3 777	1 899	1 879	3 101	1 567	1 534	538	260	278	138	71	67	401	209	192
24 years	4 040	2 031	2 008	3 332	1 686	1 645	563	271	292	145	74	71	418	219	198
25 to 29 years	21 830	10 979	10 851	18 192	9 222	8 970	2 861	1 370	1 492	777	387	389	2 193	1 164	1 030
25 years	4 242	2 136	2 106	3 519	1 784	1 735	571	275	296	152	77	75	433	229	204
26 years	4 282	2 153	2 128	3 564	1 807	1 758	566	271	295	151	75	76	442	235	207
27 years	4 400	2 210	2 191	3 666	1 855	1 811	578	277	301	157	78	79	444	236	208
28 years	4 326	2 173	2 153	3 618	1 833	1 785	555	264	291	154	76	77	441	234	207
29 years	4 580	2 307	2 273	3 825	1 943	1 882	591	282	309	164	81	82	434	230	203
30 to 34 years	22 218	11 151	11 068	18 622	9 433	9 188	2 767	1 308	1 459	830	409	421	1 964	1 030	933
30 years	4 575	2 299	2 276	3 812	1 933	1 880	590	281	309	172	85	87	423	224	199
31 years	4 483	2 251	2 233	3 764	1 907	1 857	552	261	291	168	83	85	411	217	194
32 years	4 507	2 263	2 244	3 778	1 914	1 864	561	265	296	168	83	84	395	207	187
33 years	4 297	2 149	2 147	3 602	1 819	1 782	527	248	279	168	82	86	377	196	180
34 years	4 357	2 189	2 168	3 666	1 860	1 806	536	253	283	155	76	79	358	186	173
35 to 39 years	19 676	9 782	9 894	16 664	8 378	8 286	2 273	1 046	1 226	740	358	382	1 539	782	757
35 years	4 204	2 101	2 103	3 545	1 790	1 755	504	235	268	154	75	79	340	175	165
36 years	4 033	2 008	2 025	3 417	1 720	1 697	462	213	249	154	75	79	322	165	157
37 years	3 934	1 954	1 980	3 332	1 674	1 658	456	209	247	146	71	75	306	156	151
38 years	3 744	1 853	1 891	3 183	1 595	1 588	419	190	228	142	68	74	292	147	145
39 years	3 762	1 866	1 896	3 187	1 599	1 588	431	199	233	144	69	75	278	139	139
40 to 44 years	16 908	8 319	8 589	14 571	7 249	7 322	1 731	786	945	606	284	322	1 186	583	603
40 years	3 701	1 850	1 905	3 200	1 597	1 600	419	192	227	141	67	75	265	131	133
41 years	3 583	1 768	1 815	3 091	1 542	1 549	364	166	198	128	60	68	251	124	127
42 years	3 855	1 903	1 952	3 376	1 684	1 692	357	162	195	123	57	65	237	116	121
43 years	2 825	1 381	1 444	2 430	1 201	1 229	287	129	158	107	50	57	223	109	114
44 years	2 885	1 411	1 473	2 474	1 224	1 250	303	137	167	107	51	57	209	102	107
45 to 49 years	13 528	6 608	6 921	11 678	5 763	5 915	1 396	627	769	455	218	237	884	427	457
45 years	2 846	1 391	1 455	2 447	1 207	1 240	299	136	163	101	48	53	196	95	101
46 years	3 068	1 499	1 569	2 676	1 323	1 353	296	131	165	96	45	50	184	89	95
47 years	2 748	1 339	1 409	2 359	1 161	1 198	296	133	162	93	44	48	175	84	90
48 years	2 440	1 193	1 247	2 112	1 043	1 068	246	110	136	82	40	42	168	81	87
49 years	2 427	1 185	1 241	2 083	1 028	1 055	260	117	143	84	40	43	162	78	84
50 to 54 years	11 377	5 511	5 866	9 790	4 792	4 998	1 223	544	679	363	174	189	726	346	380
50 years	2 411	1 165	1 247	2 063	1 006	1 057	267	119	148	81	39	42	156	75	81
51 years	2 312	1 123	1 189	1 991	978	1 014	245	109	136	75	37	38	150	72	78
52 years	2 209	1 070	1 139	1 896	928	968	240	107	133	73	35	37	145	69	76
53 years	2 210	1 073	1 137	1 908	937	971	234	104	130	69	33	36	140	67	73
54 years	2 235	1 079	1 155	1 931	942	988	237	106	131	67	31	35	135	64	71
55 to 59 years	10 726	5 121	5 605	9 310	4 480	4 830	1 116	508	608	300	133	167	622	293	329
55 years	2 102	1 010	1 092	1 809	877	932	228	104	125	65	30	35	131	62	69
56 years	2 076	995	1 081	1 796	868	928	219	100	119	61	27	34	127	60	67
57 years	2 176	1 039	1 137	1 886	908	978	230	105	126	60	26	34	124	58	66
58 years	2 163	1 027	1 135	1 886	902	984	219	100	119	58	26	32	122	57	65
59 years	2 209	1 049	1 160	1 933	925	1 009	219	100	119	57	25	33	119	56	64
60 to 64 years	10 867	5 079	5 788	9 569	4 498	5 071	1 035	467	567	264	113	150	540	249	291
60 years	2 229	1 053	1 176	1 937	922	1 015	234	107	127	58	25	33	117	54	62
61 years	2 235	1 053	1 182	1 970	933	1 036	212	97	115	54	23	31	113	52	61
62 years	2 114	984	1 129	1 858	870	988	203	92	111	53	23	30	109	50	59
63 years	2 103	978	1 125	1 859	870	989	194	86	107	50	22	28	104	48	56
64 years	2 187	1 010	1 176	1 945	903	1 042	192	86	106	50	22	28	98	45	53
65 to 69 years	10 170	4 631	5 538	9 029	4 130	4 899	916	402	515	224	100	125	401	181	220
70 to 74 years	8 012	3 464	4 549	7 193	3 120	4 074	661	274	386	158	69	89	264	110	153
75 to 79 years	6 033	2 385	3 648	5 430	2 147	3 282	486	187	299	117	51	66	197	77	120
80 to 84 years	3 728	1 306	2 422	3 409	1 189	2 220	256	91	165	63	26	37	121	46	74
85 to 89 years	1 962	588	1 374	1 791	531	1 260	142	45	97	29	12	17	63	23	40
90 to 94 years	790	195	594	719	174	544	61	17	43	10	4	6	20	7	14
95 to 99 years	229	53	176	200	46	155	25	7	18	4	1	3	6	2	4
100 years and over	61	13	48	50	10	41	9	3	6	1	1	0	1	0	1
16 years and over	191 570	92 156	99 414	163 456	79 015	84 440	21 898	10 134	11 763	6 216	3 006	3 210	14 074	7 048	7 026
18 years and over	184 679	88 623	96 056	157 952	76 191	81 761	20 794	9 573	11 221	5 933	2 859	3 075	13 367	6 687	6 680
65 years and over	30 984	12 636	18 348	27 822	11 347	16 475	2 555	1 025	1 529	607	264	344	1 073	447	626
85 years and over	3 042	850	2 192	2 761	761	2 000	236	72	165	44	17	27	91	32	59
Median age....years	32.6	31.5	33.8	33.6	32.4	34.7	27.7	26.3	29.1	29.0	27.9	30.1	26.1	25.7	26.5
Mean age....years	35.2	33.8	36.5	36.0	34.6	37.4	30.7	29.3	32.0	30.7	29.7	31.7	28.2	27.4	29.0

[1]Persons of Hispanic origin may be of any race.

Source: *U.S. Population Estimates by Age, Sex, Race, and Hispanic Origin: 1989*, (WDC, 1990)

TABLE 1.3

Birth Rates : 1970 to 1989

[Births per 1,000 women 15 to 44 years old in specified racial group. Live-birth order refers to number of children born alive. Figures for births of order not stated are distributed. *1970,*

LIVE-BIRTH ORDER	ALL RACES [1]					WHITE					BLACK				
	1970	1980	1985	1988	1989	1970	1980	1985	1988	1989	1970	1980	1985	1988	1989
Total	87.9	68.4	66.2	67.2	69.2	84.1	64.7	63.0	63.0	64.7	115.4	88.1	82.2	86.6	90.4

[1] Includes other races not shown separately.

Source: U.S. National Center for Health Statistics, *Vital Statistics of the United States,* annual; and unpublished data.

BIRTH AND FERTILITY RATES

The National Center for Health Statistics reports there were 4.2 million live births in the United States during 1990, the largest number since 1964. The birth rate, measured in live births per 1,000 total population, was 16.2 per 1,000 in 1990, compared with the record low level of 14.5 per 1,000 in 1976. Black and "other" race birth rates were substantially higher than that of whites. While the white birth rate has been decreasing, the black birth rate has been increasing.

The general fertility rate in 1989 was 69.2 births per 1,000 women aged 15 to 44 years (Table 1.3). In contrast, the fertility rates from 1946, the beginning of the Baby Boom, to 1964, exceeded 100 births per 1,000 women of childbearing age, peaking at 122.7 per 1,000 women in 1957.

CHAPTER II

FAMILY AND LIVING ARRANGEMENTS

MOST WANT CHILDREN

The vast majority of Americans want to have children and raise families. The 1990 *Gallup Poll Monthly* reported that nine out of 10 Americans over the age of 40 have had children and 60 percent of the remainder who had not had children indicated that they wished they had. More than half (58 percent) of the respondents under age 40 had already had children and 84 percent of those without children said they eventually wanted them. Only 4 percent of Americans polled said they did not have children, did not want any, or were glad they did not have any. Fewer than one out of 12 parents (7 percent) said they regretted having children.

Intangible Reasons

Most Americans could not specifically explain their desire for children. Gallup asked respondents to discuss the "greatest plus or the thing you gain most from having children." Most responses involved the emotional content children bring into the lives of adults. Twelve percent cited the love and affection that children bring; 11 percent found pleasure in watching them grow; 7 percent felt they created a sense of family; and 6 percent believed children were sources of fulfillment and satisfaction. Many answers were attempts to explain an instinct, such as: "Children give meaning to life," "Teaching them your values," "They help keep life interesting," and "They make life complete."

IDEAL FAMILY SIZE

Since 1936, the Gallup Poll has been asking, "What do you think is the ideal number of children for a family to have?" Immediately after World War II (1945 to 1947), almost half of Americans believed four or more children made up the ideal family. Many acted on their beliefs, and the Baby Boom followed. Through the 1960s, over one-third of Americans thought four or more children was ideal. However, as the Baby-Boomers entered their child-bearing years in the late 1960s and early

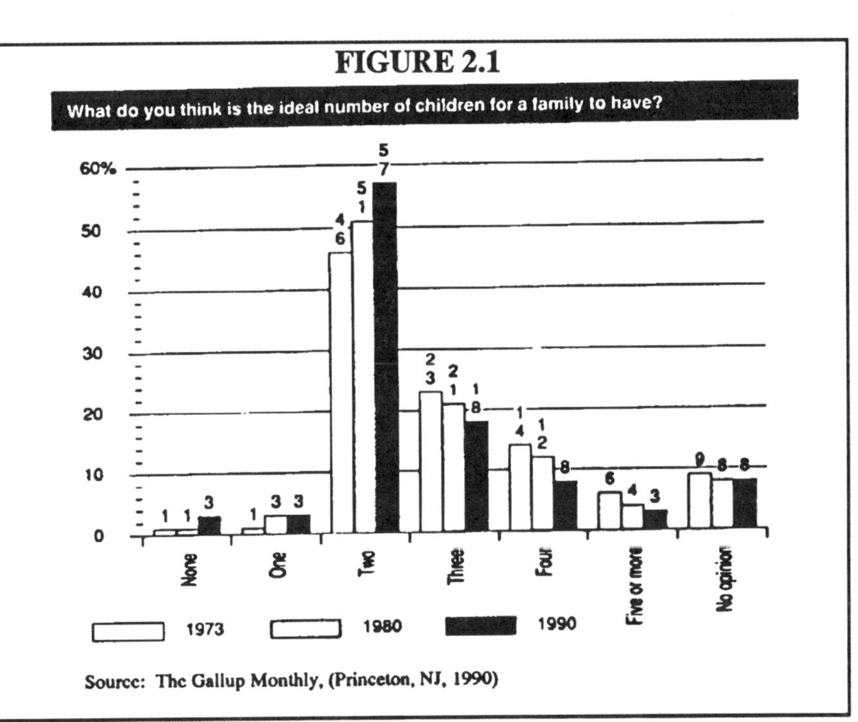

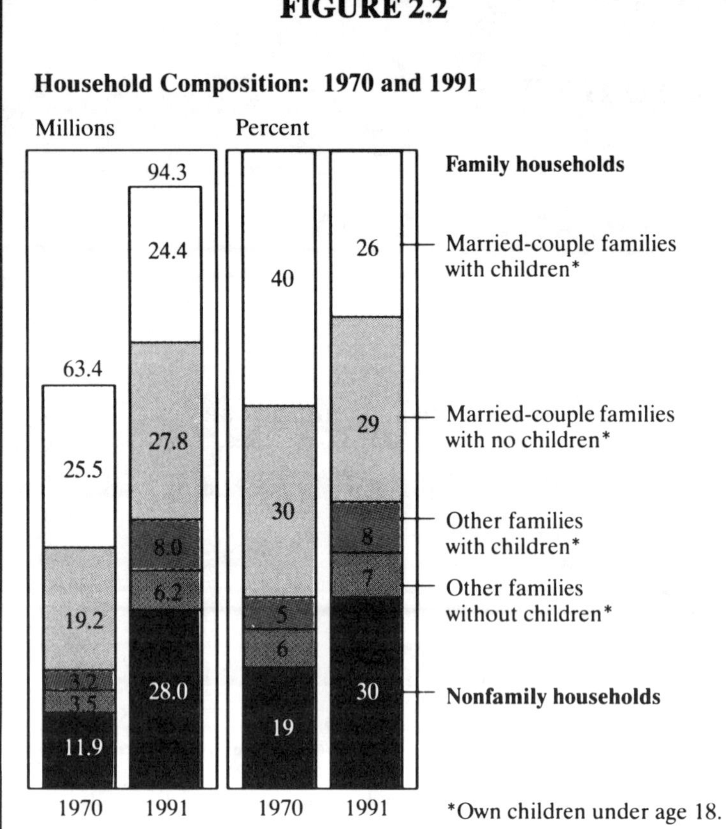

FIGURE 2.2

Household Composition: 1970 and 1991

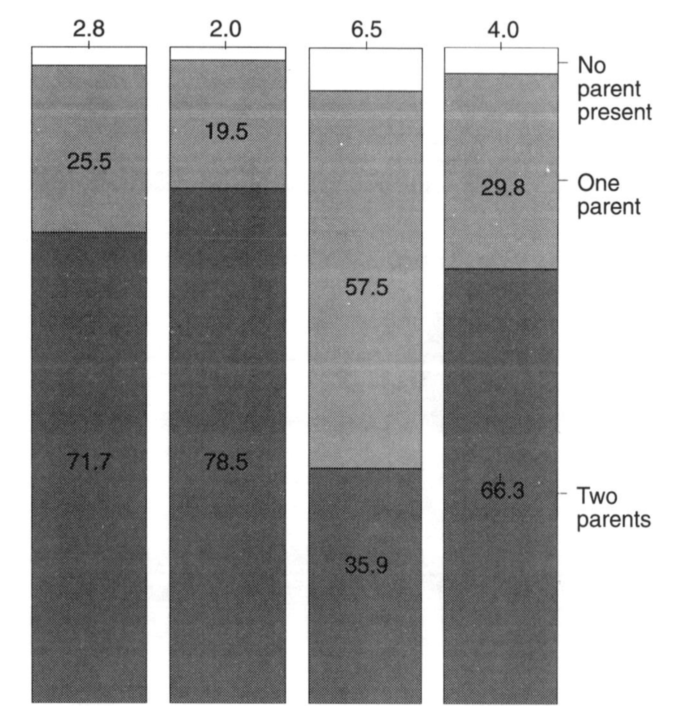

FIGURE 2.3

Children by Presence of Parents: 1991

Source of both figure: U. S. Bureau of the Census

1970s, the proportion choosing four or more children dropped significantly. In 1971, only 23 percent preferred four or more children, compared to 41 percent just three years earlier. In 1990, only 11 percent of respondents, the lowest percentage ever, found four or more children to be ideal, while more than half (57 percent) favored two children. (See Figure 2.1.)

Few Want Only One

Recent studies by social scientists and educators suggest that being an only child may have certain advantages that can lead to greater chances of success in later life. Still, only 3 percent of those Americans polled preferred to have a single child. Most parents of an only child admitted that they would have had more children if it were possible. More than two-thirds (70 percent) of Americans believed that being an only child was a disadvantage, a proportion that has remained virtually unchanged in 40 years.

FEWER TRADITIONAL FAMILIES

One of the most significant social changes of the past decades has occurred in the types of families and households. Married-couple families with children under age 18 comprised 26 percent of households in 1991, down from 40 percent in 1970. (See Figure 2.2.) On the other hand, the number of single-parent families (fathers or mothers) with children grew 30 percent during the 1980s; the number of single-parent families headed by women grew 22 percent. The number of male-headed families with children rose from 748,000 in 1970 to 2,016,000 in 1991. However, they were still the smallest household type in 1991 at 3 percent of all households. Overall,

TABLE 2.1

Living Arrangements of Children Under 18 Years, by Race and Hispanic Origin: 1991, 1980, and 1970

(Numbers in thousands. Excludes persons under 18 years old who were maintaining households or family groups and spouses)

Living arrangements	1991	1980	1970	Percent distribution		
				1991	1980	1970
ALL RACES						
Children under 18 years..................	65,093	63,427	69,162	100.0	100.0	100.0
Living with:						
Two parents.............................	46,658	48,624	58,939	71.7	76.7	85.2
One parent.............................	16,624	12,466	8,199	25.5	19.7	11.9
Mother only........................	14,608	11,406	7,452	22.4	18.0	10.8
Father only.........................	2,016	1,060	748	3.1	1.7	1.1
Other relatives........................	1,428	1,949	1,547	2.2	3.1	2.2
Nonrelatives only......................	383	388	477	0.6	0.6	0.7
WHITE						
Children under 18 years..................	51,918	52,242	58,790	100.0	100.0	100.0
Living with:						
Two parents.............................	40,733	43,200	52,624	78.5	82.7	89.5
One parent.............................	10,142	7,901	5,109	19.5	15.1	8.7
Mother only........................	8,585	7,059	4,581	16.5	13.5	7.8
Father only.........................	1,557	842	528	3.0	1.6	0.9
Other relatives........................	787	887	696	1.5	1.7	1.2
Nonrelatives only......................	256	254	362	0.5	0.5	0.6
BLACK						
Children under 18 years..................	10,209	9,375	9,422	100.0	100.0	100.0
Living with:						
Two parents.............................	3,669	3,956	5,508	35.9	42.2	58.5
One parent.............................	5,874	4,297	2,996	57.5	45.8	31.8
Mother only........................	5,516	4,117	2,783	54.0	43.9	29.5
Father only.........................	358	180	213	3.5	1.9	2.3
Other relatives........................	565	999	820	5.5	10.7	8.7
Nonrelatives only......................	101	123	97	1.0	1.3	1.0
HISPANIC ORIGIN*						
Children under 18 years..................	7,462	5,459	**4,006	100.0	100.0	100.0
Living with:						
Two parents.............................	4,944	4,116	3,111	66.3	75.4	77.7
One parent.............................	2,222	1,152	(NA)	29.8	21.1	(NA)
Mother only........................	1,983	1,069	(NA)	26.6	19.6	(NA)
Father only.........................	239	83	(NA)	3.2	1.5	(NA)
Other relatives........................	230	183	(NA)	3.1	3.4	(NA)
Nonrelatives only......................	66	8	(NA)	0.9	0.1	(NA)

NA Not available.

* Persons of Hispanic origin may be of any race.

** All persons under 18 years.

Source of Hispanic data for 1970: U.S. Bureau of the Census, 1970 Census of Population, PC(2)-1C, *Persons of Spanish Origin*, table 4.

---

the number of all families with children grew a modest 7 percent. The number of what has been known as "traditional" families is declining as the number of single-parent familes increases. (See Figure 2.3 and Table 2.1).

LIVING ARRANGEMENTS OF CHILDREN

One Parent, Two Parents

The rise in divorce, separation, and out-of-wedlock births all significantly affect children's living arrangements. In 1970, 85 percent of children in the United States lived with two parents; by 1991, 72 percent did, while the proportion living with one parent doubled from 12 to 25 percent. In 1991, 46.6 million of the 65 million children under 18 lived with two parents. About 25 percent lived with one parent, most often the mother. Minority children are less likely to live with two parents than are white children. Black children are least likely to live in a two-parent household. In 1991, fewer than 36 percent of black children lived with both parents while 79 percent of white children and 66 percent of Hispanic children did.

Many children who live in one-parent situations live under less favorable circumstances than those who live with both parents. As shown in Table 2.2, the demographic and economic characteristics of many one-parent families, especially female-headed and minority families, place the children at a disadvantage. These children are more

TABLE 2.2

Living Arrangements of Children Under 18 Years, by Marital Status and Selected Characteristics of Parent: March 1991

[Numbers in thousands. Characteristics are shown for householder or reference person in married-couple situations.

Subject	Total, living with one or both parents	Living with both parents	Living with mother only					Living with father only				
				Marital status of mother					Marital status of father			
			Total	Divorced	Married, spouse absent	Widowed	Never married	Total	Divorced	Married, spouse absent	Widowed	Never married
ALL RACES												
Children under 18 years	63 262	46 658	14 608	5 206	3 583	780	5 040	2 016	916	462	110	528
Number of siblings in household:												
None	11 936	7 268	3 922	1 369	679	193	1 682	746	334	125	34	254
One	25 405	19 453	5 162	2 186	1 224	291	1 461	790	418	178	28	166
Two	15 652	12 090	3 277	1 119	941	157	1 060	285	114	94	20	57
Three	6 258	4 869	1 277	328	429	79	441	113	32	29	23	29
Four	2 343	1 727	566	133	137	33	263	50	9	24	6	11
Five or more	1 686	1 252	404	72	172	27	133	31	10	11	-	10
Mean number of siblings	1.47	1.53	1.36	1.21	1.62	1.42	1.31	1.02	.90	1.31	1.45	.87
Age of parent:												
15 to 19 years	521	75	427	8	26	2	390	19	-	-	-	19
20 to 24 years	3 300	1 296	1 884	190	375	5	1 314	120	15	11	-	95
25 to 29 years	8 627	5 346	2 959	719	719	53	1 469	321	71	71	-	179
30 to 34 years	14 241	10 426	3 446	1 397	868	139	1 042	370	174	72	10	114
35 to 39 years	15 423	12 005	2 948	1 402	827	177	541	469	255	147	14	54
40 to 44 years	12 096	9 926	1 778	970	477	138	193	393	224	78	35	55
45 to 49 years	5 516	4 648	694	356	183	106	49	174	98	52	14	10
50 to 54 years	2 117	1 737	290	110	80	67	33	89	49	24	16	1
55 to 59 years	856	720	106	48	16	37	6	31	18	3	10	-
60 to 64 years	409	348	41	2	12	27	-	20	11	4	5	1
65 years and over	176	130	37	4	-	30	3	9	3	-	6	-
Education of parent:												
Elementary: 0 to 8 years	4 576	3 214	1 143	288	387	89	379	220	43	67	29	81
High school: 1 to 3 years	7 822	4 101	3 470	795	787	169	1 718	251	75	73	2	100
4 years	24 427	17 289	6 287	2 244	1 596	316	2 131	850	411	157	47	235
College: 1 to 3 years	12 374	9 359	2 584	1 201	552	142	689	431	219	110	26	76
4 years	7 866	6 990	710	417	172	48	74	166	114	30	3	18
5 or more years	6 216	5 705	413	261	88	16	49	98	54	24	3	17
Percent high school graduates	80.4	84.3	68.4	79.2	67.2	66.9	58.4	76.7	87.1	69.7	72.1	65.6
Employment status of parent:												
In the labor force	53 350	42 557	8 983	3 970	2 119	440	2 453	1 811	834	421	90	466
Employed	49 487	40 122	7 777	3 642	1 824	386	1 924	1 588	754	367	85	382
Both parents employed	25 144	25 144	(X)	(X)	(X)	(X)	(X)	(X)	(X)	(X)	(X)	(X)
Full time	44 995	37 393	6 121	3 040	1 390	278	1 412	1 481	722	348	77	334
Part time	4 492	2 729	1 656	602	434	108	512	107	32	18	9	48
Unemployed	3 863	2 434	1 207	328	295	54	529	222	79	54	5	84
Not in the labor force	8 905	3 112	5 610	1 227	1 458	339	2 586	182	77	31	20	54
Presence of adults other than parent:												
Other relatives present only	11 655	7 331	3 837	1 106	917	246	1 568	487	165	119	55	148
Nonrelatives present only	2 791	514	1 622	815	198	45	564	655	287	75	10	283
Other relatives and nonrelatives present	559	209	270	90	66	26	87	79	17	19	7	37
No adults other than parent	48 277	38 604	8 878	3 195	2 401	461	2 821	794	448	248	39	60
Family income:												
Under $2,500	1 289	276	938	185	354	30	369	75	25	17	2	31
$2,500 to $4,999	2 252	269	1 918	433	406	31	1 048	65	33	5	-	27
$5,000 to $7,499	2 508	667	1 739	461	477	36	765	102	28	30	2	41
$7,500 to $9,999	2 525	745	1 689	473	469	74	673	91	24	15	7	45
$10,000 to $12,499	2 618	1 218	1 318	531	316	88	383	82	35	10	6	32
$12,500 to $14,999	2 303	1 213	961	370	242	75	275	129	64	19	2	44
$15,000 to $19,999	4 736	3 063	1 449	553	409	109	378	224	89	58	15	62
$20,000 to $24,999	5 077	3 607	1 260	588	272	73	327	211	83	70	11	46
$25,000 to $29,999	4 857	3 725	920	485	144	79	213	211	120	49	-	42
$30,000 to $39,999	9 864	8 426	1 127	557	260	80	230	311	157	62	23	68
$40,000 to $49,999	7 971	7 214	535	278	81	40	136	221	123	44	24	31
$50,000 and over	17 280	16 234	752	290	152	67	243	293	135	82	18	50
Mean income	39 473	46 776	17 414	20 502	15 862	23 121	14 446	30 282	31 641	32 230	33 031	25 844
Median income	33 273	40 137	11 935	16 156	10 672	16 887	8 758	25 575	26 153	25 511	36 228	18 139
Percent below poverty level	20.1	10.1	52.1	36.7	59.4	34.9	65.6	18.7	14.1	16.2	10.0	30.7
Percent below 125 percent of poverty level	25.5	14.7	60.0	45.3	66.9	45.4	72.5	24.7	18.6	22.6	16.5	38.8
Area of residence:												
Inside metropolitan areas	48 866	35 585	11 687	4 006	2 810	603	4 268	1 593	713	381	80	418
1,000,000 or more	27 197	19 629	6 703	1 977	1 633	359	2 735	864	346	231	45	242
Inside central cities	10 475	6 378	3 732	761	883	168	1 920	366	122	84	19	141
Outside central cities	16 721	13 251	2 972	1 216	749	191	815	499	224	148	26	101
Under 1,000,000	21 669	15 956	4 984	2 029	1 178	244	1 533	729	367	150	35	176
Inside central cities	8 307	5 250	2 710	971	636	109	994	347	170	87	6	85
Outside central cities	13 362	10 706	2 274	1 058	542	134	539	381	197	63	29	92
Outside metropolitan areas	14 416	11 073	2 921	1 200	772	177	771	423	203	80	30	109
Tenure[1]:												
Owned	39 352	33 524	4 790	2 176	1 044	474	1 097	1 037	522	241	89	185
Rented	23 930	13 134	9 818	3 030	2 539	306	3 943	979	394	221	21	343
Public housing	4 000	872	3 018	728	667	58	1 574	110	21	23	1	65
Private housing	19 931	12 263	6 800	2 302	1 872	254	2 372	868	373	197	20	278

(Continued)

TABLE 2.2 Continued

Living Arrangements of Children Under 18 Years, by Marital Status and Selected Characteristics of Parent: March 1991—Con.

[Numbers in thousands. Characteristics are shown for householder or reference person in married-couple situations.

Subject	Total, living with one or both parents	Living with both parents	Living with mother only					Living with father only				
				Marital status of mother					Marital status of father			
			Total	Divorced	Married, spouse absent	Widowed	Never married	Total	Divorced	Married, spouse absent	Widowed	Never married
WHITE												
Children under 18 years	50 875	40 733	8 585	4 000	2 326	534	1 725	1 557	764	352	80	361
Number of siblings in household:												
None	9 515	6 364	2 571	1 102	461	146	862	580	280	104	32	165
One	21 088	17 216	3 280	1 773	859	206	442	592	328	132	22	110
Two	12 619	10 572	1 802	812	623	92	275	246	106	80	10	49
Three	4 893	4 204	597	205	255	47	90	91	31	15	16	29
Four	1 574	1 330	221	69	93	16	42	24	9	15	-	-
Five or more	1 186	1 047	114	39	36	27	13	24	10	7	-	7
Mean number of siblings	1.44	1.51	1.18	1.12	1.47	1.37	.87	1.01	.94	1.22	1.14	.92
Age of parent:												
.15 to 19 years	293	62	216	8	22	2	184	15	-	-	-	15
20 to 24 years	2 128	1 078	953	155	273	1	523	97	12	11	-	74
25 to 29 years	6 489	4 642	1 610	621	499	35	455	237	55	65	-	118
30 to 34 years	11 678	9 365	2 018	1 086	544	104	283	295	155	52	10	79
35 to 39 years	12 822	10 580	1 879	1 018	565	131	166	363	227	102	5	29
40 to 44 years	10 115	8 653	1 154	713	274	86	81	308	182	58	30	38
45 to 49 years	4 563	3 954	470	270	114	64	22	139	78	46	9	6
50 to 54 years	1 673	1 451	167	89	24	43	11	55	31	14	9	1
55 to 59 years	696	604	70	34	10	25	1	22	13	2	7	-
60 to 64 years	302	265	20	2	1	18	-	17	8	4	4	1
65 years and over	116	78	29	4	-	25	-	8	3	-	6	-
Education of parent:												
Elementary: 0 to 8 years	3 732	2 742	826	224	304	66	231	164	31	43	22	66
High school: 1 to 3 years	5 370	3 450	1 745	575	502	101	568	175	56	51	1	66
4 years	19 310	15 071	3 568	1 722	1 005	208	634	671	339	137	36	159
College: 1 to 3 years	10 149	8 226	1 598	832	325	111	230	325	195	73	14	43
4 years	8 821	6 137	545	348	125	36	36	139	98	24	3	14
5 or more years	5 493	5 107	302	199	66	12	25	84	45	24	3	11
Percent high school graduates	82.1	84.8	70.1	80.0	65.4	66.7	53.6	78.3	88.7	73.4	71.3	82.6
Employment status of parent:												
In the labor force	44 666	37 593	5 641	3 100	1 378	321	842	1 431	698	332	64	337
Employed	41 845	35 538	5 063	2 858	1 210	280	715	1 244	621	292	59	272
Both parents employed	22 039	22 039	(X)	(X)	(X)	(X)	(X)	(X)	(X)	(X)	(X)	(X)
Full time	38 308	33 206	3 947	2 363	918	180	486	1 155	600	274	52	229
Part time	3 537	2 332	1 117	495	292	100	229	89	22	18	7	43
Unemployed	2 820	2 055	578	242	167	42	127	187	77	40	5	66
Not in the labor force	5 506	2 452	2 939	900	945	211	862	115	64	14	16	21
Presence of adults other than parent:												
Other relatives present only	8 120	5 850	1 877	742	495	163	477	393	135	106	48	104
Nonrelatives present only	2 182	433	1 233	730	177	37	289	516	248	63	4	201
Other relatives and nonrelatives present	399	173	161	71	49	12	29	65	16	19	-	30
No adults other than parent	40 174	34 276	5 315	2 458	1 605	321	931	584	365	164	28	27
Family income:												
Under $2,500	796	217	541	140	240	19	142	38	21	7	2	8
$2,500 to $4,999	1 143	200	897	324	257	20	296	46	30	2	-	14
$5,000 to $7,499	1 570	569	929	323	299	29	277	72	18	24	2	29
$7,500 to $9,999	1 601	605	935	345	338	36	215	61	17	13	7	24
$10,000 to $12,499	1 817	971	773	370	223	68	111	73	30	10	6	28
$12,500 to $14,999	1 782	1 083	575	288	155	47	85	105	58	15	2	30
$15,000 to $19,999	3 525	2 452	905	442	234	77	152	168	56	55	12	45
$20,000 to $24,999	3 979	3 059	761	460	159	47	95	159	77	43	3	36
$25,000 to $29,999	4 113	3 326	623	415	102	42	64	164	92	41	-	31
$30,000 to $39,999	8 352	7 373	740	447	155	43	95	239	139	40	13	47
$40,000 to $49,999	6 999	6 414	407	227	64	37	79	179	105	30	21	23
$50,000 and over	15 218	14 464	500	219	101	65	115	253	121	72	12	48
Mean income	42 074	47 328	18 998	20 970	16 036	25 210	16 496	31 860	32 646	33 876	31 818	28 241
Median income	35 934	40 668	13 450	17 116	10 330	17 287	9 226	28 396	29 017	25 612	37 796	20 396
Percent below poverty level	15.5	9.2	45.1	33.1	57.8	33.0	59.5	16.6	13.6	15.4	13.9	24.7
Percent below 125 percent of poverty level	20.5	13.5	52.9	41.9	64.8	42.1	65.6	22.8	19.1	18.9	22.8	34.4
Area of residence:												
Inside metropolitan areas	38 468	30 666	6 611	2 995	1 781	411	1 423	1 191	582	276	56	277
1,000,000 or more	20 509	16 448	3 439	1 377	1 002	236	824	621	269	168	35	149
Inside central cities	6 241	4 662	1 365	412	429	76	448	214	73	46	15	80
Outside central cities	14 268	11 786	2 075	965	573	160	376	407	197	122	20	69
Under 1,000,000	17 959	14 218	3 171	1 618	779	175	599	570	313	108	21	128
Inside central cities	5 984	4 302	1 439	689	368	70	312	243	124	66	4	49
Outside central cities	11 975	9 916	1 732	929	411	105	287	327	189	42	17	79
Outside metropolitan areas	12 407	10 067	1 975	1 005	546	122	302	366	182	76	24	84
Tenure[1]:												
Owned	34 189	30 015	3 315	1 810	753	348	404	859	455	194	67	143
Rented	16 686	10 718	5 271	2 190	1 574	186	1 321	698	309	158	12	219
Public housing	1 824	609	1 172	434	323	35	381	43	16	14	1	12
Private housing	14 862	10 109	4 099	1 757	1 251	151	940	655	293	144	11	207

(Continued)

11

Living Arrangements of Children Under 18 Years, by Marital Status and Selected Characteristics of Parent: March 1991—Con.

[Numbers in thousands. Characteristics are shown for householder or reference person in married-couple situations.

Subject	Total, living with one or both parents	Living with both parents	Living with mother only					Living with father only				
			Total	Divorced	Married, spouse absent	Widowed	Never married	Total	Divorced	Married, spouse absent	Widowed	Never married
BLACK												
Children under 18 years	9 543	3 669	5 516	1 014	1 118	208	3 176	358	117	85	24	132
Number of siblings in household:												
None	1 889	544	1 212	219	200	35	757	133	44	19	2	68
One	3 183	1 322	1 712	342	314	75	980	149	65	27	6	50
Two	2 360	991	1 342	256	283	49	754	27	7	13	4	4
Three	1 073	414	638	111	144	32	351	20	1	12	7	-
Four	641	285	332	61	41	17	214	24	-	9	6	9
Five or more	398	113	281	26	135	-	120	5	-	5	-	-
Mean number of siblings	1.64	1.70	1.64	1.54	1.93	1.82	1.57	1.07	.70	1.77	(B)	.71
Age of parent:												
15 to 19 years	216	12	201	-	3	-	198	3	-	-	-	3
20 to 24 years	1 039	135	864	27	91	4	762	20	3	-	-	17
25 to 29 years	1 854	532	1 255	72	202	16	965	67	6	7	-	54
30 to 34 years	2 101	719	1 327	275	292	35	724	55	17	14	-	23
35 to 39 years	1 957	944	934	313	222	29	369	79	17	39	3	20
40 to 44 years	1 291	680	543	226	169	44	104	68	34	17	5	11
45 to 49 years	566	335	200	73	67	36	25	31	18	3	6	3
50 to 54 years	280	141	115	16	54	23	21	24	14	4	7	-
55 to 59 years	95	58	29	12	5	7	5	8	5	1	3	-
60 to 64 years	100	77	20	-	11	9	-	4	2	-	1	-
65 years and over	44	36	8	-	-	5	3	-	-	-	-	-
Education of parent:												
Elementary: 0 to 8 years	507	229	239	39	61	8	132	39	11	15	7	7
High school: 1 to 3 years	2 162	449	1 646	210	258	62	1 116	67	18	20	1	28
4 years	4 323	1 634	2 538	448	552	96	1 443	151	60	19	11	62
College: 1 to 3 years	1 738	782	884	222	201	30	432	73	11	27	6	29
4 years	553	413	124	48	33	11	32	17	11	5	-	2
5 or more years	259	163	85	48	15	2	20	11	7	1	-	4
Percent high school graduates	72.0	81.5	65.8	75.5	71.5	66.4	60.7	70.3	75.3	59.4	(B)	73.4
Employment status of parent:												
In the labor force	6 453	3 115	3 046	721	670	109	1 546	291	100	66	20	106
Employed	5 570	2 862	2 443	643	550	98	1 152	265	97	54	20	94
Both parents employed	2 031	2 031	(X)	(X)	(X)	(X)	(X)	(X)	(X)	(X)	(X)	(X)
Full time	4 781	2 577	1 955	554	424	90	887	249	90	53	18	88
Part time	789	285	488	89	126	7	265	16	7	1	2	6
Unemployed	883	254	603	78	119	11	394	26	3	12	-	12
Not in the labor force	2 868	353	2 461	285	447	99	1 630	55	13	16	4	21
Presence of adults other than parent:												
Other relatives present only	2 742	834	1 832	317	390	71	1 054	76	25	12	7	32
Nonrelatives present only	494	51	333	61	12	6	254	110	36	11	-	63
Other relatives and nonrelatives present	113	10	89	16	17	10	46	13	-	-	7	7
No adults other than parent	6 194	2 773	3 262	620	700	121	1 822	159	55	63	11	30
Family income:												
Under $2,500	410	17	369	44	99	4	222	25	4	2	-	18
$2,500 to $4,999	1 057	48	994	100	145	9	739	16	3	2	-	11
$5,000 to $7,499	816	72	730	109	164	6	451	15	5	6	-	4
$7,500 to $9,999	822	106	687	99	107	32	448	28	6	1	-	21
$10,000 to $12,499	682	161	516	148	80	17	271	5	3	-	-	2
$12,500 to $14,999	465	93	349	65	80	18	186	23	7	4	-	12
$15,000 to $19,999	941	388	502	91	164	31	216	51	31	2	3	16
$20,000 to $24,999	893	386	456	117	108	21	211	51	5	27	8	10
$25,000 to $29,999	545	244	270	66	35	32	138	31	15	5	-	10
$30,000 to $39,999	1 105	733	325	75	87	33	130	47	13	11	-	10
$40,000 to $49,999	684	534	114	45	14	3	51	37	16	13	4	18
$50,000 and over	1 122	888	205	56	36	1	113	29	8	10	3	4
											6	5
Mean income	24 162	38 477	14 620	18 236	14 961	19 052	13 055	24 470	25 845	28 793	(B)	18 279
Median income	17 278	34 202	9 923	12 767	11 407	16 530	8 478	21 158	19 953	24 299	(B)	14 570
Percent below poverty level	44.2	17.1	63.5	50.2	63.4	37.0	69.5	23.6	15.8	14.2	(B)	40.9
Percent below 125 percent of poverty level	51.7	24.0	71.5	58.2	71.9	49.9	77.1	30.6	15.8	34.6	(B)	46.7
Area of residence:												
Inside metropolitan areas	7 958	2 968	4 665	866	912	157	2 730	325	107	84	18	116
1,000,000 or more	5 030	1 835	3 005	501	558	102	1 844	190	60	46	10	75
Inside central cities	3 496	1 129	2 237	309	426	78	1 423	130	43	29	4	54
Outside central cities	1 534	705	768	192	132	24	421	61	17	17	6	21
Under 1,000,000	2 928	1 133	1 660	365	354	55	887	135	48	37	8	41
Inside central cities	1 955	661	1 199	253	249	37	660	95	43	18	2	32
Outside central cities	974	473	461	112	105	18	227	40	5	19	7	9
Outside metropolitan areas	1 585	701	851	148	206	51	446	33	10	2	6	16
Tenure[1]:												
Owned	3 612	2 164	1 309	291	252	112	654	139	53	40	16	30
Rented	5 930	1 505	4 207	723	866	96	2 522	219	63	46	8	101
Public housing	1 992	189	1 749	266	314	16	1 154	53	5	8	-	40
Private housing	3 938	1 315	2 458	457	553	80	1 368	165	58	38	8	61

(Continued)

Living Arrangements of Children Under 18 Years, by Marital Status and Selected Characteristics of Parent: March 1991—Con.

[Numbers in thousands. Characteristics are shown for householder or reference person in married-couple situations.

Subject	Total, living with one or both parents	Living with both parents	Living with mother only					Living with father only				
				Marital status of mother					Marital status of father			
			Total	Divorced	Married, spouse absent	Widowed	Never married	Total	Divorced	Married, spouse absent	Widowed	Never married
HISPANIC[2]												
Children under 18 years	7 166	4 944	1 983	482	733	124	644	239	68	46	15	111
Number of siblings in household:												
None	1 077	597	400	97	86	30	186	79	22	10	6	41
One	2 274	1 559	644	187	220	34	203	70	28	14	4	24
Two	1 909	1 369	481	125	194	25	137	59	16	14	3	26
Three	1 141	847	271	32	153	18	67	23	2	8	2	11
Four	432	311	122	27	50	6	38	-	-	-	-	-
Five or more	334	260	66	14	29	10	13	7	-	-	-	7
Mean number of siblings	1.80	1.90	1.63	1.47	1.93	1.74	1.39	1.23	(B)	(B)	(B)	1.33
Age of parent:												
15 to 19 years	69	16	48	2	6	-	40	5	-	-	-	5
20 to 24 years	585	290	267	24	77	-	166	29	3	1	-	25
25 to 29 years	1 271	873	360	65	150	5	139	39	6	5	-	27
30 to 34 years	1 670	1 158	457	116	157	28	156	55	15	8	2	30
35 to 39 years	1 440	996	413	126	171	30	86	31	15	11	1	4
40 to 44 years	1 090	813	228	75	100	18	35	49	15	8	8	18
45 to 49 years	583	431	136	55	55	8	18	17	10	7	-	-
50 to 54 years	252	210	33	10	7	12	4	9	4	2	2	1
55 to 59 years	130	100	26	8	8	9	1	4	-	2	2	-
60 to 64 years	61	50	9	-	2	7	-	1	-	1	-	-
65 years and over	15	7	7	1	-	6	-	1	-	-	1	-
Education of parent:												
Elementary: 0 to 8 years	2 422	1 756	580	124	238	39	179	86	7	27	7	45
High school: 1 to 3 years	1 520	904	584	107	211	30	235	33	6	5	-	22
4 years	1 931	1 295	554	161	202	25	166	82	30	8	4	40
College: 1 to 3 years	812	583	200	70	47	26	57	30	19	3	4	4
4 years	269	240	47	11	31	3	2	3	1	2	-	-
5 or more years	190	167	18	9	4	1	5	5	5	-	-	-
Percent high school graduates	45.0	46.2	41.3	52.0	38.7	44.2	35.7	50.3	(B)	(B)	(B)	39.6
Employment status of parent:												
In the labor force	5 379	4 271	884	289	304	69	223	224	63	44	12	104
Employed	4 750	3 805	748	253	243	58	194	197	60	43	12	81
Both parents employed	1 856	1 856	(X)	(X)	(X)	(X)	(X)	(X)	(X)	(X)	(X)	(X)
Full time	4 164	3 399	586	220	205	41	120	179	55	42	6	76
Part time	586	406	162	33	39	16	74	18	5	1	7	6
Unemployed	629	466	136	36	60	11	29	27	3	1	-	23
Not in the labor force	1 712	598	1 099	193	430	55	421	16	4	2	3	7
Presence of adults other than parent:												
Other relatives present only	1 839	1 198	557	130	205	48	174	84	12	31	6	36
Nonrelatives present only	391	134	188	69	36	9	75	69	13	1	1	54
Other relatives and nonrelatives present	160	71	67	22	35	1	9	21	3	2	-	16
No adults other than parent	4 776	3 541	1 171	260	458	66	387	65	40	12	9	4
Family income:												
Under $2,500	220	64	152	17	72	5	58	4	-	2	-	2
$2,500 to $4,999	346	95	242	47	81	12	102	9	2	-	-	7
$5,000 to $7,499	485	153	320	63	111	10	136	12	2	4	1	5
$7,500 to $9,999	566	206	332	73	132	14	113	26	1	2	6	19
$10,000 to $12,499	646	388	233	50	116	12	55	25	6	1	-	17
$12,500 to $14,999	429	325	93	24	33	15	21	10	5	2	-	4
$15,000 to $19,999	850	619	197	56	64	28	49	34	6	11	2	15
$20,000 to $24,999	662	546	109	40	36	7	27	8	3	2	-	2
$25,000 to $29,999	625	508	104	50	25	3	25	13	7	2	-	5
$30,000 to $39,999	941	789	92	30	38	9	15	60	21	11	3	25
$40,000 to $49,999	618	558	47	12	11	4	19	13	6	4	2	1
$50,000 and over	778	690	63	19	15	4	25	24	9	5	1	9
Mean income	25 933	30 564	14 132	16 883	12 956	16 607	12 936	26 085	(B)	(B)	(B)	26 050
Median income	20 287	25 746	9 596	12 073	9 426	13 949	8 104	19 267	(B)	(B)	(B)	15 204
Percent below poverty level	38.1	26.9	66.7	40.7	74.1	48.7	74.3	32.7	(B)	(B)	(B)	43.6
Percent below 125 percent of poverty level	48.2	38.5	73.2	57.9	78.2	71.4	79.4	41.8	(B)	(B)	(B)	53.1
Area of residence:												
Inside metropolitan areas	6 608	4 528	1 858	447	678	107	626	222	63	44	13	102
1,000,000 or more	4 555	3 075	1 344	279	515	75	475	136	33	27	13	84
Inside central cities	2 642	1 690	872	168	321	51	333	79	13	13	7	45
Outside central cities	1 913	1 385	471	111	194	24	142	57	20	13	5	19
Under 1,000,000	2 053	1 453	514	168	163	32	151	86	30	17	-	39
Inside central cities	1 094	724	315	103	95	27	90	55	23	13	-	19
Outside central cities	959	729	199	65	68	4	61	32	7	4	-	20
Outside metropolitan areas	558	416	125	35	56	17	18	17	4	2	2	8
Tenure[1]:												
Owned	2 552	2 111	350	150	88	44	68	91	43	11	11	26
Rented	4 614	2 833	1 633	332	645	80	576	148	24	35	4	84
Public housing	653	208	435	106	146	22	162	10	-	2	-	8
Private housing	3 961	2 625	1 196	226	500	58	414	138	24	34	4	70

Source: *Marital Status and Living Arrangements: March 1991*, Bureau of the Census, (WDC, 1992)

TABLE 2.3

**Proportion of Children in
Female-Headed Families,
1970, 1980, 1990, 1991**

	March 1970	March 1980	March 1990	March 1991
Nonmetro	10.3%	15.0%	18.1%	18.6%
Metro	12.2	20.4	21.9	22.5
City	18.9	31.1	32.5	32.8
Suburb	7.6	13.5	15.1	15.9

Source: Arloc Sherman, *Falling by the Wayside: Children in Rural America*, Children's Defense Fund, (WDC, 1992)

likely to live with a parent who has low income, is less educated, unemployed, and rents a home or lives in public housing.

The proportion of children in female-headed households has been rising faster in rural areas than in metropolitan areas. In 1991, 19 percent of rural children lived in female-headed families, slightly less than the 23 percent of children in metropolitan areas (Table 2.3).

Grandparents

In 1991, 5 percent of children under age 18 (3.3 million) lived in households maintained by their grandparent or grandparents. This does not include children whose parents maintain a household that includes a grandparent. (See Table 2.4 and Figure 2.4.)

About 17 percent of children living with grandparents also had both parents living with them, but the majority (50 percent) had only their mother present. Twelve percent of all black children under age 18 lived with their grandparents, compared with only 4 percent of white children and 6 percent of Hispanic children. Black children were also less likely to have their parents living in the household with them.

Stepchildren, Blended Families

More than one-quarter of American adults have been divorced at some point in their lives, a propor-

TABLE 2.4

Grandchildren of the Householder, by Presence of Parents, Race, and Hispanic Origin: 1991, 1980, and 1970

(Numbers in thousands)

Living arrangement	1991				1980 Census	1970 Census
	Total	White	Black	Hispanic origin*		
Grandchild of householder under 18 years	3,320	1,936	1,256	419	2,306	2,214
Percent of all children under 18 years	5.1	3.7	12.3	5.6	3.6	3.2
With both parents present...................	559	455	68	103	310	363
With mother only present....................	1,674	830	780	185	922	817
With father only present....................	151	120	28	25	86	78
With neither parent present.................	937	531	380	106	988	957
Percent	100.0	100.0	100.0	100.0	100.0	100.0
With both parents present...................	16.8	23.5	5.4	24.6	13.4	16.4
With mother only present....................	50.4	42.9	62.1	44.2	40.0	36.9
With father only present....................	4.5	6.2	2.2	6.0	3.7	3.5
With neither parent present.................	28.2	27.4	30.3	25.3	42.8	43.2

*Persons of Hispanic origin may be of any race.
Source of 1970 and 1980 data: U.S. Bureau of the Census, 1970 Census of Population, PC(2)-4B, *Persons by Family Characteristics*, table 1. 1980 Census of Population, PC80-2-4B, table 1. Excludes inmates of institutions.

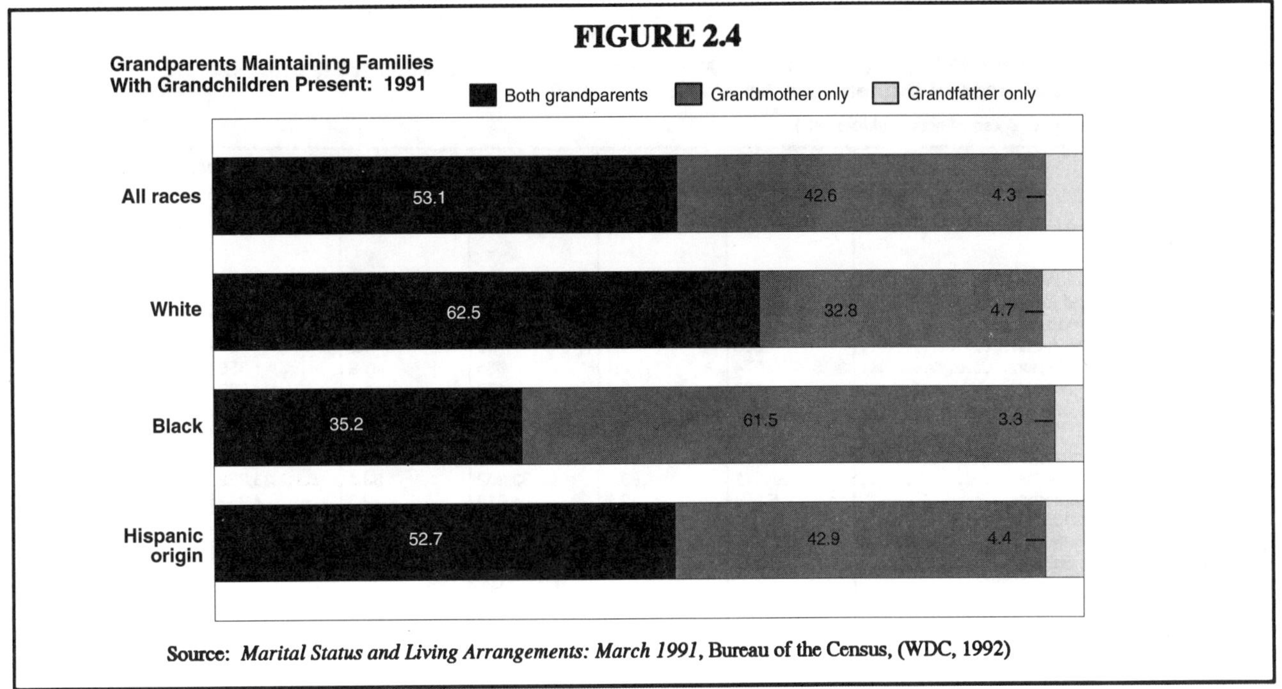

Source: *Marital Status and Living Arrangements: March 1991*, Bureau of the Census, (WDC, 1992)

tion higher than ever before. Most divorced people eventually remarry, creating situations in which adults and children are living as part of stepfamilies, or blended families, as some sociologists call them.

Of the more than 25 million married-couple families with children in 1990, 19 million, more than three-quarters (76 percent) were "natural" or "biological" families in which the children were born to both parents. About 345,000 families, or 1.4 percent of married-couple families with chil-

dren, had at least one adoptive child. The remainder (22 percent) were couples with at least one stepchild. (See Table 2.5.)

In 1990, more than one in five married-couple families (22 percent) with children had at least one stepchild living in the household, up from 18 percent in 1980. These couples could have biological children living in the household as well, but at least one spouse had a child from a previous marriage or relationship. Sixteen percent of children (7.2 mil-

TABLE 2.5

Married-Couple Family Households With Children, by Type of Family: June 1990, 1985, and 1980

(Numbers in thousands)

Type of family	1990		1985		1980	
	Number	Percent	Number	Percent	Number	Percent
Total...............................	25,314	100.0	23,868	100.0	24,091	100.0
Biological............................	19,253	76.1	18,470	77.4	19,037	79.0
Adoptive	345	1.4	303	1.3	429	1.8
Biological mother-stepfather	2,619	10.3	2,207	9.2	1,818	7.5
Biological father-stepmother	152	0.6	180	0.8	171	0.7
Joint biological-step	2,475	9.8	2,038	8.5	1,862	7.7
Joint biological-adoptive....................	324	1.3	223	0.9	429	1.8
Joint step-adoptive	8	-	15	0.1	12	-
Joint bio-step-adoptive.....................	-	-	29	0.1	25	0.1
Unknown...............................	137	0.5	403	1.7	309	1.3

- Represents zero.

Source: *Marriage, Divorce, and Remarriage in the 1990s*, Bureau of the Census, (WDC, 1992)

TABLE 2.6

Children Under 18 Years of Age Living With Biological, Step, and Adoptive Married-Couple Parents, by Race of Mother: June 1990, 1985, and 1980

(Numbers in thousands. Children of householders only)

Category	1990		1985		1980	
	Number	Percent	Number	Percent	Number	Percent
All races						
Total own children under 18 years	45,448	100.0	45,347	100.0	47,248	100.0
Biological mother and father	37,026	81.5	37,213	82.1	39,523	83.7
Biological mother-stepfather	6,643	14.6	6,049	13.3	5,355	11.3
Stepmother-biological father	608	1.3	740	1.6	727	1.5
Adoptive mother and father	974	2.1	866	1.9	1,350	2.9
Unknown mother or father	197	0.4	479	1.1	293	0.6
White						
Total own children under 18 years	39,732	100.0	39,942	100.0	42,329	100.0
Biological mother and father	32,975	83.0	33,202	83.1	35,852	84.7
Biological mother-stepfather	5,258	13.2	4,918	12.3	4,362	10.3
Stepmother-biological father	549	1.4	676	1.7	664	1.6
Adoptive mother and father	815	2.1	754	1.9	1,209	2.9
Unknown mother or father	135	0.3	391	1.0	242	0.6
Black						
Total own children under 18 years	3,671	100.0	3,816	100.0	3,775	100.0
Biological mother and father	2,336	63.6	2,661	69.7	2,698	71.5
Biological mother-stepfather	1,149	31.3	952	24.9	877	23.2
Stepmother-biological father	38	1.0	50	1.3	46	1.2
Adoptive mother and father	97	2.6	76	2.0	119	3.1
Unknown mother or father	51	1.4	77	2.0	35	0.9
Hispanic origin[1]						
Total own children under 18 years	4,568	100.0	(NA)	(NA)	(NA)	(NA)
Biological mother and father	3,703	81.1	(NA)	(NA)	(NA)	(NA)
Biological mother-stepfather	699	15.3	(NA)	(NA)	(NA)	(NA)
Stepmother-biological father	38	0.8	(NA)	(NA)	(NA)	(NA)
Adoptive mother and father	101	2.2	(NA)	(NA)	(NA)	(NA)
Unknown mother or father	27	0.6	(NA)	(NA)	(NA)	(NA)

NA Not available.

[1] Persons of Hispanic origin may be of any race.

Source: *Marriage, Divorce, and Remarriage in the 1990s*, Bureau of the Census, (WDC, 1992)

lion) in all married-couple families in 1990 were stepchildren. The proportion was considerably higher among black stepchildren, who accounted for one-third of children under age 18 living in black married-couple families (Table 2.6).

Characteristics of Stepfamilies

The most common stepfamily or blended family situation was that of children living with their biological mother and stepfather with no other children present (2.6 million stepfather families). This is due primarily to the large number of divorced women who gain custody of their children. The second most common type is the "joint biological-step family," in which there was at least one stepchild and one biological child of the couple. There were 2.5 million of these "yours-ours" fami-

lies in 1990. Fewer than 608,000 children lived with their biological fathers and stepmothers.

On the whole, stepfamilies did not fare as well, economically, as other married couple families. In 1985, the last year for which data are available, the median income for all married-couple families with children was $28,162. For those with a biological mother, stepfather, and stepchildren, the median income was $25,272. Married-couple families with at least one stepchild and at least one biological child had an even lower median income of $22,932. The highest median income for any married-couple family with children, $34,850, was in families with a biological father and stepmother. (See Table 2.7.)

Distribution of Married-Couple Families With Children, by Type of Family and Selected Characteristics: June 1980 and 1985

Characteristic	All family types[1]		1. Biological		2. Adoptive		3. Stepfather		4. Stepmother		5. Joint biological-step		6. Joint biological-adoptive	
	1980	1985	1980	1985	1980	1985	1980	1985	1980	1985	1980	1985	1980	1985
Number (thousands)	24,091	23,868	19,037	18,470	429	303	1,818	2,207	171	180	1,862	2,038	429	223
Percent	100.0	100.0	100.0	100.0	100.0	100.0	100.0	100.0	100.0	100.0	100.0	100.0	100.0	100.0
Times parents married:														
Both once	78.7	76.1	88.0	86.3	82.0	84.1	24.5	28.3	(X)	(X)	39.6	38.3	91.6	92.2
Mother once	7.1	7.7	6.6	7.1	7.3	5.5	6.4	5.5	39.6	51.6	11.2	13.3	4.7	5.5
Father once...........	6.0	7.8	3.1	3.9	5.5	5.3	22.3	28.6	(X)	(X)	19.9	21.0	2.3	1.0
Both more than once	8.2	8.4	2.3	2.7	5.2	5.1	46.8	37.6	60.4	48.4	29.3	27.4	1.4	1.3
Age of mother:														
Under 35 years	50.2	49.7	49.5	48.8	17.7	18.6	52.9	53.5	45.9	45.4	71.2	67.1	14.7	16.2
35 to 44 years..........	33.4	37.6	33.5	37.9	24.9	38.1	38.3	38.8	24.7	36.7	26.2	30.8	58.0	66.7
45 years and over	16.3	12.7	17.0	13.3	57.6	43.3	8.8	7.8	29.4	17.9	2.6	2.1	27.3	17.1
Mean age (years)	35.3	35.2	35.5	35.3	46.6	44.7	33.9	34.1	37.4	37.0	31.4	31.9	41.0	39.3
Age of father:														
Under 35 years	39.9	38.6	39.7	38.3	9.8	16.9	42.6	41.8	22.7	13.9	53.3	49.5	10.7	8.1
35 to 44 years..........	34.7	39.8	34.8	40.0	26.3	30.8	33.6	37.7	40.7	51.1	36.3	40.0	43.4	57.4
45 years and over	25.4	21.7	25.5	21.7	63.6	52.3	23.9	20.5	36.6	35.0	10.4	10.5	45.7	34.5
Mean age (years)	38.2	37.9	38.2	37.9	48.9	46.7	37.5	37.3	42.0	42.5	34.7	35.1	44.2	42.0
Duration of current marriage:														
Under 10 years	40.3	41.9	33.4	33.8	10.3	15.1	88.3	87.6	79.5	79.2	73.5	74.1	5.1	1.9
10 to 19 years..........	36.3	38.8	40.2	43.7	28.0	30.9	11.6	12.4	16.4	15.3	26.2	25.7	42.4	59.6
20 to 29 years..........	18.7	15.9	21.5	18.8	35.9	33.5	-	-	2.3	3.5	0.2	0.2	43.6	37.1
30 years or more........	4.7	3.5	4.9	3.7	25.6	20.5	-	-	1.8	1.9	-	-	8.9	1.4
Number of children:														
Total own children.......	2.0	1.9	1.9	1.8	1.3	1.2	1.6	1.5	1.4	1.4	2.8	2.8	3.8	3.9
Biological children	1.6	1.6	1.9	1.8	(X)	(X)	(X)	(X)	(X)	(X)	1.3	1.3	2.4	2.5
Adoptive children.......	0.1	-	(X)	(X)	1.3	1.2	(X)	(X)	(X)	(X)	(X)	(X)	1.4	1.4
Stepchildren...........	0.3	0.3	(X)	(X)	(X)	(X)	1.6	1.5	1.4	1.4	1.5	1.5	(X)	(X)
Mother's education:														
Less than 12 years	21.2	16.7	18.7	15.0	24.5	24.7	30.2	19.7	22.8	14.9	30.9	22.7	31.9	24.5
Exactly 12 years	48.0	46.8	48.3	46.0	41.7	43.4	47.5	51.2	43.9	45.8	49.9	51.7	43.4	44.9
More than 12 years	30.8	36.6	33.0	39.0	33.8	31.9	22.3	29.1	33.3	39.4	19.1	25.6	24.9	30.7
Father's education:														
Less than 12 years	22.9	18.3	20.9	16.8	26.8	24.2	27.2	22.7	27.6	17.3	30.3	22.1	34.0	22.9
Exactly 12 years	37.2	37.9	36.8	37.2	29.1	35.1	41.6	41.8	35.3	34.8	42.7	42.6	29.1	37.6
More than 12 years	39.9	43.9	42.3	46.1	43.8	40.7	31.1	35.5	37.1	47.9	27.0	35.3	37.1	39.5
Parents' labor force status:														
Both in labor force.......	41.2	46.0	40.5	45.0	40.6	37.4	50.4	56.3	53.7	55.9	41.0	47.1	34.5	34.8
Father in labor force	54.7	49.5	55.9	51.0	47.2	45.9	43.8	38.5	40.3	37.5	54.7	48.2	58.9	59.5
Mother in labor force.....	1.5	1.8	1.4	1.7	2.2	4.3	1.8	2.4	2.2	2.8	1.7	1.8	1.9	-
Both not in labor force ...	2.6	2.7	2.3	2.3	10.0	12.3	4.0	2.7	3.8	3.9	2.6	2.9	4.8	5.8
Family income:[2]														
Low income...........	27.5	29.2	25.4	27.1	24.9	28.1	35.7	36.0	25.9	19.7	38.7	39.9	29.8	26.0
Middle income..........	35.0	34.3	35.8	35.0	31.9	30.0	30.8	30.9	28.8	31.4	33.9	34.6	28.8	33.2
High income	32.4	32.9	33.7	34.3	41.0	36.6	26.7	28.4	39.4	48.8	22.6	22.1	35.8	38.1
Not reported	5.1	3.6	5.1	3.5	2.3	5.0	6.8	4.7	5.9	0.1	4.8	3.4	5.6	2.7
Median income (dollars)[3].	20,697	28,162	21,095	29,132	22,484	28,389	18,133	25,272	21,621	34,850	16,985	22,932	21,121	30,867

X Not applicable. - Represents zero.

[1]Includes the three family types—joint step-adoptive, joint biological-step-adoptive, and unknown—for which data are not shown separately in this table.

[2]The income intervals are as follows:

Interval	1980	1985
Low.........	Under $15,000	Under $20,000
Middle.......	$15,000-24,999	$20,000-34,999
High	$25,000 or more	$35,000 or more

The after-inflation values of the 1980 and 1985 intervals are comparable, to the extent possible, given the limitations of the intervals available on the survey form.

[3]For the median computations, the universe was restricted to families with reported incomes.

Source: Current Population Survey.

TABLE 2.8

Comparison of students whose parents divorced during last year with those whose parents did not on various risk items

(N = 1,484 and 20,222)

Item	At Risk	Not At Risk
Suspended from school	8.8	5.7
Attempted suicide	2.2	.7
Involved in pregnancy	1.6	.5
Student sold drugs	1.1	.5
Student used drugs	5.9	2.7
Family used drugs	9.5	3.0
Student used alcohol	8.6	4.3
Parent alcoholic	11.5	3.0
Student arrested	2.3	1.2
Student abused	6.4	1.5
Low grades in school	16.0	13.2
Failed courses	12.7	8.7
Overage in grade	19.3	16.1
Retained in grade	19.3	13.9
Excessive absences	12.1	6.5
Low self-esteem	20.9	11.7
Referred special education	12.1	9.6
Low reading scores	11.7	9.2
Parent sick last year	9.2	3.7
Parent died last year	1.2	.9
Parent lost job last year	12.2	3.4
Friend died last year	7.2	4.4
Student ill last year	6.2	3.0
Sibling died last year	1.9	.4
Father low-level job	19.3	16.7
Father not high school graduate	10.7	7.5
Mother low-level job	23.7	19.3
Mother not high school graduate	11.9	8.1
Parents' attitude negative	8.6	4.8
Language not English	4.7	4.9
Broken home	80.1	31.2
Moved frequently	34.5	14.4
Changed schools frequently	32.2	22.7
Parents divorced last year	100	0

Source: Jack Frymier, Growing *Up Is Risky Business, and Schools Are Not to Blame*, Phi Delta Kappa, (Bloomington, IN, 1992)

Consistent with earlier findings of the National Center for Health Statistics which showed divorced persons who remarried had fewer years of education than persons marrying for the first time, the Census Bureau found that, in general, parents in stepfamilies were less well-educated than parents in married-couple families. Almost 44 percent of fathers and 37 percent of mothers in all married-couple families had at least some college education, but only 35 percent of fathers and 29 percent of mothers in families made up of a stepfather, a biological mother, and stepchildren had at least some college. On the other hand, almost half (48 percent) of biological fathers in stepfamilies had at least some college.

America's New Orphans

The Annie Casey Foundation, Center for the Study of Social Policy, reported that in 1990, 9.7 percent of children lived in households not headed by a parent, up from 6.7 percent in 1970 and 8.3 percent in 1980. Experts say that America's new orphans are common in the inner city where fathers have long been absent and mothers are becoming victims of drugs or violence. Some are true "zero-parent" children, living permanently with relatives or in foster homes or institutions. Others are shuttled about while a drug-abusing parent is unwilling or unable to care for them.

FACTORS AFFECTING LIVING ARRANGEMENTS

Divorce

The National Center for Health Statistics (NCHS) reports that every year since 1972, more than a million children saw their parents divorce, a three-fold increased since 1950. Suzanne M. Bianchi of the Bureau of the Census, in "America's Children: Mixed Prospects," (1990, *Population Bulletin*, Vol. 45, No. 1, WDC: Population Reference Bureau, Inc.), notes that the <u>rate</u> of children whose parents divorce has risen even faster. During the 1950s, only six out of every 1,000 children experienced divorce every year, but during the 1980s, between 17 and 19 children per 1,000 experienced parental divorce.

Divorce, separation, and premarital childbearing have caused one-parent families to become much more prevalent (and accepted) in the last 20 years.

TABLE 2.9

Comparison of students who lived in broken home situation
with those who did not on various risk items

(N = 7,505 and 14,201)

Item	At Risk	Not At Risk
Suspended from school	9.6	4.0
Attempted suicide	1.3	.5
Involved in pregnancy	1.0	.4
Student sold drugs	.8	.4
Student used drugs	4.3	2.2
Family used drugs	6.0	2.1
Student used alcohol	6.4	3.7
Parent alcoholic	5.9	2.4
Student arrested	2.1	.9
Student abused	3.5	1.0
Low grades in school	18.5	10.7
Failed courses	12.8	6.9
Overage in grade	22.5	12.9
Retained in grade	21.0	10.7
Excessive absences	10.2	5.1
Low self-esteem	17.4	9.7
Referred special education	11.5	8.9
Low reading scores	12.2	7.8
Parent sick last year	5.6	3.2
Parent died last year	2.1	.3
Parent lost job last year	5.5	3.2
Friend died last year	6.0	3.9
Student ill last year	4.3	2.6
Sibling died last year	.7	.4
Father low-level job	17.3	16.6
Father not high school graduate	8.1	7.5
Mother low-level job	27.0	15.7
Mother not high school graduate	11.1	6.9
Parents' attitude negative	7.5	3.7
Language not English	4.3	5.3
Broken home	100	0
Moved frequently	25.4	10.8
Changed schools frequently	28.4	20.7
Parents divorced last year	15.8	2.1

Source: Jack Frymier, Growing *Up Is Risky Business, and Schools Are Not to Blame, Phi Delta Kappa*, (Bloomington, IN, 1992)

Although it is unclear whether these effects persist into adulthood or whether certain positive effects also result from the experience of divorce for adolescents, it is certain that increasing numbers of young people will experience divorce at some time.

Unmarried Mothers

The huge rise of births to unmarried women over the past three decades has drastically affected the living arrangements of many children. According to the Centers for Disease Control, in 1989 (the last year for which data are available), 517,989 babies were born to teenagers, up from 488,941 the year before. This is not only an increase in the number of teen births, but also an 8 percent increase in the teen birthrate (the number of births per 1,000 persons). In other words, with every minute another teenager became a mother. Nearly one-fourth of these young women were giving birth for the second, third, or more time. Every 46 minutes an adolescent 14 years or younger had a child. This represents 27 percent of all births; in 1960, only about one in 20 (5 percent) births were to unmarried women.

Now, 30 percent of families are maintained by just one parent, compared to only one out of 10 in 1970.

The Fallout of Divorce

Numerous studies have linked family instability and divorce with risk factors in adolescents. Tables 2.8 and 2.9 compare those teens in "at risk" situations (recent divorce and divorced households) to those teens not currently living in divorcing families. Those teens experiencing family dissolution were higher on all measures of risk than those not at risk.

Though the proportion of mothers who are unmarried is much higher among blacks than whites, it is increasing at a much faster rate among whites. Among white mothers, 19.2 percent were unmarried in 1989 compared with 65.7 percent of black mothers. Younger mothers were far more likely to be unmarried. Nearly all black mothers ages 15 to 19—92 percent and 55.3 percent of white mothers in that age group were unmarried. (See Table 2.10.) Of children in single-parent households, 31 percent are living with a parent who never married.

TABLE 2.10

BIRTHS TO UNMARRIED WOMEN, BY AGE OF MOTHER, 1989

	Age of Mother						
	15-19	20-24	25-29	30-34	35-39	Over 40	All Ages
Births to Unmarried Women by Race of Mother							
All races	337,268	378,122	215,477	106,344	39,030	7,316	1,094,169
White	188,253	211,815	120,640	60,344	23,730	4,841	613,543
Black	138,718	153,551	86,846	41,468	13,333	2,021	442,395
Percentage of Births to Unmarried Women by Race of Mother							
All races	66.6%	35.1%	17.1%	12.6%	13.3%	15.9%	27.1!
White	55.3	25.7	11.6	8.6	9.8	13.1	19.2
Black	92.0	71.2	51.9	43.8	40.6	37.2	65.7

SOURCE: National Center for Health Statistics. Calculations by the Children's Defense Fund.

LIVING ARRANGEMENTS OF YOUNG ADULTS

Living With Parents

In 1990, more than half the young adults between the ages of 18 and 24 lived at home with their parents. Males were more likely than females to live with their parents, primarily because males tend to marry at a later age than females. Nearly six in 10 men (58 percent) in the 18 to 24 age group lived with their parents, while 47 percent of females did. Almost all (97 percent) of both men and women in this age group who lived with their parents had never been married. In addition, both males and females are marrying later than ever before in this century (an average age of 26.1 years for men and 23.9 for women). A sagging economy, the high cost of maintaining a separate residence, and a reluctance to live within the restrictions of a tight budget all contribute to the number of young adults living with parents.

TABLE 2.11

Living Arrangements of Young Adults: 1970 to 1991

[1970 and 1980, as of April. Beginning 1985, as of March and based on Current Population Survey, see headnote, table 63]

LIVING ARRANGEMENTS AND SEX	PERSONS 18 TO 24 YEARS OLD					PERSONS 25 TO 34 YEARS OLD				
	1970	1980	1985	1990	1991	1970	1980	1985	1990	1991
Total (1,000)	22,357	29,122	27,844	25,310	24,902	24,566	36,796	40,857	43,240	42,905
Percent distribution:										
Child of householder [1]	47	48	54	53	54	8	9	11	12	12
Family householder or spouse . . .	38	29	24	22	22	83	72	68	65	64
Nonfamily householder	5	10	8	9	9	5	12	13	13	13
Other.	10	13	14	16	16	4	7	9	11	11
Male (1,000)	10,398	14,278	13,695	12,450	12,275	11,929	18,107	20,184	21,462	21,319
Percent distribution:										
Child of householder [1]	54	54	60	58	60	10	11	13	15	15
Family householder or spouse . . .	30	21	16	15	14	79	66	60	56	55
Nonfamily householder	5	11	10	10	10	7	15	16	16	17
Other.	10	13	14	17	16	5	8	11	13	14
Female (1,000)	11,959	14,844	14,149	12,860	12,627	12,637	18,689	20,673	21,779	21,586
Percent distribution:										
Child of householder [1]	41	43	48	48	49	7	7	8	8	9
Family householder or spouse . . .	45	36	32	30	29	86	78	76	73	72
Nonfamily householder	4	8	7	8	7	4	9	10	10	10
Other.	10	13	13	15	15	4	6	7	9	9

[1] Includes unmarried college students living in dormitories.
Source: U.S. Bureau of the Census. *1970* and *1980 Census of Population*, PC(2)-4B and *Current Population Reports*, series P-20, No. 461, and earlier reports.

Maintaining Households

The William T. Grant Foundation Commission on Work, Family and Citizenship, an organization concerned with problems facing America's youth, reported in *American Youth: A Statistical Snapshot* (1989, WDC) that more than 5 million youth and young adults between the ages of 15 and 24 were maintaining households. About 2.9 million were in family households in which two or more people related by marriage or blood lived together. Another 2.3 million were maintaining nonfamily households in which a person lived alone or shared a residence with unrelated persons.

Married and Unmarried Couples

In 1991, 29 percent of all young women between the ages of 18 and 24 were married and living in a family household, compared with 45 percent in 1970. During the same period, the proportion of similarly aged young men who maintained households fell by more than half from 30 percent in 1970 to 14 percent in 1991. (See Table 2.11.)

In 1991, 10 percent of young men ages 18 to 25 and 7 percent of young women age 18 to 25 were living in unmarried-couple households, which is defined as one in which two unrelated adults of the opposite sex, with or without children, reside.

HOMELESS CHILDREN AND YOUTH

Information on the number of homeless persons is based largely on estimates. There is little question, however, that the fastest-growing segment of homeless persons are families with children.

The United States Conference of Mayors, in *A Status Report on Hunger and Homelessness in America's Cities: 1991* (1991, WDC), estimated that on the average, 40 percent of the homeless persons in the 26 American cities surveyed were families with children, while 5 percent were unaccompanied youth, age 18 and under. Among homeless families, 72 percent are headed by a single parent.

CHAPTER III

CARING FOR THE CHILDREN

A 1990 Gallup Poll indicated that the majority of Americans believe that the traditional model of two children, a father who goes to work, and a mother who stays at home to care for the children is still the ideal family arrangement. Nevertheless, that arrangement has become, and will likely remain, the exception rather than the rule. The majority of mothers with children are in the labor force. Not only are women working longer in their pregnancies, they are usually returning to work after they have children, often while the children are still very young. Most working mothers and an increasing number of working fathers are at one time or another faced with the problem of who will care for their children.

WORKING MOTHERS

Earlier Return to Work

A U.S. Bureau of the Census study of women and work, *Work and Family Patterns of American Women* (1990, WDC), found that not only are women more likely to remain in the labor force during their pregnancies than they were 20 years ago, but they are also more likely to return to work sooner after the birth of their first child (Figure 3.1). The study, which describes the maternity leave and return-to-work patterns of women who had their first births between January 1961 and December 1985, found that most women in the early 1960s did not return to work after giving birth to their first child. During that period only 14 percent of mothers with newborns returned to work by the sixth month, and only 17 percent, or one mother in six, was back to work by the twelfth month. Work habits had changed dramatically by the early 1980s when 44 percent of new mothers returned to work within six months after giving birth, and more than half (53 percent) by the twelfth month. The mothers of the 1980s and 1990s were older and better educated and, therefore, more likely to be career-oriented. They may have seen their jobs as long-term careers, in which time lost would adversely affect their ability to hold a position and earn promotions. The economic recession of the 1980s and the increasing numbers of single mothers meant that more women had the financial need to work.

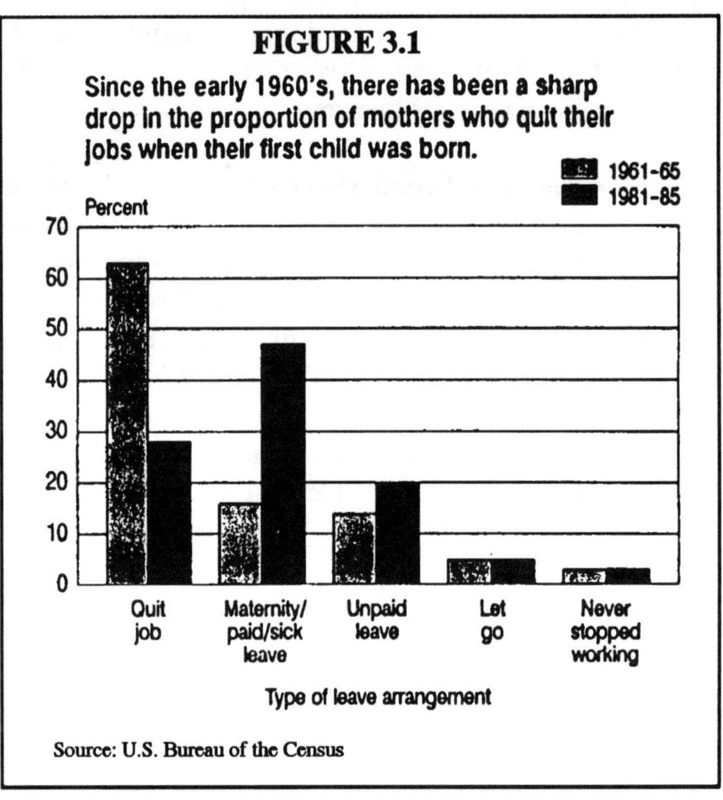

Source: U.S. Bureau of the Census

More With Young Children

The Bureau of Labor Statistics (BLS) reports that the labor force participation rate of mothers with children under age 18 increased from 47 percent in 1975 to 67 percent in 1991. The increasing need for child care programs is linked to the rise in labor force participation rates of mothers with young children. In 1970, only 30 percent of married mothers with children under age 6 were in the labor force, but by 1990, 60 percent of such mothers were in the labor force. The result has been that increasing numbers of children are cared for by someone other than a parent.

The U.S. Bureau of Labor Statistics shows that, among nonworking mothers ages 21 to 29 who had small children, about 1.1 million were not working outside the home because of child care problems. Mothers at the lower end of the economic scale were more likely than others to report difficulty finding high quality child care that was also accessible and affordable.

CHILD CARE FACILITIES

No comprehensive data exist on the numbers, types, or quality of child care facilities in the United States. The National Association for the Education of Young Children (NAEYC) counted 80,000 licensed child care centers operating in 1990. These facilities, which were most often a school-like environment, served about 4.2 million children.

Estimated numbers of licensed child care homes vary considerably. The NAEYC counted 118,000 regulated family child care homes and 550,000 to 1.1 million nonregulated providers doing business in 1990. The U.S. Department of Labor's Women's Bureau estimates that as many as 94 percent of family day care homes are "underground" and not licensed.

Regulations

More than half the states regulate family day care homes. The remaining states either do not require licensing or do not include smaller day care facilities under their guidelines. There is, in most cases, a fee for filing for a license as a regulated family day care home. Many family child care homes do not apply for licensing because of the cost and the obligation to maintain required fire prevention and health guidelines. While children generally are safe in such facilities, the fact that there are few, if any, safeguards in unlicensed homes leaves many children at risk.

Child care centers are regulated in all states, but the standards vary considerably, particularly with regard to staffing requirements. Established child/staff ratios vary by state and by the age of the children involved. Most states also set minimum educational or training requirements for staff.

In 1988, Congress passed the Family Support Act (FSA), otherwise known as the welfare reform bill (PL 100-485). This act includes several provisions that affected Aid to Families with Dependent Children (AFDC) and the regulation of child care service. The act specified that by 1990 all states were required to establish programs for AFDC recipients. States are now required to guarantee child care for families participating in the Job Opportunities and Basic Skills Training programs (JOBS). The FSA also made grants available for states to improve their child care licensing and registration requirements.

CHILD CARE ARRANGEMENTS

The Bureau of the Census, in *Who's Minding the Kids?* (1992, WDC), surveyed families using child care services during the Fall of 1988 and found the types of child care used by working mothers varied depending on the age of the child, the mother's work schedules, marital status, income levels, and racial and ethnic backgrounds.

School Age Children

The primary provider of child care (the one used most frequently, and often exclusively) for grade school age children was school. Seventy-six

TABLE 3.1

Percentage of 1988 eighth graders whose parents reported various after-school locations for their child and person present when their child returned home, by SES

| | | Where 8th grader went after school: | | | | Who was at home:* | | | |
		Neighbor sitter/ relative/ friend	After school program/ sports	Job/ other	Home	Parent	Other adult/ older sibling	Younger sibling	No one home
		(percent)				(percent)			
Total	100	7.1	13.1	2.1	77.7	63.7	33.5	37.5	10.1
Socioeconomic status									
Lower 25%	100	10.6	8.3	2.5	78.7	73.4	38.6	39.9	6.9
Middle 50%	100	7.1	12.4	2.0	78.5	60.6	33.8	37.2	10.9
High 25%	100	3.8	19.1	1.8	75.3	61.5	28.6	35.8	11.2

* Each column is independent (e.g., more than one person can be home).

SOURCE: U.S. Department of Education, National Center for Education Statistics, "National Education Longitudinal Survey of 1988: Base-Year Parent Survey."

percent (15.7 million) of the 20.8 million children between the ages of 5 and 14 years with employed mothers were either in kindergarten or grade school during most of the hours their mothers were at work. This does not mean that the remaining 24 percent were not in school but that most of the hours their mothers worked did not coincide with their school day. These school-age children needed secondary child care arrangements in addition to the time they spent in school. Almost 2.5 million of the remaining grade-school-age children were cared for in their own homes, while the remaining 3 million received care in other homes or organized facilities. About 800,000 children were left unsupervised during most of their mother's working hours.

The U.S. Department of Education reported that among eighth graders in 1988, the majority of students went home after school (78 percent). Students from higher income families were more likely to participate in after-school programs or sports (Table 3.1).

Self-Care

According to Kathleen Dwyer of the University of Southern California and the University of Illinois, over two-thirds of eighth graders care for themselves after school for at least one hour weekly. Twenty-four percent are unsupervised from one to four hours each week; 16 percent are unsupervised for five to 10 hours; and 29 percent are alone for 11 hours or longer.

Dwyer's 1990 study showed that children left alone are more likely to cite friends as their primary influence, to go to parties, and to use alcohol, cigarettes, and marijuana. Self-care was more common in higher-income families.

Children Under 5 Years

Almost one-third (30 percent) of the 10 million preschoolers with working mothers in 1990 were cared for in their own homes, primarily by their fathers while their mothers worked, while 36 percent were cared for in another person's home by a nonrelative. About one-quarter (24 percent) of preschoolers were enrolled in organized child care centers, such as day care centers and preschools, as their primary source of child care service. About 9 percent of younger children were cared for by their mothers while working, either at home, or away from home. Of the 724,000 working mothers with preschool children who cared for them while they

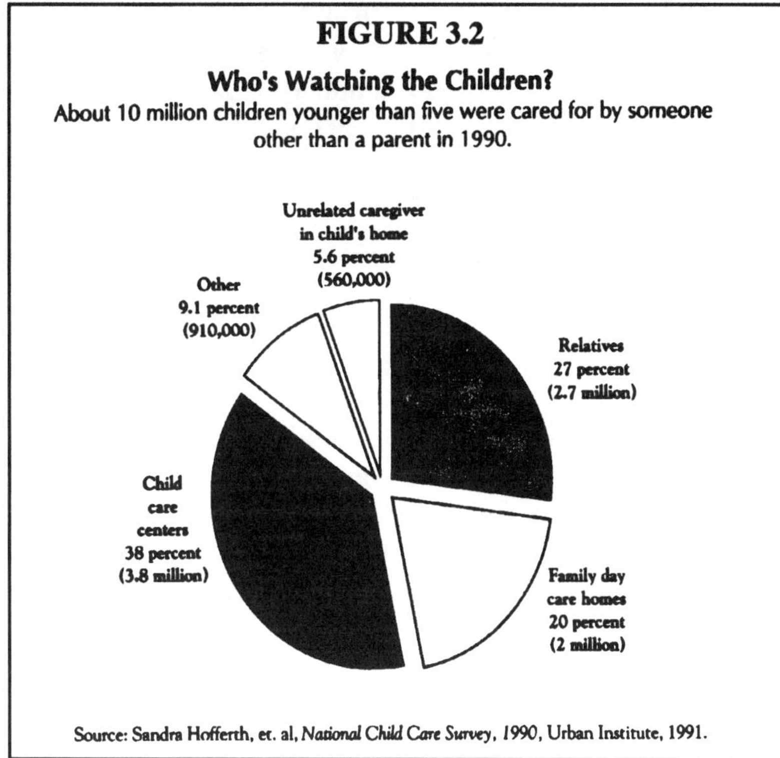

percent of 3- and 4-year-olds were cared for in homes, while 34 percent were in organized child care facilities, an indication of the increased availability of facilities for these ages.

The Urban Institute reports that of the children under the age of five who were not cared for by a parent, 38 percent stayed in child care centers. Relatives cared for children 27 percent of the time; family day care accounted for 20 percent; and unrelated caretakers or others cared for the remaining 15 percent of the children. (See Figure 3.2.)

What Happens to Children in Child Care?

As more and more children go into child care at younger ages, child care experts have expressed concern about the quality of that care and whether or not day care at an early age imperils children's inner security and development. Some studies have suggested that early child care is harmful to children. But while the debate continues, the experts largely agree on these items:

• The debate is largely over care in the first year of life;

• Any negative effects from early nonmaternal care itself are small;

• For children from poor families, early, high-quality day care often means improved test scores;

• Even if early outside care does no harm, having a parent at home for at least the first three or four months is an intrinsically good thing for both parents and children.

In response to these concerns, a federally-sponsored study, one of the most complex projects ever undertaken in the behavioral sciences, is now under way to study learning and development in

worked, about 26 percent were private household workers or child care workers.

Infants and Preschoolers

Child care arrangements vary greatly among preschoolers according to their age. As their children grow from infancy to school age, working mothers often make changes in child care arrangements to meet the needs of their children, their families, and their employers. Making child care arrangements for preschoolers is often more difficult because fewer organized child care facilities admit infants and very young children. This is due primarily to the cost involved in hiring a sufficient number of workers and adapting facilities to suit younger children.

Seventy percent of infants (under one year) were cared for either in the child's home or a caregiver's home. Another 12 percent were in day/group care centers, while only 2 percent were in nursery/preschools. Like the infants, almost three-quarters (74 percent) of 1- and 2-year-olds whose mothers worked were cared for in homes, and 18 percent were in organized child care. However, 56

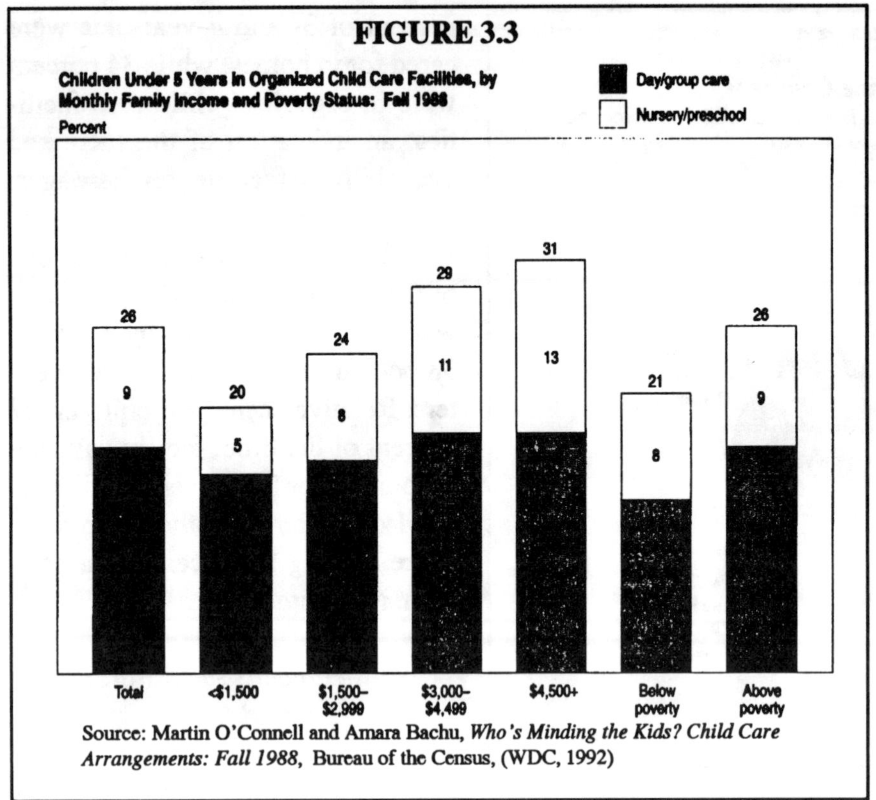

Source: Martin O'Connell and Amara Bachu, *Who's Minding the Kids? Child Care Arrangements: Fall 1988*, Bureau of the Census, (WDC, 1992)

than $54,000 per year) were more likely to use organized child care facilities (31 percent) as children whose family incomes were less than $1,500 per month (less than $18,000 per year). (See Figure 3.3.)

About 15 percent of children whose families lived in poverty in fall 1988 ($900 monthly income for all families with children under age 15) or near poverty (125 percent of the poverty level) used organized child care facilities as the primary child care arrangement while their mothers worked. In contrast, about one-quarter of children living in families that were "not poor" used organized child care facilities (Figure 3.4). Children living in poverty were more likely to be cared for in their own homes by relatives.

early child care. The new federal study, sponsored by the National Institute of Child Health and Human Development, was begun in 1991 and is scheduled to continue for five years. Experts believe the project may provide a better understanding of the effects of child care on children.

Arrangements By Fathers

The Census Bureau also asked about child care arrangements of the 1.9 million children under age 15 who lived with their fathers (and not their mothers) or male legal guardians. As with mothers, kindergarten/grade school provided the primary child care for 71 percent of grade-school-age children living with fathers. Almost one in four preschool-age children living with their fathers were in organized day care facilities.

Economic Characteristics of Child Care Users

The economic status of the family significantly affected the use of organized child care facilities as the primary child care arrangement. Children whose family income exceeded $4,500 per month (more

SECONDARY CHILD CARE ARRANGEMENTS

About 28 percent of those children under age 15 with employed mothers used a secondary child care arrangement in fall 1987. A secondary child care arrangement is one used frequently (after the primary arrangement) during a typical work week for the mother. Twelve percent of preschool-age children and 35 percent of school-age children ages 5 to 15 years needed secondary arrangements.

Three-quarters (6 million) of those who used secondary arrangements were children 5 years and over who attended kindergarten or grade school. The most frequently used arrangement was in the child's homes (38 percent). One-quarter were cared for in someone else's homes, and 10 percent in organized child care facilities. Another 22 percent (1.3 million) cared for themselves after school while their mothers worked.

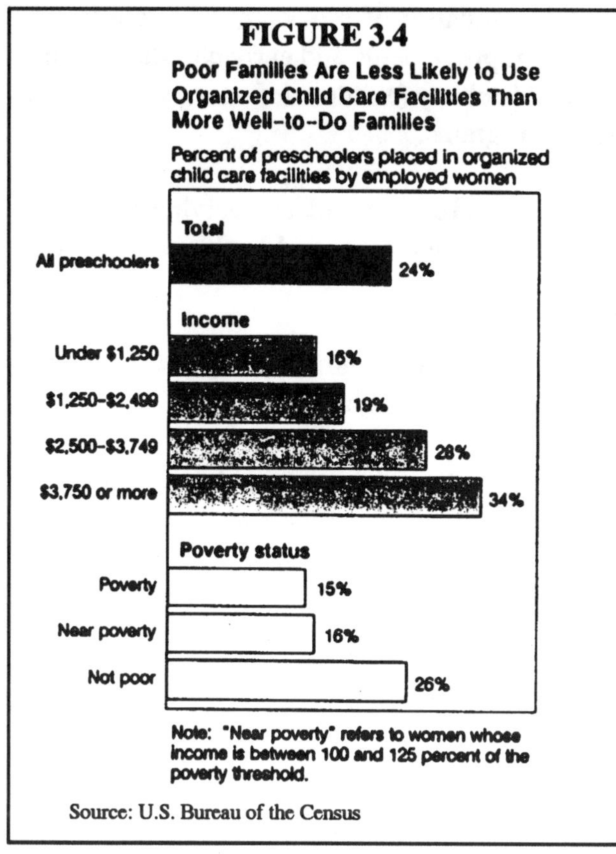

COST OF CHILD CARE

Of the 18.5 million working women with children under age 15 in 1987, one-third reported that they had made cash payments for child care services for at least one of their children. Average child care costs were $49 per week per family. The average monthly family income of women who paid for child care services was $3,200. The costs for child care were usually 7 percent of their total income.

Child care costs vary greatly by the age of the child, region of the country, and type of care. Women with preschool children were more likely to make cash payments, to make higher payments ($51 to $58), and to spend a higher proportion of their monthly income on child care (7 to 8 percent) than their counterparts with older children ($35 per week for child care or 4.5 percent of family income).

The Women's Bureau of the U.S. Labor Department, in *Employers and Child Care: Benefiting Work and Family* (1989, WDC), reported that full-time care in an organized day care center can vary from $40 a week for a preschool child in the South to $175 a week for an infant in a Northeastern city. Census Bureau figures show that child care is about $14 per week higher in the Northeast ($57) than in the South ($43). Fees for full-time care in a family day care home can range from $30 to $140 a week. Few parents can afford a full-time nanny or child care provider to care for the child in the parent's home, but those who can are required by federal law to pay at least minimum wage and Social Security insurance to those who work more than 20 hours per week.

Poverty and Income Status

In 1987, about 8 percent of working women (1.4 million) with children under age 15 were living in poverty. About one-quarter of these women made cash payments for child care services, compared with one-third of women who were not poor. Women living in poverty paid an average of $35 per week, while women living in more affluent households paid an average of $50 per week. However, those living in poverty paid a significantly higher proportion of their income (25 percent) on child care services than women who were not poor (6 percent) (Figure 3.5). Women living in poor households who paid for child care had an estimated average family income of $610 per month.

GOVERNMENT INVOLVEMENT

Perhaps the best known and most successful government endeavor in child care is Head Start, a federal program established to provide social, educational, and nutritional services for disadvantaged preschoolers. Head Start operates in every state and serves almost half a million children. Eligibility is determined by family income and federal poverty guidelines.

Block Grant

In 1990, the 101st Congress, after considerable lobbying by child-advocate groups, passed what

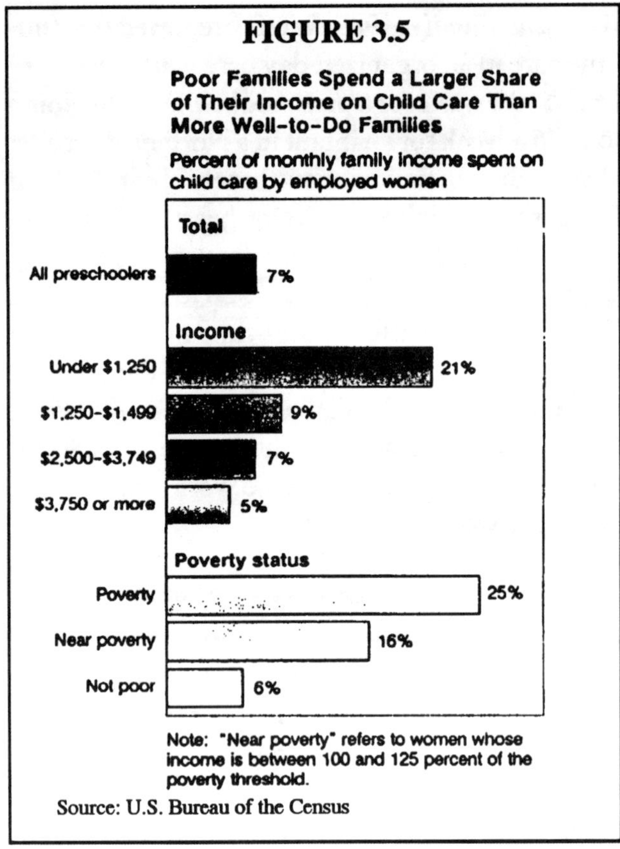

many consider the nation's first comprehensive child care legislation. The Child Care and Development Block Grant (PL 101-508) authorized $2.5 billion to the states over three years ($750 million in 1991, $825 million in F(iscal) Y(ear) 1992, $925 million in FY 1993, and "necessary" amounts for FY 1994 and FY 1995). This new legislation does not require matching state funds and allocates money to the states based on per capita income, the number of children under age 5, and the number of children receiving free or reduced-price lunch through the School Lunch Program (See Chapter IV). Following are highlights of the new law:

• States will use three-quarters of grant funds to assist families in paying for care or improve quality or availability of child care.

• Working parents qualify for assistance if they have children under age 13 and family income is 75 percent less than state's median income.

• States must offer parents vouchers to help pay for child care of parents' choice.

• One-quarter of block grant is reserved for quality improvements and early childhood education and latchkey (children left alone while parents work) programs.

• All child care providers receiving grant funds must meet state-established health and safety requirements.

• Parents have unlimited access to children while in care funded by the act.

• States must establish parental complaint procedures.

EMPLOYER INVOLVEMENT

In "Child day care services: an industry at a crossroads" (*Monthly Labor Review*, December 1990, WDC), Darrel Patrick Wash and Liesel E. Brand reported that, in 1978, only 110 employers provided some kind of child care support. By 1982, the number grew to 600; to 2,000 by 1984; 2,500 by 1985; and 3,500 by 1988.

A 1987 Bureau of Labor Statistics study of child care benefits provided by employers found that about 25,000, or 2 percent, of all business with at least 10 employees sponsored day care centers. An additional 35,000 businesses, or 3 percent, provided some sort of financial assistance for child care. However, 60 percent of all businesses offered some benefit for working parents, such as flex-time (adjusting work hours to fit the parents needs), part-time work options, and flexible leave policies.

The growth in employer involvement is related to several factors, including the increased demand for labor, the nontaxable nature of child care benefits, the positive public relations value, and the increased number of women in the labor force. A U.S. Department of Health and Human Services (HHS) study of 415 hospitals and mid-sized companies in 1978 to 1981 that had newly-established child care programs, found improved morale, an attraction for recruiting new employees, lower turnover, and less absenteeism among employees.

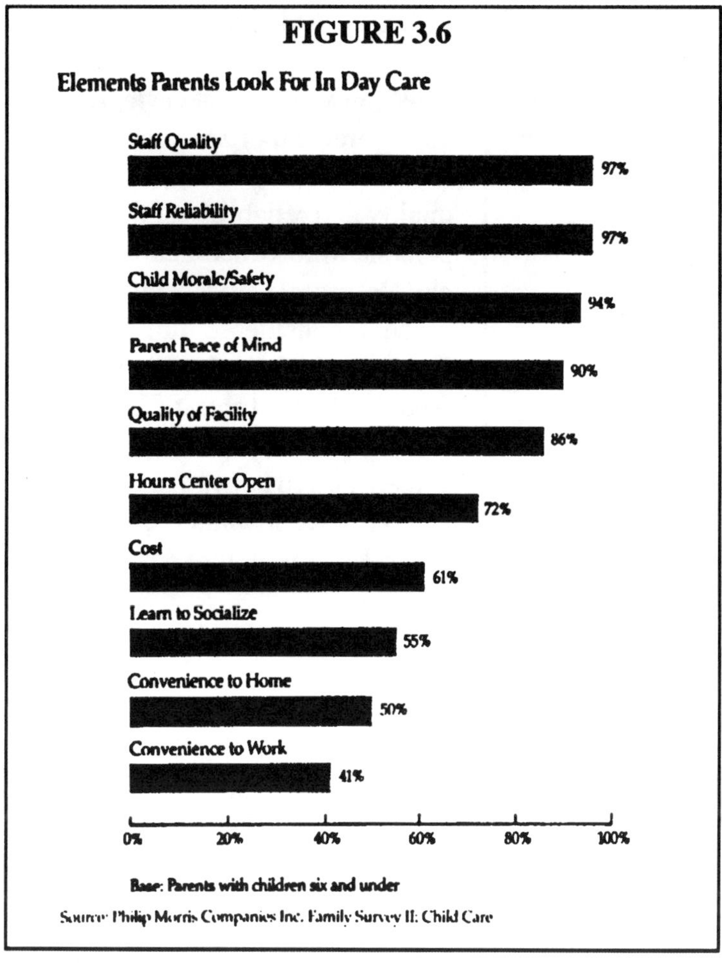

In 1992, 11 of the nation's leading corporations, joining with more than 100 smaller businesses and private organizations, collaborated on a $25-million project to help provide their employees with care for their children and aging relatives. Among the programs to be funded were day care centers, vacation programs for school-age children, and training for women who care for children in their own homes. The 11 large corporations, which provided most of the money, are IBM, American Express, Exxon Corporation, Eastman Kodak, Xerox, Travelers Corporation, Johnson and Johnson, Amoco Corporation, Allstate Insurance, Motorola, and AT&T.

Experts on the family believe this collaboration, the most comprehensive effort in American business, reflects the growing awareness that family responsibilities can interfere with job performance. Ted Childs, director of work-force programs for IBM, explained, "We're doing this be- cause we have to. We have to attract and retain the best people we can find, more and more of whom have issues regarding their family lives. If we don't address those issues, they're going to be distractions."

A FAMILY SURVEY

The *Family Survey II: Child Care survey,* conducted by the Philip Morris Companies and Louis Harris and Associates, Inc., found that most Americans, both parents and non-parents, believed that children in this country are neglected and that the situation is worsening. They were especially concerned about the quality of care received by children under age six while their parents worked. In general, those polled called for a national child care policy that would involve both the public and private sectors, provide better wages for child care providers in order to attract more competent professionals, address the issue of care for children of welfare mothers to break their cycle of poverty, and offer financial assistance with child care expenses for needy parents. While the public favors federal legislation to deal with child care issues by a three to one margin, it is evenly divided on the question of new federal expenditures to support the programs.

What Parents Would Choose

If given their choice, three-quarters of parents polled would choose a relative to care for their children six years or under while they worked, while 13 percent preferred a day care group, and 12 percent selected a nonrelative. However, many of those who chose relatives as caretakers for their small children admitted that it was not a realistic alternative given the mobility of many American families who live far from their own parents and siblings. The Harris Poll noted that this ideal may become even less realistic as many elderly people, including grandparents, hope to re-enter the labor force in the 1990s.

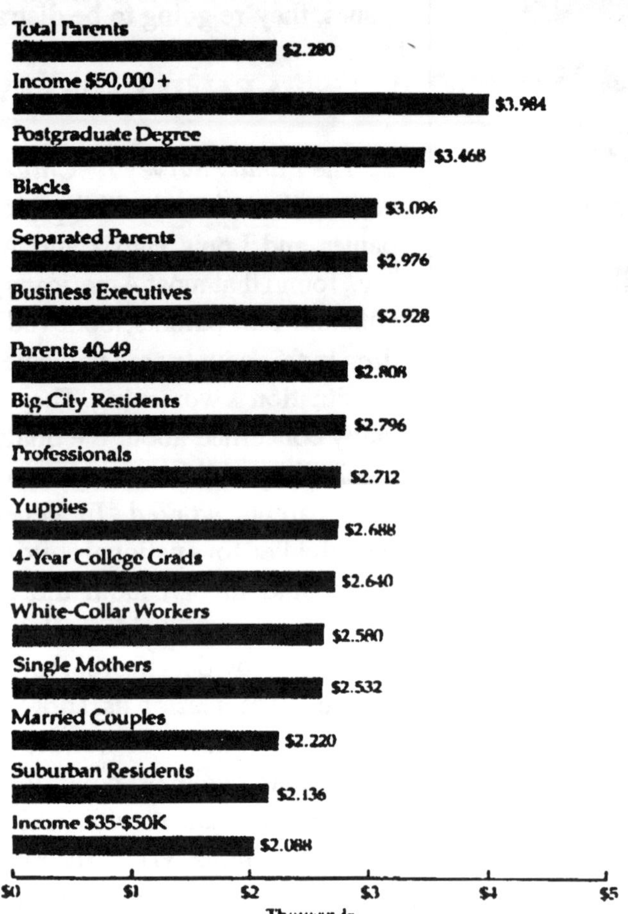

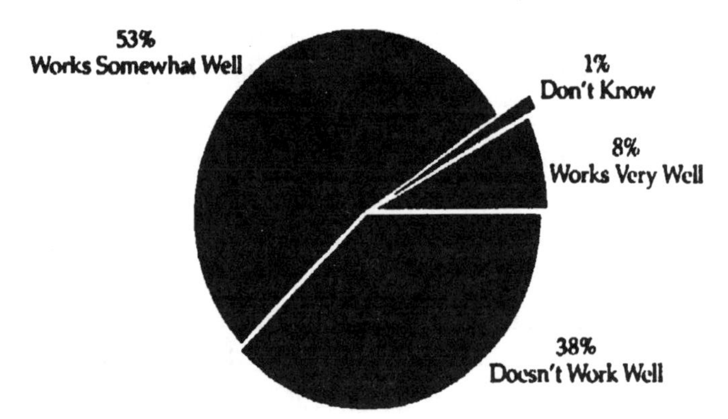

A Desirable Day Care Center

When asked about the factors they considered important in an organized day care center, 97 percent cited the quality and reliability of the staff, 94 percent were concerned about their child's morale and safety, and 90 percent considered not having to worry about their child as important factors. About three-fifths (61 percent) cited cost as an issue, half (50 percent) listed convenience to home, and 41 percent wanted convenience to work. (See Figure 3.6.)

Cost

Parents of children six years and under were asked about their child care expenditures. The mean (average) total was $190 per month, or $2,280 per year. Figure 3.7 shows annual payments based on various demographic characteristics.

Satisfaction

Fewer than 10 percent of all parents with children six years and under felt that the present day care system in this country was working well (Figure 3.8). While more than half (53 percent) felt it was working "somewhat well," 38 percent responded "not very well," or "not well at all." College graduates, professionals, those with post graduate degrees, parents with incomes of $50,000 and more, Easterners, Westerners, big-city residents, those who regularly vote, and working mothers were those most likely to express negative views on child care.

One of the major problems affecting the present child care system is the shortage of qualified child care workers. Low wages, lack of public esteem, inadequate work environments, and high turnover rates negatively affect not only the workers, but the well-being of the children in their care. *Who Cares? Child Care Teachers and the Quality of Care in America: A National Child Care Staffing Study* (Child Care Employee Project, Oakland, CA, 1989) examined child care as a work environment for adults, in which, like all work environments, the working conditions affect the quality of the product or service.

The Child Care Employee Project found that care workers, in general, were well educated. In 1988, half of all women in the labor force had attended college, but more than half of the assistant teachers and roughly three-quarters of the teachers in the study had some college background.

Wages

In 1988, the average hourly wage for child care teaching staff was $5.35, resulting in an annual income of $9,363 for full-time (35 hours/50 weeks) employment. This income did not meet the 1988 poverty threshold for a family of three ($9,431). More than half of workers sampled made less than $5 per hour, with few receiving annual cost-of-living merit increases.

The formal education and experience of child care teachers has increased between a 1977 sample and 1988, but when adjusted for inflation, teachers'

TABLE 3.2
What Does America Value?

Children's experiences during their earliest years are the foundation for much of their future learning and development. For children cared for outside the home, child care workers make an enormous difference in children's daily experience. Despite child care teachers' critical importance to the development and well-being of millions of American children, they earn among the lowest wages of American workers.

	Average Annual Earnings (1988)*
Child care teaching staff	$9,363
Laundry workers	$11,095
Amusement park/recreation service workers	$12,968
Sanitation workers	$19,163
Workers in cigarette factories	$30,590

*Full-time, based on 35 hours per week, 50 weeks per year. Data on child care workers' salaries from Child Care Employee Project, Who Cares? Child Care Teachers and the Quality of Care in America, National Child Care Staffing Study, 1989. Data on other occupations from the Bureau of the Census, Statistical Abstract of the United States, 1990.

---

earnings fell by 27 percent and assistants' earnings by 20 percent.

When compared with other comparably educated women, child care teaching staff earn considerably less. In 1988, a child care teacher with at least a baccalaureate degree (four years of college) earned an average of $11,603, while other degreed women in the civilian work force earned $26,066. Similarly educated men (there are very few in the child care teaching profession) earned $42,422. Despite the importance of teachers to the development and well-being of American children, they earn among the lowest wages of American workers (Table 3.2).

Working Conditions

About two-thirds of full-time teaching staff were paid for a 40 hour week, but on the average, they spent another four hours a week preparing curriculum, meeting with parents, and fundraising for no additional pay. Almost three-quarters worked without a contract agreement, 40 percent lacked a written job description, and only 4 percent were protected by collective bargaining.

Turnover

In 1988, the annual turnover reported by child care center directors was an extraordinarily high 41 percent, compared with 15 percent in 1977. In the 1977 sample, 40 percent of centers reported no turnover within the preceding 12 months, but by 1988, only 7 percent had had no turnover. Those who left were more likely to be new to the career and to have less specialized training. Teachers who earned $4 per hour or less were twice as likely to leave as those who earned $6 or more per hour.

Several studies have found that high rates of turnover are damaging for children in both their social activities and their vocabulary development.

FOSTER CARE

Welfare officials report that there are more than 360,000 children in foster care nationwide, and they expect the number to surpass 500,000 by 1995. The National Commission on Family Foster Care believes that two-thirds of such children are in family foster care, while the rest are in institutions, halfway houses, and other residential settings.

In foster care, officials place children who are taken from their parents because of neglect or abuse in the homes of families who volunteer to care for them temporarily, with financial assistance from the government. Foster care is supposed to be a short-term solution for children who are either returned to their parents when the situation improves or put up for adoption, but many children remain in the system for years. The average length of stay in foster care for a child is nearly five years. Children placed in emergency care custody, which by law is supposed to last no longer than 90 days, often spend years in that status, living in an institution.

At the same time that the number of children in need of foster care is increasing, there has been a decrease in the number of families with wage-earning fathers and at-home mothers, the couples who have traditionally provided foster care. In addition, the children in family foster care today are more troubled than those of a decade or two ago, placing strains on the nation's 125,000 foster homes.

CHAPTER IV

CHILDREN, YOUTH, AND MONEY

FAMILY INCOME

Because most children are dependent upon their parents, their financial conditions are tied directly to how much money their parents earn. The U.S. Bureau of the Census reports that, in both 1990 and 1991, households in the United States experienced a significant decline (3.5 percent) in real income. The median family income was $30,126; for married-couple families, which represented 74 percent of all families, it was $40,995. (See Table 4.1.)

Families with female heads-of-house, no husband present, had a 1991 median income of $16,692, a 7.6 percent decline from 1990. White female householders had a median income of $19,547; the black female householder earned $11,414; and Hispanic female heads-of-households made $12,132.

Children living in white, married-couple households were most likely to be in the best financial situation. The median family income for white, married-couple families was $41,506; for black, married-couple families, $33,307; and for Hispanic, married-couple families, $28,594.

CHILDREN IN POVERTY

Children have become America's poor. In 1975, they replaced the elderly as the poorest age group. Table 4.2 provides a profile of poor children. In 1991, 40 percent of the nation's poor were children under age 18. The poverty rate for all children under 18 years was 21.8 percent. Eighteen percent of families with children under 18 had incomes below the 1991 poverty threshold (Table 4.3).

A large number of young children (under the age of 6) are poor because many young adults, those most likely to have young children, have had decreased earnings over the past 15 years. In 1991, half (49 percent) the families in which the householder was younger than age 25 were living in poverty. (See Table 4.4.)

Racial and Ethnic Differences

There is a strong relationship between poverty rates and race/ethnicity, regardless of age. In 1991, the poverty rate for white children was 14 percent, 35 percent for Hispanic children, and 43 percent for black children. The poverty rates for Asian or Pacific Islander children was 14 percent and 22 percent for children of "other races."

Although the poverty rates for whites were lower than for the other groups, the majority of poor persons (66 percent), including children, in 1991, were white. (See Table 4.5.) Blacks made up almost 33 percent of all persons below the poverty level, and the remaining 5 percent were persons of "other" races, primarily Asians or Pacific Islanders, who together represented 3 percent of the nation's poor. More than half the children in female-headed households were poor. Among Hispanic and black children in such households, more than two-thirds were poor.

TABLE 4.1

Comparison of Income Summary Measures by Selected Characteristics: 1989 to 1991

(Households, families, and persons as of March 1992)

Characteristic	1991		Median income (in 1991 dollars)		Percent change in real income	
	Number (thous.)	Median income (dols.)	1990	1989	1990 to 1991	1989 to 1991
HOUSEHOLDS						
All households	95,669	$30,126	$31,203	$31,750	*-3.5	*-5.1
Region:						
Northeast	19,314	33,467	34,051	35,855	-1.7	*-6.7
Midwest	23,327	29,927	31,155	31,579	*-3.9	*-5.2
South	33,073	27,178	28,076	28,415	*-3.2	*-4.4
West	19,955	32,253	33,098	34,144	*-2.6	*-5.5
Residence:						
Inside metropolitan areas	74,535	31,975	33,162	34,186	*-3.6	*-6.5
1 million or more	47,675	34,472	35,249	36,426	*-2.2	*-5.4
Inside central cities	18,851	26,891	27,857	28,612	*-3.5	*-6.0
Outside central cities	28,824	39,996	40,465	42,299	-1.2	*-5.4
Under 1 million	26,859	28,551	29,782	30,565	*-4.1	*-6.6
Inside central cities	11,461	24,959	25,948	27,460	*-3.8	*-9.1
Outside central cities	15,399	31,255	32,716	33,437	*-4.5	*-6.5
Outside metropolitan areas	21,134	24,691	24,707	24,623	-0.1	0.3
Race and Hispanic origin of householder:						
White	81,675	31,569	32,545	33,398	*-3.0	*-5.5
Black	11,083	18,807	19,462	19,862	-3.4	*-5.3
Other races	2,911	32,207	35,285	34,311	*-8.7	*-6.1
Asian and Pacific Islander	2,094	36,449	40,068	39,654	*-9.0	*-8.1
Hispanic origin[1]	6,379	22,691	23,270	24,078	-2.5	*-5.8
FAMILIES						
All families	67,173	35,939	36,841	37,579	*-2.4	*-4.4
Race and Hispanic origin of householder:						
White	57,224	37,783	38,468	39,514	*-1.8	*-4.4
Black	7,716	21,548	22,325	22,197	-3.5	-2.9
Hispanic origin[1]	5,177	23,895	24,417	25,753	-2.1	*-7.2
Type of family:						
All races:						
Married-couple families	52,457	40,995	41,574	42,340	*-1.4	*-3.2
Female householder, no husband present	11,692	16,692	17,645	18,060	*-5.4	*-7.6
White:						
Married-couple families	47,124	41,506	42,028	43,066	*-1.2	*-3.8
Female householder, no husband present	7,726	19,547	20,350	20,810	*-3.9	*-6.1
Black:						
Married-couple families	3,631	33,307	35,206	33,666	*-5.4	-1.1
Female householder, no husband present	3,582	11,414	12,635	12,774	*-9.7	*-10.6
Hispanic origin[1]:						
Married-couple families	3,532	28,594	29,174	30,076	-2.0	-4.9
Female householder, no husband present	1,261	12,132	12,415	12,901	-2.3	-6.0
Age of Householder:						
15 to 24 years	2,642	16,848	16,902	18,743	-0.3	*-10.1
25 to 34 years	14,379	31,539	32,822	33,911	*-3.9	*-7.0
35 to 44 years	17,533	41,859	42,789	44,157	*-2.2	*-5.2
45 to 54 years	12,187	49,606	49,150	50,637	0.9	-2.0
55 to 64 years	9,296	40,014	40,678	41,347	-1.6	*-3.2
65 years and over	11,135	24,805	26,103	25,354	*-5.0	-2.2
EARNINGS OF YEAR-ROUND, FULL-TIME WORKERS						
Male	47,888	29,421	28,843	30,020	*2.0	*-2.0
Female	32,436	20,553	20,656	20,616	-0.5	-0.3
PER CAPITA INCOME						
All races	251,434	14,617	14,992	15,439	*-2.5	*-5.3
White	210,246	15,510	15,907	16,362	*-2.5	*-5.2
Black	31,438	9,170	9,396	9,608	-2.4	*-4.6
Hispanic origin[1]	22,095	8,662	8,778	9,215	-1.3	*-6.0

*Statistically significant change at the 90-percent confidence level.
[1]Persons of Hispanic origin may be of any race.

Source: *Money, Income of Households, Families, and Persons in the United States*: 1991, Bureau of the Census, (WDC, 1992)

TABLE 4.2

A Profile of Poor Children in America

Out of 100 poor children in America:

40   are white, non-Latino.
34   are black.
22   are Latino.
 5   are Asian, Pacific Islander, Native American, or Alaskan Native.

37   live in married-couple families.
59   live in female-headed families.
 4   live in male-headed families.

62   live in families with at least one worker.
17   live in families with two or more workers.
22   live in families with at least one full-time, year-round worker.

45   live in central cities.
32   live in suburban areas.
24   live in rural areas.

44   live in families with incomes of less than half the poverty level ($6,962 for a family of four).

40   are younger than six.

11   live in families headed by persons younger than 25.

Ten States With the Worst Child Poverty Rates

Mississippi	33.5%
Louisiana	31.2
New Mexico	27.5
West Virginia	25.9
Arkansas	25.0
Kentucky	24.5
Alabama	24.0
Texas	24.0
Arizona	21.7
Oklahoma	21.4

Ten Cities With the Worst Child Poverty Rates

Detroit, MI	46.6%
Laredo, TX	46.4
New Orleans, LA	46.3
Flint, MI	44.6
Miami, FL	44.1
Hartford, CT	43.8
Gary, IN	43.0
Cleveland, OH	43.0
Atlanta, GA	42.9
Dayton, OH	40.9

Note: National data are for 1991. State and city data are for 1989.

Source: *The State of America's Children, 1992*, Children Defense Fund, (WDC, 1992)

TABLE 4.3

Poverty Status of Families, by Type of Family, Presence of Related Children, Race, and Hispanic Origin: 1959 to 1991

(Numbers in thousands. Families as of March of the following year.

Year and characteristic	All families			Married-couple families			Male householder, no wife present			Female householder, no husband present		
		Below poverty			Below poverty			Below poverty			Below poverty	
	Total	Number	Percent	Total	Number	Percent	Total	Number	Percent	Total	Number	Percent
ALL RACES												
With & Without Children Under 18 Years												
1991	67 173	7 712	11.5	52 457	3 158	6.0	3 024	393	13.0	11 692	4 161	35.6
1990	66 322	7 098	10.7	52 147	2 981	5.7	2 907	349	12.0	11 268	3 768	33.4
1989	66 090	6 784	10.3	52 317	2 931	5.6	2 884	348	12.1	10 890	3 504	32.2
1988	65 837	6 874	10.4	52 100	2 897	5.6	2 847	336	11.8	10 890	3 642	33.4
1987	65 204	7 005	10.7	51 675	3 011	5.8	2 833	340	12.0	10 696	3 654	34.2
1986	64 491	7 023	10.9	51 537	3 123	6.1	2 510	287	11.4	10 445	3 613	34.6
1985	63 558	7 223	11.4	50 933	3 438	6.7	2 414	311	12.9	10 211	3 474	34.0
1984	62 706	7 277	11.6	50 350	3 488	6.9	2 228	292	13.1	10 129	3 498	34.5
1983	62 015	7 647	12.3	50 081	3 815	7.6	2 038	268	13.2	9 896	3 564	36.0
1982	61 393	7 512	12.2	49 908	3 789	7.6	2 016	290	14.4	9 469	3 434	36.3
1981	61 019	6 851	11.2	49 630	3 394	6.8	1 966	205	10.3	9 403	3 252	34.6
1980	60 309	6 217	10.3	49 294	3 032	6.2	1 933	213	11.0	9 082	2 972	32.7
1979	59 550	5 461	9.2	49 112	2 640	5.4	1 733	176	10.2	8 705	2 645	30.4
1978	57 804	5 280	9.1	47 692	2 474	5.2	1 654	152	9.2	8 458	2 654	31.4
1977	57 215	5 311	9.3	47 385	2 524	5.3	1 594	177	11.1	8 236	2 610	31.7
1976	56 710	5 311	9.4	47 497	2 606	5.5	1 500	162	10.8	7 713	2 543	33.0
1975	56 245	5 450	9.7	47 318	2 904	6.1	1 445	116	8.0	7 482	2 430	32.5
1974	55 698	4 922	8.8	47 069	2 474	5.3	1 399	125	8.9	7 230	2 324	32.1
1973	55 053	4 828	8.8	46 812	2 482	5.3	1 438	154	10.7	6 804	2 193	32.2
1972	54 373	5 075	9.3	46 314	(NA)	(NA)	1 452	(NA)	(NA)	6 607	2 158	32.7
1971	53 296	5 303	10.0	45 752	(NA)	(NA)	1 353	(NA)	(NA)	6 191	2 100	33.9
1970	52 227	5 260	10.1	44 739	(NA)	(NA)	1 487	(NA)	(NA)	6 001	1 952	32.5
1969	51 586	5 008	9.7	44 436	(NA)	(NA)	1 559	(NA)	(NA)	5 591	1 827	32.7
1968	50 511	5 047	10.0	43 842	(NA)	(NA)	1 228	(NA)	(NA)	5 441	1 755	32.3
1967	49 835	5 667	11.4	43 292	(NA)	(NA)	1 210	(NA)	(NA)	5 333	1 774	33.3
1966	48 921	5 784	11.8	42 553	(NA)	(NA)	1 197	(NA)	(NA)	5 171	1 721	33.1
1965	48 278	6 721	13.9	42 107	(NA)	(NA)	1 179	(NA)	(NA)	4 992	1 916	38.4
1964	47 836	7 160	15.0	41 648	(NA)	(NA)	1 182	(NA)	(NA)	5 006	1 822	36.4
1963	47 436	7 554	15.9	41 311	(NA)	(NA)	1 243	(NA)	(NA)	4 882	1 972	40.4
1962	46 998	8 077	17.2	40 923	(NA)	(NA)	1 334	(NA)	(NA)	4 741	2 034	42.9
1961	46 341	8 391	18.1	40 405	(NA)	(NA)	1 293	(NA)	(NA)	4 643	1 954	42.1
1960	45 435	8 243	18.1	39 624	(NA)	(NA)	1 202	(NA)	(NA)	4 609	1 955	42.4
1959	45 054	8 320	18.5	39 335	(NA)	(NA)	1 226	(NA)	(NA)	4 493	1 916	42.6
With Children Under 18 Years												
1991	34 861	6 170	17.7	25 357	2 106	8.3	1 513	297	19.6	7 991	3 767	47.1
1990	34 503	5 676	16.4	25 410	1 990	7.8	1 386	260	18.8	7 707	3 426	44.5
1989	34 279	5 308	15.5	25 476	1 872	7.3	1 358	246	18.1	7 445	3 190	42.8
1988	34 251	5 373	15.7	25 598	1 847	7.2	1 292	232	18.0	7 361	3 294	44.7
1987	33 996	5 465	16.1	25 464	1 963	7.7	1 316	221	16.8	7 216	3 281	45.5
1986	33 801	5 516	16.3	25 571	2 050	8.0	1 136	202	17.8	7 094	3 264	46.0
1985	33 536	5 586	16.7	25 496	2 258	8.9	1 147	197	17.1	6 892	3 131	45.4
1984	32 942	5 662	17.2	25 038	2 344	9.4	1 072	194	18.1	6 832	3 124	45.7
1983	32 787	5 871	17.9	25 216	2 557	10.1	949	192	20.2	6 622	3 122	47.1
1982	32 565	5 712	17.5	25 276	2 470	9.8	892	184	20.6	6 397	3 059	47.8
1981	32 587	5 191	15.9	25 278	2 199	8.7	822	115	14.0	6 488	2 877	44.3
1980	32 773	4 822	14.7	25 671	1 974	7.7	802	144	18.0	6 299	2 703	42.9
1979	32 397	4 081	12.6	25 615	1 573	6.1	747	116	15.5	6 035	2 392	39.6
1978	31 735	4 060	12.8	25 199	1 495	5.9	699	103	14.7	5 837	2 462	42.2
1977	31 637	4 081	12.9	25 284	1 602	6.3	644	95	14.8	5 709	2 384	41.8
1976	31 434	4 060	12.9	25 515	1 623	6.4	609	94	15.4	5 310	2 343	44.1
1975	31 377	4 172	13.3	25 704	1 855	7.2	554	65	11.7	5 119	2 252	44.0
1974	31 319	3 789	12.1	25 857	1 558	6.0	545	84	15.4	4 917	2 147	43.7
1973	30 977	3 520	11.4	25 983	(NA)	(NA)	397	(NA)	(NA)	4 597	1 987	43.2
1972	30 807	3 621	11.8	26 085	(NA)	(NA)	401	(NA)	(NA)	4 321	1 925	44.5
1971	30 725	3 683	12.0	26 201	(NA)	(NA)	447	(NA)	(NA)	4 077	1 830	44.9
1970	30 070	3 491	11.6	25 789	(NA)	(NA)	444	(NA)	(NA)	3 837	1 680	43.8
1969	29 827	3 226	10.8	26 083	(NA)	(NA)	360	(NA)	(NA)	3 384	1 519	44.9
1968	29 325	3 347	11.4	25 684	(NA)	(NA)	372	(NA)	(NA)	3 269	1 459	44.6
1967	29 032	3 586	12.4	25 482	(NA)	(NA)	360	(NA)	(NA)	3 190	1 418	44.5
1966	28 592	3 734	13.4	25 197	(NA)	(NA)	436	(NA)	(NA)	2 959	1 410	47.1
1965	28 100	4 379	15.6	24 829	(NA)	(NA)	398	(NA)	(NA)	2 873	1 499	52.2
1964	28 277	4 771	16.9	25 017	(NA)	(NA)	367	(NA)	(NA)	2 893	1 439	49.7
1963	28 317	4 991	17.6	25 084	(NA)	(NA)	400	(NA)	(NA)	2 833	1 578	55.7
1962	28 174	5 460	19.4	24 990	(NA)	(NA)	483	(NA)	(NA)	2 701	1 613	59.7
1961	27 600	5 500	19.9	24 509	(NA)	(NA)	404	(NA)	(NA)	2 687	1 505	56.0
1960	27 102	5 328	19.7	24 164	(NA)	(NA)	319	(NA)	(NA)	2 619	1 476	56.3
1959	26 992	5 443	20.3	24 099	(NA)	(NA)	349	(NA)	(NA)	2 544	1 525	59.9

Source: *Poverty in the United States: 1991*, Bureau of the Census, (WDC, 1992)

36

TABLE 4.4

Number of Children and Type of Family, by Poverty Status of Families, Subfamilies, and Persons in Families in 1991

[Numbers in thousands. Families and persons in families as of March of the following year. For meaning of symbols, see text]

Characteristic	All races			White			Black			Hispanic Origin[1]		
		Below poverty level			Below poverty level			Below poverty level			Below poverty level	
	Total	Number	Percent of total	Total	Number	Percent of total	Total	Number	Percent of total	Total	Number	Percent of total
ALL FAMILIES												
Householders of All Ages												
Total	67 173	7 712	11.5	57 224	5 022	8.8	7 716	2 343	30.4	5 177	1 372	26.5
Mean number of persons in families	3.17	3.52	(B)	3.11	3.47	(B)	3.43	3.59	(B)	3.81	4.05	(B)
Standard error	.01	.03	(B)	.01	.03	(B)	.02	.05	(B)	.03	.07	(B)
Without related children under 18 years	32 312	1 542	4.8	28 856	1 142	4.0	2 573	327	12.7	1 556	153	9.9
With related children under 18 years	34 861	6 170	17.7	28 368	3 880	13.7	5 143	2 016	39.2	3 621	1 219	33.7
One	14 547	1 950	13.4	11 863	1 256	10.6	2 105	589	28.0	1 243	309	24.8
Two or more	20 314	4 220	20.8	16 505	2 624	15.9	3 036	1 427	47.0	2 378	910	38.3
Mean number of related children	1.86	2.21	(B)	1.83	2.17	(B)	1.95	2.26	(B)	2.12	2.45	(B)
Standard error	.01	.03	(B)	.01	.03	(B)	.02	.05	(B)	.03	.06	(B)
Mean no. of persons in families with related children	3.91	3.83	(B)	3.90	3.84	(B)	3.84	3.76	(B)	4.33	4.28	(B)
Standard error	.01	.03	(B)	.01	.04	(B)	.03	.06	(B)	.04	.06	(B)
With related children under 6 years	16 883	3 753	22.2	13 522	2 354	17.4	2 666	1 244	46.7	2 033	816	40.1
One	11 706	2 308	19.7	9 392	1 446	15.4	1 814	754	41.6	1 335	484	36.3
Two or more	5 177	1 445	27.9	4 129	908	22.0	852	490	57.6	698	331	47.5
Householder Under 25 Years												
Total	2 642	937	35.5	2 070	577	27.9	490	328	66.9	391	181	46.3
Mean number of persons in families	2.80	2.94	(B)	2.76	2.95	(B)	2.96	2.95	(B)	3.35	3.37	(B)
Standard error	.03	.06	(B)	.03	.06	(B)	.06	.11	(B)	.09	.16	(B)
Without related children under 18 years	870	70	8.0	787	54	6.8	46	8	(B)	100	23	23.3
With related children under 18 years	1 771	867	49.0	1 283	523	40.8	444	319	72.0	292	158	54.2
One	1 044	432	41.4	812	280	34.4	206	135	65.7	155	75	48.2
Two or more	727	435	59.8	471	243	51.7	238	184	77.5	137	84	61.0
Mean number of related children	1.51	1.86	(B)	1.44	1.58	(B)	1.72	1.80	(B)	1.88	1.81	(B)
Standard error	.03	.06	(B)	.03	.06	(B)	.07	.10	(B)	.07	.10	(B)
Mean no. of persons in families with related children	3.13	2.99	(B)	3.17	3.03	(B)	3.02	2.94	(B)	3.70	3.57	(B)
Standard error	.04	.07	(B)	.04	.09	(B)	.09	.12	(B)	.11	.17	(B)
With related children under 6 years	1 656	830	50.1	1 216	505	41.5	398	301	75.6	265	153	57.6
One	1 100	468	42.5	847	302	36.7	219	145	66.1	165	82	49.8
Two or more	556	362	65.1	369	203	54.9	179	156	87.2	100	71	70.4

Source: *Poverty in the United States: 1991*, Bureau of the Census, (WDC, 1992)

FORMS OF AID TO CHILDREN

Aid to Families With Dependent Children

Aid to Families with Dependent Children (AFDC), the nation's largest cash assistance program for needy families, is funded jointly by the federal and state governments. AFDC is limited to families in which a child is deprived of parental care or support due to parental death, parental disability, or parental absence from the home. Eighty-eight percent of recipient children have an absent parent, usually the father. (See Figure 4.1.)

In the past, households with both able-bodied parents present could not qualify for AFDC payments. As a result, many out-of-work fathers left home so their children could receive benefits. In 1961, acting on the concerns of sociologists and others who felt these eligibility requirements were

TABLE 4.5

Persons Below Poverty Level, by Detailed Race: 1990-91

(Numbers in thousands)

Characteristic	1991			1990			1991-90 difference	
		Below poverty level			Below poverty level			
	Total	Number	Percent	Total	Number	Percent	Number of poor	Poverty rate
PERSONS								
Total	251,179	35,708	14.2	248,644	33,585	13.5	*2,123	*0.7
White	210,121	23,747	11.3	208,611	22,326	10.7	*1,421	*0.6
Not of Hispanic origin[1]	189,106	17,741	9.4	188,129	16,622	8.8	*1,119	*0.6
Black	31,312	10,242	32.7	30,806	9,837	31.9	405	0.8
Other races	9,746	1,719	17.6	9,227	1,422	15.4	*297	*2.2
Asian and Pacific Islander	7,192	996	13.8	7,014	858	12.2	138	1.6
Hispanic origin[1]	22,068	6,339	28.7	21,405	6,006	28.1	*333	0.7

*Statistically significant change at the 90-percent confidence level.
[1] Persons of Hispanic origin may be of any race.

Source: *Poverty in the United States: 1991*, Bureau of the Census, (WDC, 1992)

FIGURE 4.1

RECIPIENT CHILDREN BY REASON FOR DEPRIVATION
OCTOBER 1989 - SEPTEMBER 1990

Unemployment (6.4%)

Incapacity (3.6%)

Death (1.6%)

Absent parent - Divorced or legally separated (16.1%)

Absent parent - Never married (54.1%)

Absent parent - Other (18.2%)

TOTAL RECIPIENT CHILDREN = 7,674,517

Source: *Characteristics and Financial Circumstances of AFDC Recipients, FY 1990*, Family Support Administration, (WDC, 1992)

TABLE 4.6
Federal Aid to Families

Persons receiving Aid to Families with Dependent Children (AFDC) and federal income tax exemptions per dependent: 1950 to 1990

| Year | Number of recipients of AFDC[1] payments, in thousands | | Percent of children under 18 receiving AFDC payments | Average monthly payment | | | | Federal income tax exemption per dependent | |
| | | | | Current dollars | | Constant 1990 dollars | | | |
	Total[2]	Children under 18		Per family	Per recipient	Per family	Per recipient	Current dollars	Constant 1990 dollars
1950	2,233	1,661	3.9	$71	$21	$385	$114	$600	$3,254
1955	2,192	1,661	3.0	85	23	415	112	600	2,926
1960	3,073	2,370	3.7	108	28	477	124	600	2,649
1965	4,396	3,316	5.0	137	33	568	137	600	2,490
1970	9,659	7,033	10.5	190	50	640	168	625	2,105
1975	11,404	8,106	12.9	229	72	556	175	750	1,822
1980	11,101	7,599	13.2	288	100	457	159	1,000	1,586
1981	10,613	7,125	12.1	302	103	434	148	1,000	1,438
1982	10,504	6,972	12.0	310	106	420	144	1,000	1,354
1983	10,865	7,130	12.4	321	110	421	144	1,000	1,312
1984	10,740	7,114	12.4	335	115	421	145	1,000	1,258
1985	10,924	7,247	12.6	341	118	414	143	1,040	1,263
1986	11,065	7,374	12.7	358	122	427	145	1,080	1,288
1987	10,862	7,296	12.6	358	123	412	142	1,900	2,186
1988	10,920	7,325	12.7	369	126	408	139	1,950	2,154
1989	10,934	7,370	12.5	378	130	398	137	2,000	2,108
1990	11,464	7,761	13.2	379	131	379	131	2,050	2,050

[1] The Aid to Families with Dependent Children (AFDC) program provides cash support for low-income families with dependent children who have been deprived of parental support due to death, disability, continued absence of a parent, or unemployment.

[2] Includes the children and one or both parents or one caretaker other than a parent in families where the needs of such adults were considered in determining the amount of assistance.

NOTE: Some data have been revised from previously published figures.

SOURCE: U.S. Department of Commerce, Bureau of the Census, *Statistical Abstract of the United States;* Current Population Reports, Series P-20, *Household and Family Characteristics,* various years; and unpublished data. U.S. Department of Health and Human Services, Social Security Administration and Family Support Administration, unpublished data. U.S. Department of the Treasury, Internal Revenue Service, *Your Federal Income Tax,* various years; and public information.

---

contributing to family instability, Congress enacted changes which gave states the option of providing AFDC to two-parent families if one parent had a recent work history but was then unemployed. With the passage of the Omnibus Budget Reconciliation Act of 1981 (PL 97-35), the program could cover two-parent families in which the father or mother was unemployed. As of October 1990, all states offer benefits to two-parent families for at least part of the year. The two-parent program is called AFDC for Unemployed Parents (AFDC-UP).

The National Association of State Budget Officers reported that, based on the new law, half the states increased AFDC grants in FY (fiscal year) 1990 between 1.0 and 7.5 percent. These increases, however, did not equal the cost of inflation. In only five states did the real value of AFDC grants for a family of three keep up with the rate of inflation.

Characteristics of Recipients

About 11.5 million adults and children received AFDC benefits in 1990. The average payment for the typical AFDC family was $379 a month (Table 4.6). Fewer than 10 percent of AFDC families had earned income in 1990, which was usually wages from the mother. Figure 4.2 shows the increase in the percentage of children receiving AFDC payments from 1950.

In 1990, 37 percent of AFDC families had a child under age 3, 60 percent had children under age 6, and 84 percent had a child under age 12. The median age for a child receiving AFDC benefits was 7 years and 9 months. Only 11 percent of AFDC children were

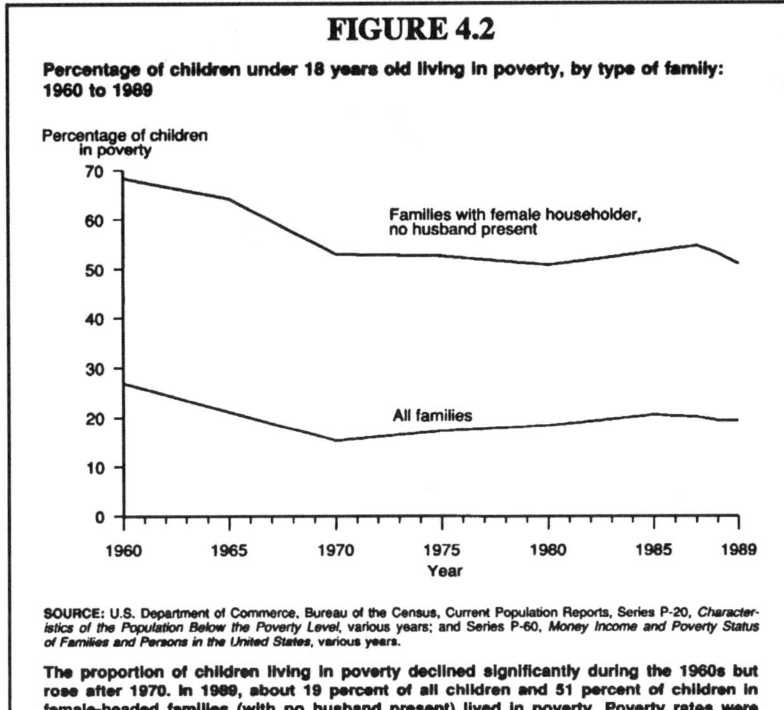

FIGURE 4.2

Percentage of children under 18 years old living in poverty, by type of family: 1960 to 1989

SOURCE: U.S. Department of Commerce, Bureau of the Census, Current Population Reports, Series P-20, *Characteristics of the Population Below the Poverty Level*, various years; and Series P-60, *Money Income and Poverty Status of Families and Persons in the United States*, various years.

The proportion of children living in poverty declined significantly during the 1960s but rose after 1970. In 1989, about 19 percent of all children and 51 percent of children in female-headed families (with no husband present) lived in poverty. Poverty rates were relatively high for minority children. About 43 percent of all black children and 36 percent of all Hispanic children lived in poverty in 1989. The proportion of poor children coming from female-headed households has risen dramatically, from 24 percent in 1960 to 57 percent in 1989 for all children, and from 29 to 76 percent for black children.

Black families were 40 percent of all AFDC families, followed by white (39 percent) and Hispanic (16 percent) families. Most of the remainder were Asian (2 percent) and Native American (1 percent) families.

Government benefit payments lifted 9 percent of children younger than 6, and 12 percent of those younger than 18, out of poverty (Figure 4.3).

Earned Income Tax Credit (EITC)

The Earned Income Tax Credit (EITC), a provision of the Tax Reform Act of 1986 (PL 99-514), is an income subsidy for working parents with incomes of less than $20,000. The EITC, administered by the Internal Revenue Service (IRS), is a

15 years of age or over. By the time a child has reached that age, the mother often finds it easier to work outside the home, and the child is also at an age where he/she might find part-time employment to help out financially.

dollar amount that working parents of dependent children can subtract from their income tax. Those who owe no income tax, or a tax smaller than the credit, receive a check from the U.S. Treasury Department.

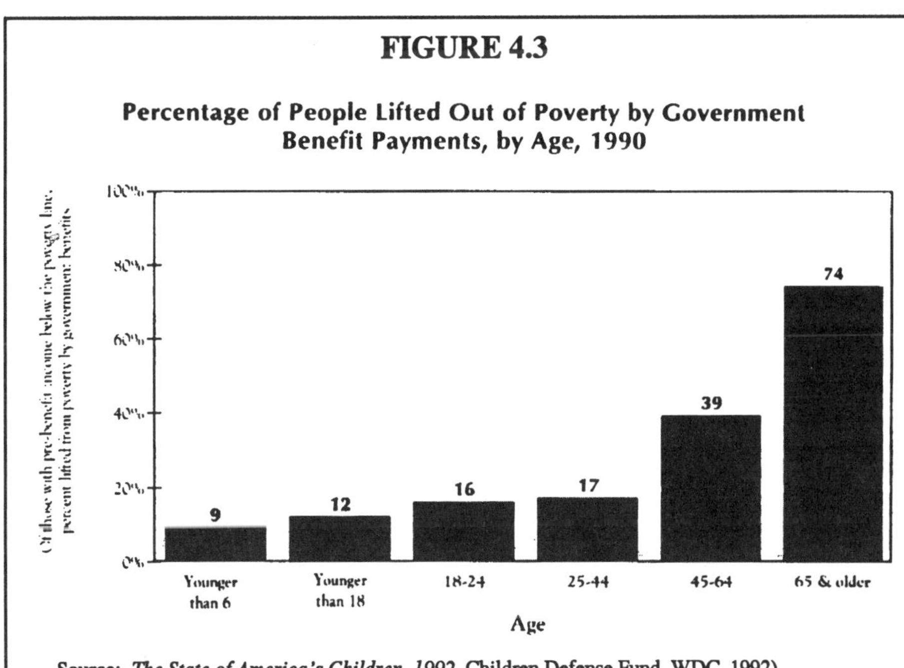

FIGURE 4.3

Percentage of People Lifted Out of Poverty by Government Benefit Payments, by Age, 1990

Source: *The State of America's Children, 1992*, Children Defense Fund, WDC, 1992)

The Child Care and Development Block Grant (see Chapter III), passed by the 101st Congress in 1990, increased the maximum credit to $1,852 for a family with one child and $2,013 for a family with two or more children from the present $1,127 maximum for all families regardless of size. EITC is expected to cost $12.36 billion over the next five years.

The Grant also provided for a Supplemental

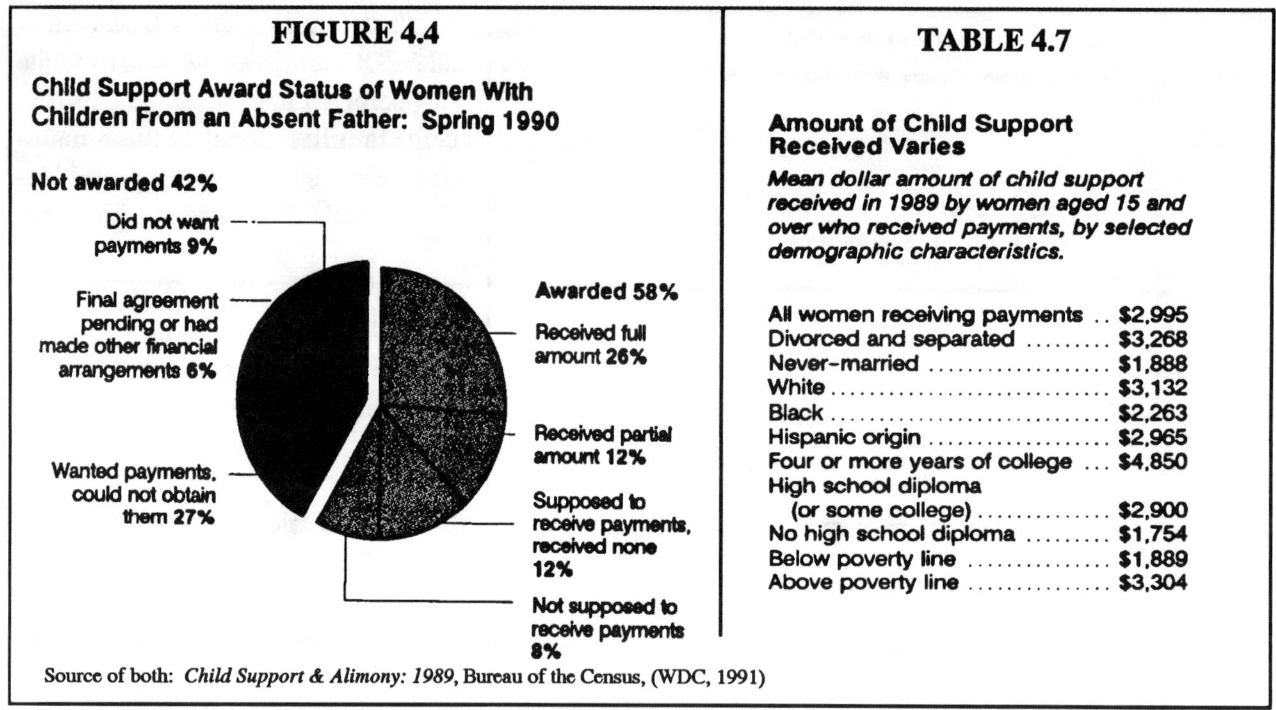

All women receiving payments	$2,995
Divorced and separated	$3,268
Never-married	$1,888
White	$3,132
Black	$2,263
Hispanic origin	$2,965
Four or more years of college	$4,850
High school diploma (or some college)	$2,900
No high school diploma	$1,754
Below poverty line	$1,889
Above poverty line	$3,304

Source of both: *Child Support & Alimony: 1989*, Bureau of the Census, (WDC, 1991)

Credit for Newborns to low-income families with children younger than one year. The projected maximum credit in 1994 is $403.

Other Forms of Assistance

The federal government spends billions of dollars on behalf of low-income children. Most services are spread over several major income-tested programs (meaning the family income cannot exceed a certain limit), many of which are for noncash assistance. These include food stamps, Medicaid, free or reduced-price lunch and breakfast programs, and subsidized housing. The federal government also provides Supplemental Security Income (SSI) for blind and disabled children.

CHILD SUPPORT

Children who live in homes without a father present are far more likely to be poor. More and more children are living in homes without fathers. Providing financial support is the responsibility of all fathers, including absent fathers, but many fathers do not fulfill this responsibility. In 1990, 10 million women lived with children under 21 years of age whose father was not living in the household. Only 57 percent of these were awarded child support.

Poverty

More than 3 million women (32 percent) living with minor children whose fathers were absent had incomes below the poverty level in 1990. The poverty rate (54 percent) was highest for never-married women. At least half of minority women with children present from an absent father were living in poverty (53 percent of black women, 50 percent of Hispanic women), while 26 percent of white women were. Mothers with child support awards had a significantly lower poverty rate (24 percent) than those without awards (43 percent).

Those with only one child present were less likely to be poor than those with two or more children. The poverty rate for women with one child was 28 percent, but 41 percent for women with two or more.

Award and Receipt of Payments

One-half of women (51 percent) who were awarded support actually received the full amount in 1990. The remainder were about equally di-

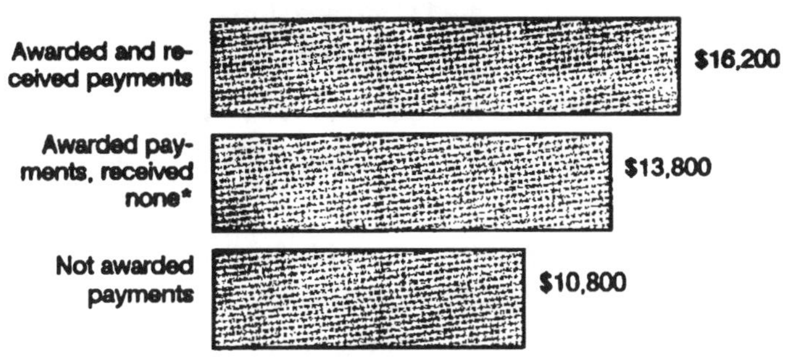

vided between those who received partial payment (24 percent) and those receiving no payment at all (25 percent. (See Figure 4.4.)

The mean amount of child support received in 1989 was $2,252. If the full amount due had been paid, the mean amount would have been $3,292. Divorced and separated women received the highest mean child support payments ($3,268), while never-married women had the lowest ($1,888). White women ($3,132) received payments greater than black women ($2,263). Women with four years of college received payments of $4,850, about two-thirds higher than women with at least a high school education (or some college) ($2,900) and more than twice that of women with less than a high school education ($1,754). (See Table 4.7.) The mean income of women who were not awarded child support payments was $10,800, lower than the average income of those due payment, whether they received them or not. (See Figure 4.5.)

Reasons for Non-Award

Almost 4 million women, or 42 percent of all women with children from absent fathers, were not awarded child support in 1990. Among the reasons cited for not receiving child support are: father unable to pay, unable to locate father, mother did not want, or mother decided not to seek it. (See Figure 4.6.)

Help in Collecting Child Support

In 1988, 2.6 million women had, at some time, made 3.5 million contacts with government agencies for assistance in collecting child support. These contacts included seeking help in finding the father and establishing paternity or support obligation (proving that the child belongs to the father, making him obligated to support it). These women also sought help in enforcing the support order or obtaining collection.

THE COST OF RAISING A CHILD

USDA Estimates

The expenses associated with rearing a child use a large proportion of a family's income. For the

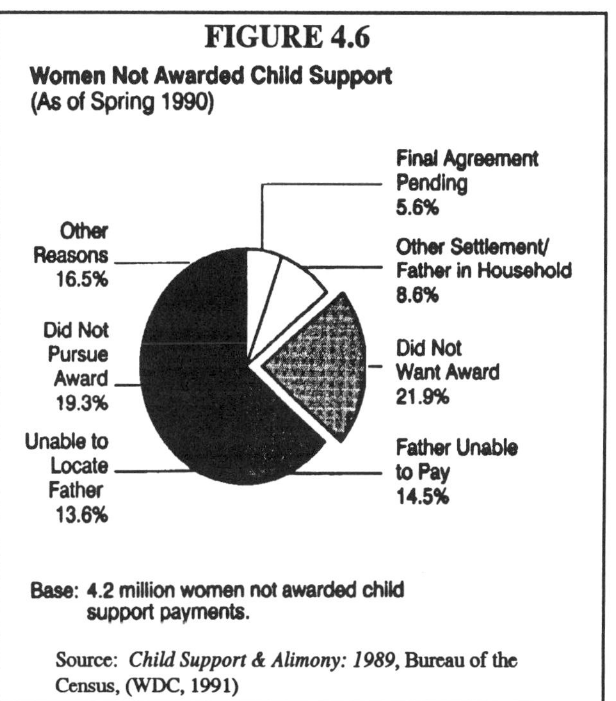

past two decades, the Family Economics Research Group of the U.S. Department of Agriculture (USDA) has provided estimates on child-rearing expenses. These estimates are used by attorneys and judges in determining child support awards in divorce cases as well as cases involving the wrongful death of a parent. Public officials use the estimates to determine payments for the support of children in foster care. Financial planners and consumer educators use these estimates in helping people determine their life insurance needs.

The estimates presented are for a child in a husband-wife household with two children and are categorized by age of child, three family income levels, and region of the country. Table 4.8 defines the categories of housing, food, transportation, clothing, health care, and education.

Income Levels

The annual family expenditures on a child varied widely by the income level of the household. Depending on the age of the child, the 1991 cost ranged from $4,520 to $5,700 for married couple households in the lowest-income group (less than $31,200), from $6,400 to $7,780 for middle-income married households, and $9,160 to $10,690 for highest-income households (more than $50,400). (See Table 4.9.)

Single-parent families generally spend less on child expenses because they have lower incomes. In families with incomes less than $31,200, from $3,930 to $5,860 will likely be spent on the child each year. Above the income level of $31,200, a family is expected to spend $8,150 to $10,410. (See Table 4.10.)

Despite the fact that highest-income households spent about twice the amount spent by lowest-income households in each age group, this difference varied by budgetary expense. Amounts spent on necessities varied considerably less than those expenses considered optional. For example, the food expenditure for a child age 15-17 in the highest-income group was $1,950, compared to $1,360 in the lowest-income group for the same child. However, the annual expense for education, child care, and other related expenses for a child

TABLE 4.9

Estimated Annual Expenditures on a Child by Husband–Wife Families, Overall United States, 1991[1]

Age of Child	Total	Housing	Food	Transpor-tation	Clothing	Health Care	Education, Child Care, and Other
Income: Less than $31,200							
0 - 2	4,520	1,830	690	610	330	250	810
3 - 5	4,820	1,770	770	660	360	230	1,030
6 - 8	4,810	1,770	990	710	390	250	700
9 - 11	4,660	1,640	1,120	640	400	260	600
12 - 14	5,350	1,580	1,200	970	650	260	690
15 - 17	5,700	1,550	1,360	1,220	610	280	680
Total	89,580	30,420	18,390	14,430	8,220	4,590	13,530
Income: $31,200 to $50,400							
0 - 2	6,400	2,420	850	1,020	420	320	1,370
3 - 5	6,800	2,360	990	1,080	450	300	1,620
6 - 8	6,760	2,370	1,250	1,160	490	320	1,170
9 - 11	6,570	2,230	1,410	1,080	500	330	1,020
12 - 14	7,320	2,170	1,490	1,410	820	330	1,100
15 - 17	7,780	2,150	1,660	1,670	780	350	1,170
Total	124,890	41,100	22,950	22,260	10,380	5,850	22,350
Income: More than $50,400							
0 - 2	9,160	3,630	1,040	1,400	520	400	2,170
3 - 5	9,640	3,570	1,250	1,450	560	370	2,440
6 - 8	9,500	3,570	1,500	1,570	590	400	1,870
9 - 11	9,310	3,440	1,690	1,500	610	410	1,660
12 - 14	10,160	3,380	1,850	1,820	970	410	1,730
15 - 17	10,690	3,350	1,950	2,080	930	430	1,950
Total	175,380	62,820	27,840	29,460	12,540	7,260	35,460

[1]Estimates are for the younger child in a two-child family.

Source: *Expenditures on a Child by Families: 1991*, U.S. Department of Agriculture, (WDC, 1992)

were second, third, or fourth, depending on the age of the child and economic position. Clothing expenses averaged 7 to 9 percent of all household expenses, while health care expenditures were 4 to 5 percent. These estimates are of monies spent on the child not covered or paid for by health insurance.

Age of Child

Family expenditures on a child increase with the child's age, although housing costs declined with the age of the child. Also, households with young children are more likely to have been more recently purchased, at higher prices, and until recently, with higher interest rates.

Although food, transportation, and clothing expenditures increased for children in all three income groups, transportation was highest for children age 15-17, when a child starts driving and incurs automobile costs, such as an additional vehicle or car insurance. Clothing expenses declined after age 12-14. This lower cost may mean that the importance of clothes to this age group is overestimated, or they are buying their own clothes with allowances or their own earnings, or they have simply stopped outgrowing their clothes so fast.

Education, child care, and related expenses were highest for preschoolers (under age 6) in all income groups. Many women with children this age are in the labor force, so much of this expense is for child care. Once the child enters school, this cost decreases.

age 15-17 in the highest-income group was nearly triple that for a child the same age in the lowest-income group.

Budgetary Component

Regardless of income level, the largest share of child-related expenditures goes for housing. The lowest-income, middle-income, and highest-income household expense for housing were 34 percent, 33 percent, and 36 percent of total expenses, respectively. Food, transportation, and education, child care, and related expenditures

TABLE 4.10

Estimated Annual Expenditures on a Child by Single-Parent Families, Overall United States, 1991[1]

Age of Child	Total	Housing	Food	Transpor-tation	Clothing	Health Care	Education, Child Care, and Other
Income: Less than $31,200							
0 - 2	3,930	1,410	730	1,010	190	90	500
3 - 5	4,960	1,640	760	1,270	260	150	880
6 - 8	5,390	1,880	1,000	1,220	300	160	830
9 - 11	5,690	1,880	1,070	1,340	330	190	880
12 - 14	5,550	1,730	1,210	1,310	630	220	450
15 - 17	5,860	1,830	1,270	1,480	620	200	460
Total	94,140	31,110	18,120	22,890	6,990	3,030	12,000
Income: $31,200 or more							
0 - 2	8,150	3,110	1,090	1,770	280	240	1,660
3 - 5	9,500	3,340	1,190	2,120	370	340	2,140
6 - 8	9,840	3,580	1,470	2,000	410	360	2,020
9 - 11	10,240	3,580	1,670	2,150	450	410	1,980
12 - 14	10,020	3,430	1,780	2,110	820	460	1,420
15 - 17	10,410	3,530	1,840	2,330	810	430	1,470
Total	174,480	61,710	27,120	37,440	9,420	6,720	32,070

[1]Estimates are for the younger child in a two-child family.

Source: *Expenditures on a Child by Families: 1991*, U.S. Department of Agriculture, (WDC, 1992)

Region

Child-related expenses increased by income level and age of child. Among all three household income groups, child-rearing expenses were highest in the urban West, followed by the urban Northeast, urban South, and urban Midwest. Costs were lower in rural areas regardless of income. Housing costs accounted for much of the variation among the regions.

Future Costs

USDA estimates of future child-related costs are shown in Table 4.11, based on a child born in 1991, reaching age 17 in the year 2008, with the average annual inflation rate over this time of 6 percent (the average annual inflation rate over the past 20 years). Total family expenses for a child through age 17 would be $157,230, $216,260, and $305,330 for lowest-, middle-, and highest-income groups, respectively. In 1991 dollar values, these amounts would be $89,580, $124,890, and $175,380.

CHILDREN AS CONSUMERS

Children ages 4 to 12 spent $14.4 billion of their own money in 1991. The average female child's income in 1991 was $7.66 weekly, for a boy, $8.87. James McNeal, professor of marketing at Texas A&M University (College Station, TX), found that children have access to more money at a younger age than in the past and that their income increases dramatically as they enter elementary and middle school. About one-half (46 percent) of children's income comes from the home in the form of allowances, one-fifth from performing household chores, 16 percent from parental gifts, 8 percent from relatives and other, and 10 percent from part-time jobs.

Saving and Spending

When compared to a similar 1984 survey, McNeal found that children ages 4 to 12 saved almost 40 percent of their income in 1991, more than twice the proportion in 1984. However, the saving rate declined as children grew older.

Children spent an avarage of $4.87 a week, 50 percent more than in 1989. During the 1991 Christmas season, children spent more than $2 billion, at least half of which came from their savings.

In 1991, children ages 4 to 12 spent about $2 billion on candy, soft drinks, frozen desserts, fruits, and other snacks. They also spent $1.9 billion on toys, games, and crafts (including toy cars, board games, skateboards, and video games). They spent about $700 million on clothes, often choosing brands or styles their parents considered too expensive. Children spent $600 million on movies, spectator events, and live entertainment. Video arcades and video games captured $486 million a

TABLE 4.11

Estimated annual expenditures of a child born in 1991, by income group[1]

Year	Age	Income group		
		Lowest	Middle	Highest
1991	<1	$4,520	$6,400	$9,160
1992	1	4,790	6,780	9,710
1993	2	5,080	7,190	10,290
1994	3	5,740	8,100	11,480
1995	4	6,090	8,580	12,170
1996	5	6,450	9,100	12,900
1997	6	6,820	9,590	13,480
1998	7	7,230	10,160	14,280
1999	8	7,670	10,770	15,140
2000	9	7,870	11,100	15,730
2001	10	8,350	11,770	16,670
2002	11	8,850	12,470	17,670
2003	12	10,770	14,730	20,440
2004	13	11,410	15,610	21,670
2005	14	12,100	16,550	22,970
2006	15	13,660	18,650	25,620
2007	16	14,480	19,760	27,160
2008	17	15,350	20,950	28,790
Total		$157,230	$218,260	$305,330

[1]Estimates are for the younger child in a two-child family for the overall United States.

Source: *Expenditures on a Child by Families: 1991*, U.S. Department of Agriculture, (WDC, 1992)

independently while shopping with parents. McNeal's survey found that a 10-year-old averages 180 store visits a year.

Good Feelings

To find out how they felt about shopping, McNeal's interviews asked 112 children, ages 8 to 10, to draw themselves shopping. The overall result was that children were willing consumers and showed great attention to detail. In two-thirds of the drawings, the children could reproduce store fixtures and counters. Some even depicted exact floor coverings, shopping carts, and even piped-in music.

Almost three-quarters of the children drew themselves smiling, showing that shopping was a positive experience. All children drew themselves shopping for things they wanted, but about 60 percent also shopped for the household. Children were clearly label-conscious and paid attention to the advertisements marketed directly at them. All the food brands and 90 percent of the nonfood brands drawn were those which are marketed to children. There were few differences by age or gender, although boys and girls drew gender-stereotyped items, such as toys and clothes.

year from children. More than a quarter of a million dollars went for "other expenditures," such as electronic equipment, cosmetics, and stamp and coin collections.

About half of children over the age of 6 make a purchase from at least one store a week. By the time they are 10, most children buy items at least twice weekly in at least two different stores. Many parents view these independent purchases as educational experiences. Most purchases are made

CHAPTER V

HEALTH AND SAFETY

LIFE EXPECTANCY

Today's young people can look forward to long lives. The average life expectancy for both sexes, of all races, is 75.4 years, although it varies with race and gender. White males born in 1990 can expect to live 72.6 years, five and a half years more than those born in 1950. White females born in 1990 have a life expectancy of 79.3 years, a seven year increase from 1950. Black females can expect to live 74.5 years, a 12 year advantage over their 1950 counterparts. Black males have the lowest life expectancy, which at 66 years is seven years longer than black males born in 1950. (See Table 5.1.)

INFANT MORTALITY

The National Center for Health Statistics defines the infant mortality rate as the number of deaths of infants under one year per 1,000 live births. Neonatal deaths occur within 28 days; post-neonatal deaths occur 28 to 165 days after birth. After leveling off through the mid-1950s and 1960s, the infant mortality rate for both whites and blacks dropped steadily after 1965.

TABLE 5.1

Expectation of Life at Birth, 1970 to 1990, and Projections, 1995 to 2010

In years. Excludes deaths of nonresidents of the United States.

YEAR	TOTAL			WHITE			BLACK AND OTHER			BLACK		
	Total	Male	Female	Total	Male	Female	Total	Male	Female	Total	Male	Female
1970	70.8	67.1	74.7	71.7	68.0	75.6	65.3	61.3	69.4	64.1	60.0	68.3
1975	72.6	68.8	76.6	73.4	69.5	77.3	68.0	63.7	72.4	66.8	62.4	71.3
1976	72.9	69.1	76.8	73.6	69.9	77.5	68.4	64.2	72.7	67.2	62.9	71.6
1977	73.3	69.5	77.2	74.0	70.2	77.9	68.9	64.7	73.2	67.7	63.4	72.0
1978	73.5	69.6	77.3	74.1	70.4	78.0	69.3	65.0	73.5	68.1	63.7	72.4
1979	73.9	70.0	77.8	74.6	70.8	78.4	69.8	65.4	74.1	68.5	64.0	72.9
1980	73.7	70.0	77.4	74.4	70.7	78.1	69.5	65.3	73.6	68.1	63.8	72.5
1981	74.2	70.4	77.8	74.8	71.1	78.4	70.3	66.1	74.4	68.9	64.5	73.2
1982	74.5	70.9	78.1	75.1	71.5	78.7	71.0	66.8	75.0	69.4	65.1	73.7
1983	74.6	71.0	78.1	75.2	71.7	78.7	71.1	67.2	74.9	69.6	65.4	73.6
1984	74.7	71.2	78.2	75.3	71.8	78.7	71.3	67.4	75.0	69.7	65.6	73.7
1985	74.7	71.2	78.2	75.3	71.9	78.7	71.2	67.2	75.0	69.5	65.3	73.5
1986	74.8	71.3	78.3	75.4	72.0	78.8	71.2	67.2	75.1	69.4	65.2	73.5
1987	75.0	71.5	78.4	75.6	72.2	78.9	71.3	67.3	75.2	69.4	65.2	73.6
1988	74.9	71.5	78.3	75.6	72.3	78.9	71.2	67.1	75.1	69.2	64.9	73.4
1989	75.3	71.8	78.6	76.0	72.7	79.2	71.2	67.1	75.2	69.2	64.8	73.5
1990, prel.	75.4	72.0	78.8	76.0	72.6	79.3	72.4	68.4	76.3	70.3	66.0	74.5
Projections:[1] 1995	76.3	72.8	79.7	76.8	73.4	80.2	(NA)	(NA)	(NA)	72.4	68.8	76.0
2000	77.0	73.5	80.4	77.5	74.J	80.9	(NA)	(NA)	(NA)	73.5	69.9	77.1
2005	77.6	74.2	81.0	78.1	74.6	81.5	(NA)	(NA)	(NA)	74.6	71.0	78.1
2010	77.9	74.4	81.3	78.3	74.9	81.7	(NA)	(NA)	(NA)	75.0	71.4	78.5

NA Not available. [1] Based on middle mortality assumptions; for details, see source. Source: U.S. Bureau of the Census, *Current Population Reports*, series P-25, No. 1018.

Source: Except as noted, U.S. National Center for Health Statistics, *Vital Statistics of the United States*, annual; *Monthly Vital Statistics Report*; and unpublished data.

In 1990, the U.S. infant mortality rate was 9.1 per 1,000 live births, one-third the rate in 1950 (29.2). The rate for white infants was 8.2 per 1,000 live births, half the 17.7 rate for black infants. (See Table 5.2.) The overall decline, attributed to several factors, including better socioeconomic conditions, improved nutrition, increased availability of prenatal care, and advances in technology of neonatal (during the first month of life) intensive care units, have not benefitted all infants equally. The main reason black babies are less likely to survive is that they are more likely to be born smaller (less than 5 1/2 pounds) than white babies. Despite the decline in mortality rates over the past several

TABLE 5.2
INFANT MORTALITY RATES[1], BY RACE, 1940-1989

Year	All Races	White	Black	Nonwhite	Ratio of Black to White
		(Race of child)			
1940	47.0	43.2	72.9	73.8	1.69
1941	45.3	41.2	74.1	74.8	1.80
1942	40.4	37.3	64.2	64.6	1.72
1943	40.4	37.5	61.5	62.5	1.64
1944	39.8	36.9	59.3	60.3	1.61
1945	38.3	35.6	56.2	57.0	1.58
1946	33.8	31.8	48.8	49.5	1.53
1947	32.2	30.1	47.7	48.5	1.58
1948	32.0	29.9	45.7	46.5	1.53
1949	31.3	28.9	46.8	47.3	1.62
1950	29.2	26.8	43.9	44.5	1.64
1951	28.4	25.8	44.3	44.8	1.72
1952	28.4	25.5	46.9	47.0	1.84
1953	27.8	25.0	44.5	44.7	1.78
1954	26.6	23.9	42.9	42.9	1.79
1955	26.4	23.6	43.1	42.8	1.83
1956	26.0	23.2	42.4	42.1	1.83
1957	26.3	23.3	44.2	43.7	1.90
1958	27.1	23.8	46.3	45.7	1.95
1959	26.4	23.2	44.8	44.0	1.93
1960	26.0	22.9	44.3	43.2	1.93
1961	25.3	22.4	41.8	40.7	1.87
1962	25.3	22.3	42.6	41.4	1.91
1963	25.2	22.2	42.8	41.5	1.93
1964	24.8	21.6	42.3	41.1	1.96
1965	24.7	21.5	41.7	40.3	1.94
1966	23.7	20.6	40.2	38.8	1.95
1967	22.4	19.7	37.5	35.9	1.90
1968	21.8	19.2	36.2	34.5	1.89
1969	20.9	18.4	34.8	32.9	1.89
1970	20.0	17.8	32.6	30.9	1.83
1971	19.1	17.1	30.3	28.5	1.77
1972	18.5	16.4	29.6	27.7	1.80
1973	17.7	15.8	28.1	26.2	1.78
1974	16.7	14.8	26.8	24.9	1.81
1975	16.1	14.2	26.2	24.2	1.85
1976	15.2	13.3	25.5	23.5	1.92
1977	14.1	12.3	23.6	21.7	1.92
1978	13.8	12.0	23.1	21.1	1.93
1979	13.1	11.4	21.8	19.8	1.91
1980	12.6	11.0	21.4	19.1	1.95
1981	11.9	10.5	20.0	17.8	1.90
1982	11.5	10.1	19.6	17.3	1.94
1983	11.2	9.7	19.2	16.8	1.98
1984	10.8	9.4	18.4	16.1	1.96
1985	10.6	9.3	18.2	15.8	1.96
1986	10.4	8.9	18.0	15.7	2.02
1987	10.1	8.6	17.9	15.4	2.08
1988	10.0	8.5	17.6	15.0	2.07
1989	9.8	8.2	17.7	15.2	2.16
		(Race of mother)			
1989	9.8	8.1	18.6	16.3	2.30

[1] Deaths per 1,000 live births.

SOURCE: National Center for Health Statistics. Calculations by the Children's Defense Fund.

TABLE 5.3
INFANT MORTALITY RATES, SELECTED COUNTRIES, 1990

Rank	Nation	Rate[1]
1	Japan	5
2	Finland	6
2	Sweden	6
4	Canada	7
4	Germany	7
4	Hong Kong	7
4	Netherlands	7
4	Switzerland	7
9	Australia	8
9	Austria	8
9	Belgium	8
9	Denmark	8
9	France	8
9	Ireland	8
9	Norway	8
9	Singapore	8
9	Spain	8
9	United Kingdom	8
19	Italy	9
20	United States	10
20	Greece	10
20	Israel	10
20	New Zealand	10
24	Cuba	11
24	Czechoslovakia	11
26	Portugal	13
27	Bulgaria	14
28	Hungary	15
28	Trinidad & Tobago	15
30	Jamaica	16
30	Poland	16
32	Kuwait	17
33	Costa Rica	18
	U.S., Black	18
34	Chile	20
34	Yugoslavia	20
36	Malaysia	22
36	Mauritius	22
36	Panama	22
36	Uruguay	22
40	South Korea	23
40	Soviet Union	23
42	United Arab Emirates	24
43	North Korea	26
43	Sri Lanka	26
43	Thailand	26
46	Romania	27
47	China	30

[1] Infant deaths per 1,000 live births.

SOURCE: UNICEF, *State of the World's Children, 1992.* U.S. data are 1989 data from NCHS.

decades, the United States still lags behind other industrialized nations. (See Table 5.3.)

IMMUNIZATIONS

The proportion of preschool-age children who have been immunized against communicable and potentially dangerous childhood diseases, including diphtheria, pertussis (whooping cough), tetanus (DTP), polio, and measles dropped during the 1980s. Health officials estimate that as many as 80 percent of adults may not be properly immunized. Minority children and those living in poverty areas within the inner city are less likely to be vaccinated than those in other parts of metropolitan areas. According to UNICEF, the United States, with 95

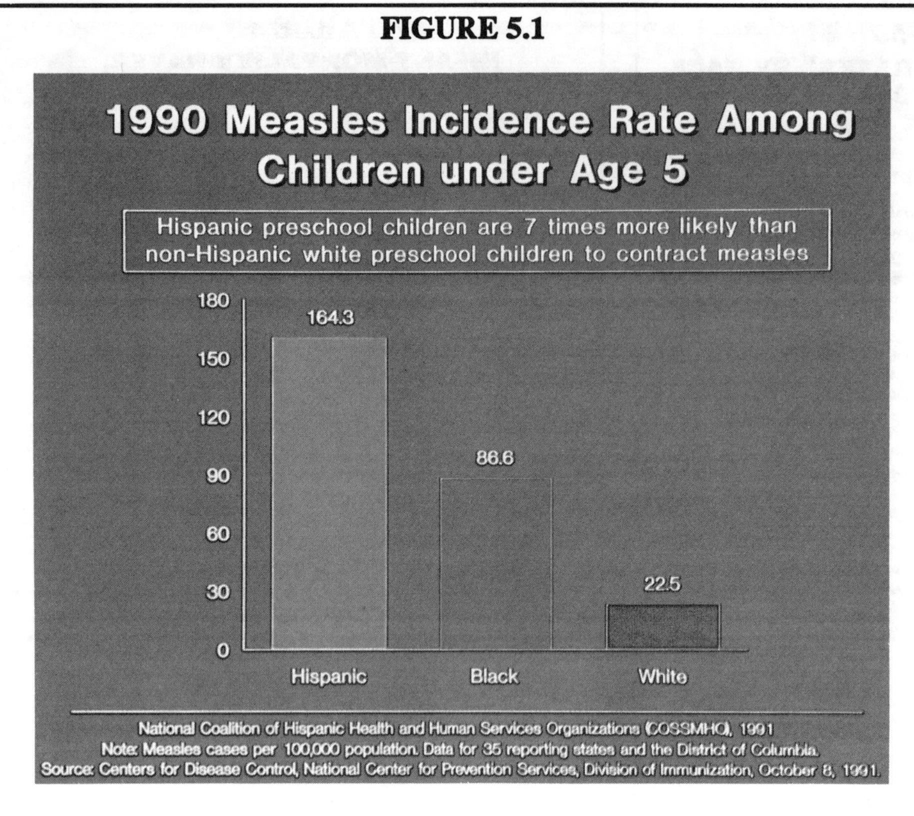

Authorities attribute the relatively low level of immunization to the fact that although American children must be immunized before entering school, there is no requirement that they be immunized before then, and no authority is held responsible for immunizing pre-schoolers and keeping track of their medical histories.

Health officials say that school entry is too late for immunization, since most children contracting diseases are under 5. Officials believe that U.S. rates are the result of poverty and the lack of a state or federal commitment that all children be properly immunized.

percent of its one-year-old children immunized against polio, ranks 17th behind such countires as Denmark, Bulgaria, Greece, Sweden, and Mexico in percentage of children immunized; U.S. non-white children rank even further behind with only 82 percent of one-year-olds being immunized.

An unexpected measles outbreak in 1990 caught many city health officials without adequate vaccine on hand and many low-income families with

TABLE 5.4
USE OF HEALTH SERVICES BY CHILDREN YOUNGER THAN 18, BY RACE AND FAMILY INCOME, 1990

	Race		Family Income			
	White	Black	Under $10,000	$10,000–$19,999	$20,000–$34,999	$35,000 or More
Average Annual Number of Physician Contacts						
Total	4.6	3.2	4.2	3.9	3.9	5.2
Physician's Office	2.9	1.5	1.9	2.0	2.4	3.4
Hospital	0.5	0.9	1.1	0.7	0.5	0.5
Percentage With No Physician Contact in Past Year						
	17.4%	21.5%	20.5%	20.9%	19.3%	14.2%
Percentage Hospitalized in Past Year						
	3.4%	4.1%	4.9%	4.1%	3.7%	2.7%
Number of Hospital Days in Past Year per Hospitalized Child						
	6.7	9.4	10.3	8.5	6.2	4.6

SOURCE: National Center for Health Statistics, National Health Interview Survey.

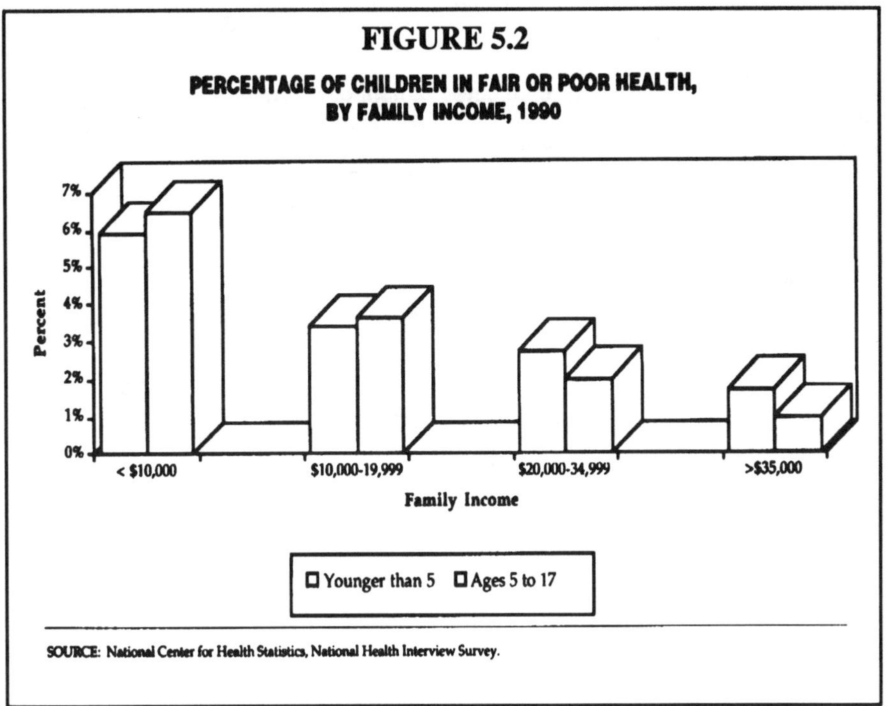

increases, the percentage of children in poor health drops, with 6 to 7 percent being in poor health in the $10,000 family income group and only 1 to 2 percent being in poor health in the $35,000 income group. (See Figure 5.2.)

While most parents were taking relatively good care of their children's bodies, many were neglecting their teeth. In 1989, one-fifth of all children under 15 years of age and 55 percent of those under 5 years of age, had never visited a dentist. Children under 15 years averaged 2.5 visits to the dentist, while those under age 5 had fewer than one visit per year to the dentist. (See Table 5.5.)

no resources to pay for the vaccine that was available. Figure 5.1 shows the racial breakdown of the cases. California enacted legislation authorizing $10 million in new funds to pay for additional vaccine to prevent shortages, finance local clinics, and provide additional outreach to low-income families. Hawaii enacted laws that encouraged health insurance providers to cover the full cost of immunizations. Other states tried to improve immunization services and prevent the spread of the disease by requiring proof of a second measles immunization before entry to high school or college.

PHYSICIAN AND DENTIST VISITS

The National Center for Health Statistics (NCHS) reports that in 1990, 83 percent of white children under age 18 and 78 percent of black children had seen a physician within the past year (Table 5.4). Hospitalizations were highest among blacks and among females with incomes below $10,000, presumably because they receive less primary health care and delay proper medical attention.

A strong relationship exists between the health of a child and family income. As the family income

HEALTH INSURANCE

Coverage

Having health insurance is a major factor in whether or not and what type of medical care a child receives. In 1991, 87 percent of children in this country ages 18 and under were covered by an insurance plan, either a private plan or Medicaid (Table 5.6). The Children's Defense Fund, in *The Health of America's Children* (1992, WDC), reports that, overall, 88 percent of white children and 85 percent of black children were covered by some type of insurance plan. Seventy-three percent of Hispanic children were enrolled in a health insurance plan.

Workers are often eligible, through their employment, for free or low-cost health insurance as an employee benefit. Therefore, it is not surprising that children in families with two parents who are both employed are more likely to have insurance coverage than those in families with only one employed parent (Figure 5.3).

TABLE 5.5

Dental visits and interval since last visit, according to selected patient characteristics: United States, 1964, 1983, and 1989

[Data are based on household interviews of a sample of the civilian noninstitutionalized population]

| Characteristic | Dental visits | | | Interval since last dental visit[1] | | | | | | | | |
| | | | | Less than 1 year | | | 2 years or more | | | Never visited dentist | | |
	1964	1983	1989	1964	1983	1989	1964	1983	1989	1964	1983	1989
	Number per person			Percent of population								
Total [2,3,4]	1.6	1.9	2.1	42.7	55.3	57.7	28.7	24.1	21.4	15.5	7.7	6.4
Age												
2–14 years [4]	1.3	2.0	2.1	39.6	57.9	60.5	5.4	7.6	6.6	46.6	23.5	19.7
2–4 years [4]	0.3	0.7	0.9	11.1	28.4	32.1	0.3	1.0	1.0	87.0	64.2	55.0
5–14 years	1.9	2.5	2.5	55.1	67.3	69.5	8.2	9.7	8.4	24.6	10.5	8.6
15–44 years	1.9	1.9	2.0	51.8	58.5	59.7	26.9	24.3	22.8	4.0	1.7	1.4
45–64 years	1.7	2.0	2.4	39.1	53.1	56.8	46.3	34.3	28.9	1.3	0.6	0.4
65 years and over	0.8	1.5	2.0	21.5	38.6	43.2	69.0	51.3	43.7	1.5	0.9	0.5
65–74 years	0.9	1.8	2.2	24.9	43.2	47.6	65.2	46.9	39.7	1.1	0.8	0.4
75 years and over	0.6	1.1	1.8	14.9	31.1	36.3	76.3	58.4	50.0	2.4	1.0	0.6
Sex [2]												
Male	1.4	1.7	2.0	40.9	53.3	55.4	29.6	25.7	23.2	16.1	7.9	6.7
Female	1.7	2.1	2.3	44.4	57.2	60.0	28.0	22.7	19.6	15.0	7.6	6.1
Race [2]												
White	1.7	2.0	2.3	45.3	57.5	60.0	27.8	23.0	20.2	13.8	7.2	6.1
Black [5]	0.8	1.2	1.2	22.3	41.1	44.0	37.6	32.2	29.5	28.0	10.3	7.7
Family income [2,6]												
Less than $14,000	0.9	1.2	1.3	26.4	40.4	41.9	35.4	35.2	33.7	27.4	11.2	9.6
$14,000–$24,999	0.9	1.5	1.6	30.0	46.7	49.5	35.2	29.7	27.5	22.0	9.8	7.8
$25,000–$34,999	1.4	2.2	2.2	39.7	58.4	60.3	30.6	22.2	20.3	15.8	7.2	6.3
$35,000–$49,999	1.9	2.5	2.7	50.1	68.2	69.7	25.3	16.2	15.1	10.9	4.5	4.5
$50,000 or more	2.7	2.9	3.1	63.9	75.3	76.1	16.8	12.2	10.6	7.2	3.6	3.4
Geographic region [2]												
Northeast	2.1	2.4	2.2	48.5	61.5	61.4	26.1	20.9	17.9	12.5	5.7	4.8
Midwest	1.6	1.9	2.1	44.6	58.0	62.2	29.3	23.4	20.1	12.9	6.1	5.0
South	1.2	1.6	1.8	35.8	49.2	52.5	30.9	27.3	25.4	20.9	10.0	8.0
West	1.7	2.0	2.4	43.8	55.9	58.0	27.9	23.3	19.7	14.3	8.0	6.7
Location of residence [2]												
Within MSA	1.8	2.1	2.2	44.9	57.4	58.8	27.5	22.4	20.2	14.4	7.2	6.2
Outside MSA	1.2	1.6	1.7	37.8	51.0	54.2	31.8	27.6	25.5	17.9	8.6	6.8

[1]Percent not shown for an interval of 1 year–less than 2 years. Denominators exclude persons with unknown interval (5.2 percent in 1989).
[2]Age adjusted.
[3]Includes all other races not shown separately and unknown family income.
[4]Data for 1983 and 1989 are shown for ages 2 years and over because children under 2 years of age rarely visit a dentist. For 1964, data for children under 2 years of age are included.
[5]1964 data are for all other races.
[6]Family income categories for 1989. Income categories in 1964 are: less than $2,000; $2,000–$3,999; $4,000–$6,999; $7,000–$9,999; and $10,000 or more; and, in 1983 are: less than $10,000; $10,000–$18,999; $19,000–$29,999; $30,000–$39,999; and $40,000 or more.

SOURCE: Division of Health Interview Statistics, National Center for Health Statistics: Data from the National Health Interview Survey.

TABLE 5.6

HEALTH INSURANCE COVERAGE STATUS OF ALL CHILDREN YOUNGER THAN 18, BY RACE/ETHNICITY, 1991

	Total	Covered by Public or Private Insurance	Covered by Any Private Insurance	Covered by Employer-Based Insurance	Covered by Medicaid	Uninsured Throughout the Year
All Races						
Number (thousands)	65,918	57,625	46,075	39,682	13,374	8,293
Percentage		87.4%	69.9%	60.2%	20.3%	12.6%
White						
Number (thousands)	52,523	46,219	39,318	34,099	8,122	6,304
Percentage		88.0%	74.9%	64.9%	15.5%	12.0%
Black						
Number (thousands)	10,350	8,791	4,744	3,932	4,511	1,559
Percentage		84.9%	45.8%	38.0%	43.6%	15.1%
Latino						
Number (thousands)	7,648	5,609	3,283	2,745	2,618	2,039
Percentage		73.3%	42.9%	35.9%	34.2%	26.7%

NOTE: Persons of Latino origin may be of any race.

SOURCE: March 1992 Current Population Survey, Bureau of the Census.

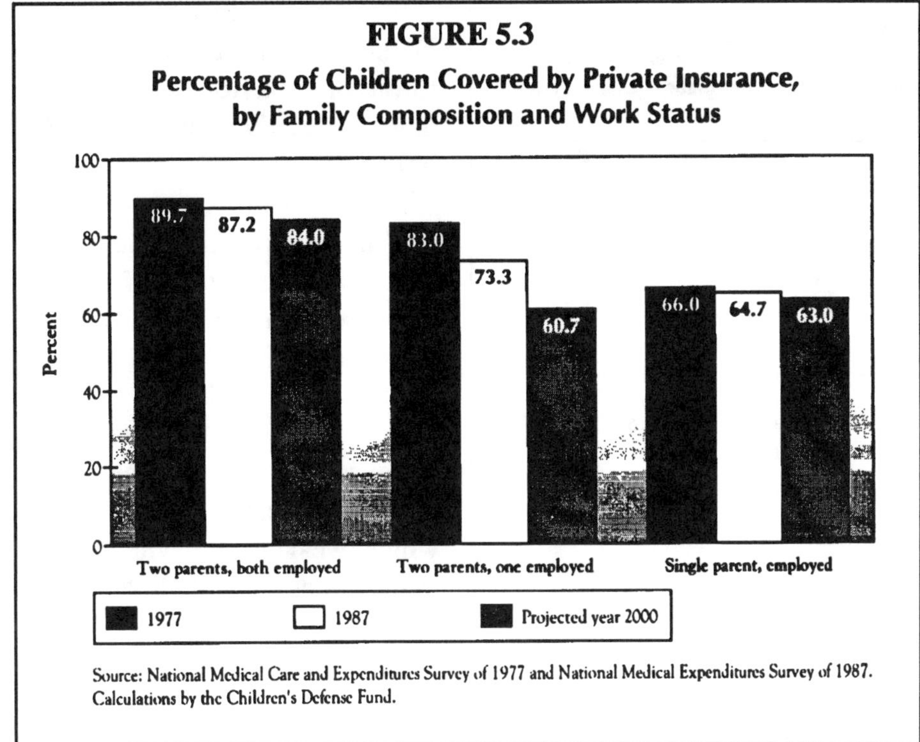

Source: National Medical Care and Expenditures Survey of 1977 and National Medical Expenditures Survey of 1987. Calculations by the Children's Defense Fund.

HEALTH OF HOMELESS CHILDREN

Recent studies suggest that homeless children suffer from frequent health problems. They are at high risk for illness because they experience problems such as parental loss, poverty, violence, drug use, and danger. The stress of homelessness on the family increases the child's likelihood for physical and mental impairment. They are less likely to receive regular, nutritious meals and health care— preventive, routine, and emergency.

PHYSICAL EDUCATION

Physical activity patterns established during youth may extend into adulthood and increase the risk for chronic diseases, such as coronary heart disease, diabetes, and cancer. Mental health experts also correlate increased physical activity with improved mental health and overall improvement in life satisfaction. The Center for Disease Control (CDC), in its *Youth Risk Behavior Survey*, found that the percentage of students in grades 9 through 12 who participated in physical education (PE) classes varied considerably. Males were somewhat more likely than females to enroll in and participate in such classes (Table 5.7). Table 5.8 shows that white high school students participated in vigorous physical activity to a greater degree than blacks and Hispanics. Younger stu-

TABLE 5.7

Percentage of high school students attending physical education classes, by gender and grade of student – United States, Youth Risk Behavior Survey, 1990*

	Male				Female				Total			
	Not enrolled		Attend daily		Not enrolled		Attend daily		Not enrolled		Attend daily	
Grade	%	(95% CI[†])	%	(95% CI)	%	(95% CI)	%	(95% CI)	%	(95% CI)	%	(95% CI)
9th	24.1	(16.9–31.4)	38.9	(30.3–47.5)	33.1	(22.1–44.1)	30.8	(23.6–38.0)	28.9	(20.1–37.8)	34.4	(27.3–41.5)
10th	36.6	(27.2–46.0)	26.7	(19.6–33.8)	46.2	(34.8–57.6)	24.8	(18.1–31.5)	41.4	(31.5–51.3)	25.7	(19.5–31.9)
11th	52.4	(42.2–62.7)	19.6	(13.2–26.0)	62.9	(51.2–74.7)	11.1	(7.2–15.0)	58.0	(47.4–68.6)	15.1	(10.4–19.8)
12th	58.1	(46.1–70.1)	13.5	(6.9–20.1)	68.2	(56.3–80.0)	7.8	(2.9–12.7)	62.7	(51.6–73.8)	10.9	(6.2–15.6)
Total	43.5	(35.2–51.8)	24.1	(18.5–29.7)	52.0	(42.4–61.6)	19.0	(15.3–22.6)	47.8	(39.1–56.5)	21.5	(17.1–25.8)

*Unweighted sample size – 11,631 students. Categories do not total 100% because students who reported taking PE less than daily are not included in this table.

[†]Confidence interval.

Source: "Participation of High School Students in School Physical Education—United States, 1990," *1990 Youth Risk Behavior Surveillance System*, Centers for Disease Control, (Atlanta, GA, 1991)

TABLE 5.8

Percentage of high school students who participated in vigorous physical activity 3 or more days per week, by sex, race/ethnicity, and grade – United States, Youth Risk Behavior Survey, 1990*

Category	Female %	Female (95% CI†)	Male %	Male (95% CI)	Total %	Total (95% CI)
Race/Ethnicity						
White	27.5	(±2.9)	51.4	(±2.7)	39.3	(±2.7)
Black	17.4	(±3.5)	42.7	(±6.7)	29.2	(±4.3)
Hispanic	20.9	(±4.5)	49.9	(±6.1)	34.5	(±4.1)
Grade						
9th	30.6	(±2.9)	51.1	(±5.1)	40.1	(±3.7)
10th	27.1	(±4.7)	54.6	(±4.1)	40.7	(±3.5)
11th	23.4	(±3.1)	50.2	(±3.9)	36.0	(±3.3)
12th	17.3	(±2.9)	43.8	(±6.1)	31.7	(±4.1)
Total	24.8	(±2.4)	49.6	(±2.5)	37.0	(±2.4)

*Unweighted sample size = 11,631 students.
†Confidence interval.

FIGURE 5.4

Percentage of high school students enrolled in physical education classes, by student grade and by survey – United States, 1984 and 1990

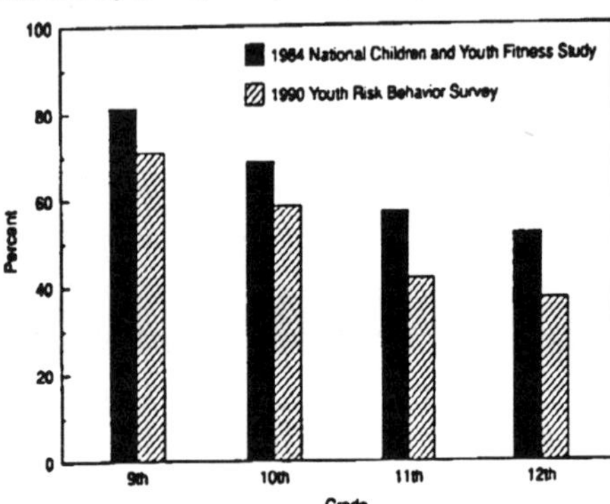

Source of both: "Participation of High School Students in School Physical Education—United States, 1990," *1990 Youth Risk Behavior Surveillance System*, Centers for Disease Control, (Atlanta, GA, 1991)

dents were involved in PE classes more frequently than the older students. Youth are participating in PE activities at a lower level than in the past (Figure 5.4).

CHILDREN, ADOLESCENTS, AND AIDS*

Young children with AIDS had the virus transmitted to them either by an infected parent or through contaminated transfusions. Adolescents are at a stage in their lives when they may be exploring their sexuality and possibly experimenting with drugs, two forms of behavior that can make them especially vulnerable to HIV infection.

AIDS, or acquired immune deficiency syndrome, was identified as a new disease in 1981. By 1992, more than 230,000 cases, resulting in over 150,000 deaths, had been reported in the United States. AIDS is caused by a virus, the human immunodeficiency virus (HIV), which weakens the victim's immune system making it vulnerable to other illnesses, often called opportunistic infections. In adults, the most common AIDS opportunistic infections are Kaposi's sarcoma, a rare skin cancer, and *pneumocystis carinii* pneumonia.

In infants and children the disease is characterized by a failure to thrive and unusually severe bacterial infections. With the exception of *pneumocystis carinii* pneumonia, children with symptomatic HIV infection do not often develop opportunistic infections as adults do. More often, they are plagued by recurrent bacterial infections, persistent oral thrush (a common fungal infection of the mouth or throat), and chronic and recurrent diarrhea. They may also suffer from enlarged lymph nodes, chronic pneumonia, developmental delays, and neurological abnormalities. Because of these differences, in 1987, the Centers for Disease Control (CDC) designed a specific definition for HIV characteristics in infants and children. (See Table 5.9.)

---

*For a detailed discussion of AIDS, including AIDS in children and adolescents, see *AIDS*, Information Plus, (1992, Wylie, TX)

TABLE 5.9

Summary of the definition of HIV infection in children

Infants and children under 15 months of age with perinatal infection

1) Virus in blood or tissues

     or

2) HIV antibody

     and

     evidence of both cellular and humoral immune deficiency

     and

     one or more categories in Class P-2

     or

3) Symptoms meeting CDC case definition for AIDS

Older children with perinatal infection and children with HIV infection acquired through other modes of transmission

1) Virus in blood or tissues

     or

2) HIV antibody

     or

3) Symptoms meeting CDC case definition for AIDS

Summary of the classification of HIV infection in children under 13 years of age

Class P-0. Indeterminate infection

Class P-1. Asymptomatic infection

    Subclass A. Normal immune function
    Subclass B. Abnormal immune function
    Subclass C. Immune function not tested

Class P-2. Symptomatic infection

    Subclass A. Nonspecific findings
    Subclass B. Progressive neurologic disease
    Subclass C. Lymphoid interstitial pneumonitis
    Subclass D. Secondary infectious diseases
      Category D-1. Specified secondary infectious diseases listed in the CDC surveillance definition for AIDS
      Category D-2. Recurrent serious bacterial infections
      Category D-3. Other specified secondary infectious diseases
    Subclass E. Secondary cancers
      Category E-1. Specified secondary cancers listed in the CDC surveillance definition for AIDS
      Category E-2. Other cancers possibly secondary to HIV infection
    Subclass F. Other diseases possibly due to HIV infection

Source: *Reports on AIDS, June 1986-May 1987*, Centers for Disease Control, (Atlanta, GA, 1987)

The CDC estimated that, in 1992, 7,000 to 10,000 children were infected with HIV due to the growing number of women who are in or reaching their childbearing years. Of the 24,323 women with AIDS in June 1992, 79 percent were between the childbearing years of 13 and 44 years. While these 20,587 women were re-ported with AIDS, there are countless unreported cases as well as women who are HIV-infected but have not yet developed AIDS.

Means of Transmittal

Table 5.10 also shows that 85 percent of children with AIDS, under age 13, had a mother infected with or at risk for AIDS; 8 per-cent received a contami-nated transfusion; 5 percent regularly received blood products because of a he-mophilia/coagulation dis-order; and 3 percent were of an undetermined origin.

How Many Are Infected?

In 1992 the CDC reported a cumulative total of 3,898 pediatric AIDS cases in children under age 13 since record-keeping began in 1981 (Table 5.10). Of these children with AIDS, 51 percent (2,100) were black, 24 percent (961) were His-panic, 24 percent (810) were white, and fewer than 1 percent (19) were Asian or Native American. More than 2,039 have died since 1981. Pediatric AIDS accounts for about 2 percent of all AIDS cases in the United States.

Adolescent AIDS

Currently, the number of AIDS cases among adolescents is comparatively low. By June 1992, the CDC reported 872 cases among young people 13 to 19 years, about 0.4 percent of the total AIDS cases. There were 8,911 cases among those ages 20 to 24 years, about 4 percent of AIDS cases. Due to the lengthy incubation period between the time of infection and the onset of symptoms, it is highly probable that many in their early 20s were infected as teenagers. (See Table 5.11.)

TABLE 5.10

AIDS cases by age group, exposure category, and race/ethnicity, reported through June 1992, United States

Adult/adolescent exposure category	White, not Hispanic No.	White, not Hispanic (%)	Black, not Hispanic No.	Black, not Hispanic (%)	Hispanic No.	Hispanic (%)	Asian/Pacific Islander No.	Asian/Pacific Islander (%)	American Indian/ Alaska Native No.	American Indian/ Alaska Native (%)	Total[a] No.	Total[a] (%)
Pediatric (<13 years old) exposure category												
Hemophilia/coagulation disorder	123	(15)	25	(1)	28	(3)	3	(16)	—		179	(5)
Mother with/at risk for HIV infection:	515	(64)	1,944	(93)	831	(87)	9	(47)	11	(100)	3,315	(85)
Injecting drug use	241		919		393		3		4		1,561	
Sex with injecting drug user	101		303		264		2		1		673	
Sex with bisexual male	29		27		15		1		—		72	
Sex with person with hemophilia	11		4		2		—		—		17	
Born in Pattern-II country	1		260		3		—		—		264	
Sex with person born in Pattern-II country	—		15		1		—		—		17	
Sex with transfusion recipient with HIV infection	5		5		7		—		—		17	
Sex with HIV-infected person, risk not specified	36		85		47		1		2		172	
Receipt of blood transfusion, blood components, or tissue	23		31		16		—		—		70	
Has HIV infection, risk not specified	68		295		83		2		4		452	
Receipt of blood transfusion, blood components, or tissue	157	(19)	66	(3)	69	(7)	7	(37)	—		300	(8)
Undetermined	15	(2)	65	(3)	23	(2)	—		—		104	(3)
Pediatric subtotal	810	(100)	2,100	(100)	951	(100)	19	(100)	11	(100)	3,898	(100)

Source: *HIV/AIDS Surveillance*, Centers for Disease Control, (Atlanta, GA, July, 1992)

TABLE 5.11

Number of cases and rate* of sudden infant death syndrome, by race of child, age period, and year of death — United States, 1980–1988

Age period at death/race	1980 No.	1980 Rate	1988 No.	1988 Rate	1980–1988 No.	1980–1988 Rate
Neonatal[†]						
White	271	9.4	248	8.1	2,255	8.5
Black	135	22.9	108	16.1	1,084	19.8
Other	12	9.7	12	6.3	124	8.9
All races	418	11.6	368	9.4	3,463	10.4
Postneonatal[§]						
White	3,448	119.0	3,523	115.7	30,828	116.0
Black	1,516	257.1	1,412	210.1	12,238	223.3
Other	128	103.3	173	90.4	1,403	101.1
All races	5,092	141.0	5,108	130.7	44,469	132.9
Total						
White	3,719	128.3	3,771	123.8	33,083	124.5
Black	1,651	280.0	1,520	226.2	13,322	243.1
Other	140	112.9	185	96.7	1,527	110.0
All races	5,510	152.5	5,476	140.1	47,932	143.3

*Per 100,000 live-born infants.

[†]Aged <28 days.

[§]Aged 28–364 days.

Source: *HIV/AIDS Surveillance*, Centers for Disease Control, (Atlanta, GA, July 1992)

TABLE 5.12

Number of cases and rate* of sudden infant death syndrome, by race of child, age period, and year of death — United States, 1980–1988

Age period at death/race	1980		1988		1980–1988	
	No.	Rate	No.	Rate	No.	Rate
Neonatal[†]						
White	271	9.4	248	8.1	2,255	8.5
Black	135	22.9	108	16.1	1,084	19.8
Other	12	9.7	12	6.3	124	8.9
All races	418	11.6	368	9.4	3,463	10.4
Postneonatal[§]						
White	3,448	119.0	3,523	115.7	30,828	116.0
Black	1,516	257.1	1,412	210.1	12,238	223.3
Other	128	103.3	173	90.4	1,403	101.1
All races	5,092	141.0	5,108	130.7	44,469	132.9
Total						
White	3,719	128.3	3,771	123.8	33,083	124.5
Black	1,651	280.0	1,520	226.2	13,322	243.1
Other	140	112.9	185	96.7	1,527	110.0
All races	5,510	152.5	5,476	140.1	47,932	143.3

*Per 100,000 live-born infants.
[†]Aged <28 days.
[§]Aged 28–364 days.

Source: "Sudden Infant Death Syndrome—United States, 1980-1988," *Morbidity and Mortality Weekly Report*, Massachusetts Medical Society, (Waltham, MA, July 17, 1992)

ILLNESS

Sudden Infant Death Syndrome (SIDS)

Sudden infant death syndrome (SIDS) is the second leading cause of infant mortality in the United States. Although the exact illness or dysfunction is still unknown and is being researched, the definition of SIDS is the "abrupt and unexplained death of an apparently healthy infant." From 1980 to 1988, the most recent year for which data are available, 47,932 infants born to U.S. residents died from SIDS. SIDS rates (per 1,000 infants) were higher for black infants than for whites. (See Table 5.12.)

Asthma

Childhood asthma is on the rise in the United states, causing 10 million missed days of school each year and 200,000 hospitilizations annually. According to the Federal Center for Disease Control, asthma is the leading cause of days lost from school.

In 1988, the most recent year for which data are available, 2.7 million children, or 4.3 percent of all children under the age of 18, suffered asthma. In 1981, 3.2 percent had the illness. Asthmatic children who are black suffered more impairment of daily activities and more frequent hospitilizations than youngsters of other ethnic groups. Experts suggest that is because more blacks lack health insurance than whites, are more likely to postpone treatment, and rely on emergency room care rather than preventive medications and treatment.

Hunger

The Food Research and Action Center, a non-profit anti-hunger group, estimates that 5.5 million people in the United States under the age of 12 years of age are hungry. The group defined hunger as periodic food shortages resulting from limited economic resources. The findings suggest that one in eight children in the United States experiences hunger at some time during each year. The study reported that hungry children were two to three times as likely as other children to experience health problems such as weight loss, fatigue, irritability, and headaches.

Lead Poisoning

Lead poisoning is one of the most common environmental pediatric health problems in the United States. Lead exposure comes primarily from leaded paints that have worn off or been scraped from older homes. It may also be found in lead plumbing and emitted by factory smokestacks. Because they are growing, children suffer the effects of lead more acutely than adults. Exposure to lead causes nervous system disorders, reduction in intelligence, fatigue, inhibited infant growth, and hearing loss. Toxic levels of lead in a parent can also affect unborn children. The federal government estimates that each year there are 400,000 cases of toxic lead levels in newborns. The Environmental Protection Agency (EPA) claims that lead exposure is the most dangerous and widespread contamination threat to the nation's children.

YOUTH MENTAL HEALTH

Marital Conflict and Divorce

Marital conflict hurts children whether it results in the breakup of marriages or not. Nearly all the studies on children of divorce have focused on the period after the parents separated. Recent studies suggest that the effects are not so much from divorce itself as from marital discord. In fact, research suggests that some problems reported with troubled teens not only began during the marriage, but may have contributed to the breakup of the marriage. Children raised in discord and marital instability often experience a variety of problems.

Marital disruption is more traumatic in the long term to children who are pre-adolescents or teenagers at the time of the breakup. Parental conflict seems to have a more immediate, obvious adverse effect on boys than on girls, but females may encounter problems with depression and sexuality later in life.

Adoption

Adolescence is a time of establishing oneself as an individual, of resolving issues of identity, sexuality, and separation. For adopted children, those issues often have frightening implications. Increasing numbers of adoptees are challenging the American system of secrecy in adoptions.

As teenagers experience puberty and the possibility of becoming parents themselves, they often begin to wonder about their own biological parents and the decisions that led to giving up their child. They may also have questions about biological and genetic conditions.

Studies have found that adopted children are two to five times as likely to be referred for mental health treatment as non-adopted children. According to Dr. Anu Sharma, psychologist at the Search Institute, an independent research organization studying the mental health needs of adolescents who were adopted as infants, adoption is harder on teenage boys than on girls. Adopted teenage boys are significantly more likely to have attempted suicide, to have been involved in gang activity, and to drop out of high school.

Eating Disorders

Youths who are overweight and remain overweight as adults may increase their risk for certain diseases in adulthood. However, over-emphasis on thinness during childhood may contribute to eating disorders such as anorexia nervosa and bulimia. The *Youth*

TABLE 5.13

Body-weight perceptions of high school students, by race/ethnicity and gender — United States, Youth Risk Behavior Survey, 1990*

Race/ Ethnicity	Female						Male					
	Underweight		Right weight		Overweight		Underweight		Right weight		Overweight	
	%	(95% CI[†])	%	(95% CI)	%	(95% CI)	%	(95% CI)	%	(95% CI)	%	(95% CI)
White	5.4	(±0.9)	58.0	(±2.6)	36.7	(±2.1)	15.6	(±1.4)	68.6	(±2.3)	15.8	(±1.8)
Black	12.7	(±3.0)	62.0	(±5.0)	25.3	(±4.3)	19.8	(±3.9)	72.5	(±4.4)	7.8	(±2.0)
Hispanic	10.5	(±3.8)	53.0	(±5.7)	36.5	(±4.7)	18.5	(±2.8)	66.6	(±2.5)	14.8	(±2.8)
Total	7.2	(±0.7)	58.5	(±2.0)	34.3	(±1.7)	16.5	(±1.1)	68.8	(±1.8)	14.7	(±1.4)

*Unweighted sample size = 11,631 students.
[†]Confidence interval.

Source: "Body-Weight Perceptions and Selected Weight-Management Goals and Practices of High School Students—United States, 1990," *1990 Youth Risk Behavior Surveillance System*, Centers for Disease Control, (Atlanta, GA, 1991)

TABLE 5.14

Trends in Annual Prevalence of Various Types of Drugs

Percent who used in last twelve months

	Class of 1975	Class of 1976	Class of 1977	Class of 1978	Class of 1979	Class of 1980	Class of 1981	Class of 1982	Class of 1983	Class of 1984	Class of 1985	Class of 1986	Class of 1987	Class of 1988	Class of 1989	Class of 1990	Class of 1991	'90–'91 change
Approx. N =	9400	15400	17100	17800	15500	15900	17500	17700	16300	15900	16000	15200	16300	16300	16700	15200	15000	
Any Illicit Drug Use[a]	45.0	48.1	51.1	53.8	54.2	53.1	52.1	50.8	49.1	—	—	—	—	—	—	—	—	
Adjusted Version[b]	—	—	—	—	—	—	—	49.4	47.4	45.8	46.3	44.3	41.7	38.5	35.4	32.5	29.4	-3.1sss
Any Illicit Drug Other Than Marijuana[c]	26.2	25.4	26.0	27.1	28.2	30.4	34.0	33.8	32.5	—	—	—	—	—	—	—	—	
Adjusted Version[b]	—	—	—	—	—	—	—	30.1	28.4	28.0	27.4	25.9	24.1	21.1	20.0	17.9	16.2	-1.7s
Marijuana/Hashish	40.0	44.5	47.6	50.2	50.8	48.8	46.1	44.3	42.3	40.0	40.6	38.8	36.3	33.1	29.6	27.0	23.9	-3.1ss
Inhalants[d]	NA	3.0	3.7	4.1	5.4	4.6	4.1	4.5	4.3	5.1	5.7	6.1	6.9	6.5	5.9	6.9	6.6	-0.3
Inhalants Adjusted[e]	NA	NA	NA	NA	8.9	7.9	6.1	6.6	6.3	7.2	7.5	8.9	8.1	7.1	6.9	7.5	6.9	-0.6
Amyl/Butyl Nitrites[f,g]	NA	NA	NA	NA	6.5	5.7	3.7	3.6	3.6	4.0	4.0	4.7	2.6	1.7	1.7	1.4	0.9	-0.5
Hallucinogens	11.2	9.4	8.8	9.6	9.9	9.3	9.0	8.1	7.3	6.5	6.3	6.0	6.4	5.5	5.6	5.9	5.8	-0.1
Hallucinogens Adjusted[h]	NA	NA	NA	NA	11.8	10.4	10.1	9.0	8.3	7.3	7.6	7.6	6.7	5.8	6.3	6.0	6.1	+0.1
LSD[g]	7.2	6.4	5.5	6.3	6.6	6.5	6.5	6.1	5.4	4.7	4.4	4.5	5.2	4.8	4.9	5.4	5.2	-0.2
PCP[f,g]	NA	NA	NA	NA	7.0	4.4	3.2	2.2	2.6	2.3	2.9	2.4	1.3	1.2	2.4	1.2	1.4	+0.2
Cocaine[i]	5.6	6.0	7.2	9.0	12.0	12.3	12.4	11.5	11.4	11.6	13.1	12.7	10.3	7.9	6.5	5.3	3.5	-1.8sss
"Crack"[j]	NA	NA	NA	NA	NA	NA	NA	NA	NA	NA	NA	4.1	3.9	3.1	3.1	1.9	1.5	-0.4
Other cocaine[j]	NA	NA	NA	NA	NA	NA	NA	NA	NA	NA	NA	NA	9.8	7.4	5.2	4.6	3.2	-1.4sss
Heroin	1.0	0.8	0.8	0.8	0.5	0.5	0.5	0.6	0.6	0.5	0.6	0.5	0.5	0.5	0.6	0.5	0.4	-0.1
Other opiates[k]	5.7	5.7	6.4	6.0	6.2	6.3	5.9	5.3	5.1	5.2	5.9	5.2	5.3	4.6	4.4	4.5	3.5	-1.0ss
Stimulants[k]	16.2	15.8	16.3	17.1	18.3	20.8	26.0	26.1	24.6	NA	NA	NA	NA	NA	NA	NA	NA	NA
Stimulants Adjusted[b,k]	NA	NA	NA	NA	NA	NA	NA	20.3	17.9	17.7	15.8	13.4	12.2	10.9	10.8	9.1	8.2	-0.9
Crystal Methamphetamine[l]	NA	NA	NA	NA	NA	NA	NA	NA	NA	NA	NA	NA	NA	NA	NA	1.3	1.4	+0.1
Sedatives[k,m]	11.7	10.7	10.6	9.9	9.9	10.3	10.5	9.1	7.9	6.6	5.8	5.2	4.1	3.7	3.7	3.6	3.6	0.0
Barbiturates[k]	10.7	9.6	9.3	8.1	7.5	6.8	6.6	5.5	5.2	4.9	4.6	4.2	3.6	3.2	3.3	3.4	3.4	0.0
Methaqualone[k,m]	5.1	4.7	5.2	4.9	5.9	7.2	7.6	6.8	5.4	3.8	2.8	2.1	1.5	1.3	1.3	0.7	0.5	-0.2
Tranquilizers[k]	10.6	10.3	10.8	9.9	9.6	8.7	8.0	7.0	6.9	6.1	6.1	5.8	5.5	4.8	3.8	3.5	3.6	+0.1
Alcohol	84.8	85.7	87.0	87.7	88.1	87.9	87.0	86.8	87.3	86.0	85.6	84.5	85.7	65.3	82.7	80.6	77.7	-2.9ss
Cigarettes	NA	NA	NA	NA	NA	NA	NA	NA	NA	NA	NA	NA	NA	NA	NA	NA	NA	NA
Steroids[l]	NA	NA	NA	NA	NA	NA	NA	NA	NA	NA	NA	NA	NA	NA	1.9	1.7	1.4	-0.3

NOTES: Level of significance of difference between the two most recent classes: s =.05, ss =.01, sss =.001. NA indicates data not available.

[a] Use of "any illicit drugs" includes any use of marijuana, hallucinogens, cocaine, and heroin, or any use of other opiates, stimulants, barbiturates, methaqualone (excluded since 1990), or tranquilizers not under a doctor's orders.

[b] Based on the data from the revised question, which attempts to exclude the inappropriate reporting of non-prescription stimulants.

[c] Use of "other illicit drugs" includes any use of hallucinogens, cocaine, and heroin, or any use of other opiates, stimulants, barbiturates, methaqualone (excluded since 1990), or tranquilizers not under a doctor's orders.

[d] Data based on four questionnaire forms in 1976–1988; N is four-fifths of N indicated. Data based on five questionnaire forms in 1989–1991; N is five-sixths of N indicated.

[e] Adjusted for underreporting of amyl and butyl nitrites. See text for details.

[f] Data based on a single questionnaire form; N is one-fifth of N indicated in 1979–1988 and one-sixth of N indicated in 1989–1991.

[g] Question text changed slightly in 1987.

[h] Adjusted for underreporting of PCP. See text for details.

[i] Data based on a single questionnaire form in 1986; N is one-fifth of N indicated. Data based on two questionnaire forms in 1987–1989; N is two-fifths of N indicated in 1987–1988 and two-sixths of N indicated in 1989. Data based on six questionnaire forms in 1990–1991.

[j] Data based on a single questionnaire form in 1987–1989; N is one-fifth of N indicated in 1987–1988 and one-sixth of N indicated in 1989. Data based on four questionnaire forms in 1990–1991; N is four-sixths of N indicated.

[k] Only drug use which was not under a doctor's orders is included here.

[l] Data based on two questionnaire forms; N is two-sixths of N indicated. Steroid data based on a single questionnaire form in 1989–1990.

[m] Data based on five questionnaire forms in 1975–1988, six questionnaire forms in 1989, and one questionnaire form in 1990–1991. N is one-sixth of N indicated in 1990–1991.

Source: Lloyd D. Johnston, *Monitoring the Future: A Continuing Study of the Lifestyles and Values of Youth*, University of Michigan, School of Social Research, (Ann Arbor, MI, 1992)

Behavior Risk Survey questioned youth in grades 9 through 12 regarding their self-perceptions of their body weights. Male adolescents were more likely to consider themselves the right weight or underweight than were female students (Table 5.13). Thirty-four percent of the females thought they were overweight; 15 percent of males believed they were. Blacks were much less likely to consider themselves overweight than other races. (For more extensive information on bulimia and anorexia, see *Health—A Concern for Every American*, Information Plus, Wylie, Texas, 1993.)

DRUGS, ALCOHOL, AND SMOKING

Few factors influence a young person's health more than the use of drugs, alcohol, and tobacco. Since 1975, the University of Michigan, under a grant from the National Institute of Drug Abuse, annually surveys the senior classes of over 100 public and private high schools to determine the extent of illicit drug and tobacco use. Several years ago, they extended the study to include college students and those recently graduated from high school and, in 1991, added eighth and tenth grade students. Their annual publication, *Monitoring the Future: A Continuing Study of the Lifestyles and Values of Youth*, is considered the most comprehensive source of statistical information on drug use by young people in America.

Dr. Lloyd D. Johnston, principal investigator, noted that illicit drug use by young Americans in high school and college continued a gradual decline. Use of crack cocaine (an inexpensive, but highly addictive smokeable form of cocaine) by all segments of young adults also dropped. Despite signs of declining use of many drugs in the young adult populations that were active users, Johnston observed that drug use by students in the eighth and tenth grades is surprisingly close to that of twelvth graders.

High School Trends

In 1991, 29 percent of all high school seniors admitted to have taken at least one illicit drug during the past year, down from a peak of 54 percent in 1978 and 1979. Almost one-fourth (24 percent) reported marijuana use (51 percent in 1979), while one in 12 (8 percent) used prescription-type stimulants without medical supervision (compared to a 20 percent peak in 1982). One in 25 high school seniors (4 percent) had used cocaine sometime in the past year (down from a 1986 peak of 13 percent), while only 1.5 percent of seniors had used crack that year (down from a high of 4 percent in 1987). (See Table 5.14.)

Dr. Jack Frymier, in *Growing Up is Risky Business* (1992, Phi Delta Kappa), compared students who used drugs to those who did not on various risk items. Students who used drugs were found to be much higher on measures of alcohol use, being from broken homes, low self-esteem, low grades, and school suspensions. They were also higher than the non-using students for many other risk factors. (See Table 5.15.)

Alcohol Use Still High

Although alcohol use remained high among young people under age 21 years, its use has

TABLE 5.15

Comparison of students who used drugs with students who did not use drugs on various risk items

(N = 632 and 21,074)

Item	At Risk	Not At Risk
Suspended from school	40.7	4.9
Attempted suicide	11.4	.5
Involved in pregnancy	3.6	.5
Student sold drugs	15.8	.1
Student used drugs	100	0
Family used drugs	36.2	2.5
Student used alcohol	75.2	2.5
Parent alcoholic	29.6	2.8
Student arrested	20.4	.7
Student abused	14.6	1.5
Low grades in school	44.0	12.5
Failed courses	36.7	8.1
Overage in grade	32.8	15.7
Retained in grade	32.9	13.7
Excessive absences	28.8	6.2
Low self-esteem	41.9	11.5
Referred special education	17.6	9.6
Low reading scores	14.6	9.2
Parent sick last year	10.8	3.8
Parent died last year	1.7	.9
Parent lost job last year	9.8	3.8
Friend died last year	18.4	4.2
Student ill last year	12.3	2.9
Sibling died last year	2.1	.5
Father low-level job	21.0	16.7
Father not high school graduate	16.8	7.5
Mother low-level job	24.4	19.5
Mother not high school graduate	18.8	8.0
Parents' attitude negative	19.3	4.6
Language not English	7.4	4.8
Broken home	51.1	34.1
Moved frequently	26.9	15.5
Changed schools frequently	28.3	23.2
Parents divorced last year	13.9	6.6

Source: Jack Frymire, *Growing Up is Risky Business, and Schools Are Not to Blame*, Phi Delta Kappa, (Bloomington, IN, 1992)

steadily declined since 1981. Investigators attribute that, in part, to the fact that alcohol is not legally obtainable for most of them since the adoption of a 21-year-old drinking age in many states. Alcohol use among high school seniors reached a peak of 88 percent in 1980, but had fallen to 78 percent by 1991. More than one-third of high school seniors reported at least one heavy drinking occasion (having five or more drinks in a row) in the two weeks prior to the survey.

College students also report high levels of drinking. Three-quarters of college students had consumed alcohol in the month prior to the survey, down from a high of 83 percent in 1982. More than two out of five (43 percent) had had at least one heavy drinking occasion (five drinks) during the previous two weeks.

Teenage Drinking and Driving

Although traffic fatalities linked to teenage drinking have fallen 33 percent since 1982, drunk driving is still the leading cause of death for Ameri-cans under age 21. The U.S. Department of Justice reported a decline in the number of drivers ages 16 to 21 arrested for driving under the influence (DUI) in 1989, reportedly due to enforcement of 21-year-old drinking age laws.

Smoking Levels Changing

Cigarette smoking rates among young people declined gradually since 1976. According to the University of Michigan study, almost three out of ten seniors (29 percent) reported smoking at least some in the prior month. However, the 1990 *Youth Risk Behavior Survey* reported that while one-third of high school students report having tried smoking at some time, only 13 percent reported use within the previous month (frequent use). Smoking increased with age, and frequent use was much more common among white students than other races. Smokeless tobacco use is a predominantly white male activity (Table 5.16).

Secondhand Smoke and Children

The Environmental Protection Agency (EPA), in its 1992 report on environmental tobacco smoke (ETS), concluded that ETS is a major hazard for children whose respiratory, immune, and other systems are not as well developed as those of adults. According to the EPA, second-hand smoke (the smoke produced by other people's cigarettes) causes as many as one million attacks of asthma and more than 25,000 new cases of asthma each year. It also results in hundreds of thousands of lower respiratory infections each year in children, resulting in as many as 15,000 hospitalizations. "Passive" smoking is also responsible for many cases of middle ear disease and reduction in lung function in children

TABLE 5.16

Percentage of current tobacco use among high school students, by gender, race/ethnicity, and grade — United States, Youth Risk Behavior Survey, 1990*

Category	Any tobacco use		Cigarette use[†]		Frequent cigarette use[§]		Smokeless tobacco use	
	%	(95% CI[‡])	%	(95% CI)	%	(95% CI)	%	(95% CI)
Gender								
Female	31.7	(±3.1)	31.3	(±3.1)	12.5	(±2.3)	1.4	(±0.5)
Male	40.4	(±5.1)	33.2	(±4.9)	13.0	(±3.6)	19.1	(±5.1)
Race/Ethnicity								
White	41.2	(±4.2)	36.4	(±3.9)	15.9	(±3.1)	12.6	(±3.5)
Female	36.5	(±3.1)	36.0	(±3.1)	16.6	(±2.7)	1.5	(±0.6)
Male	46.0	(±6.1)	36.8	(±5.6)	15.2	(±4.1)	23.9	(±6.9)
Black	16.8	(±2.9)	16.1	(±2.9)	2.3	(±1.0)	1.9	(±0.9)
Female	15.9	(±4.8)	15.7	(±4.8)	1.8	(±0.9)	0.8	(±0.6)
Male	18.0	(±3.3)	16.8	(±3.6)	3.0	(±1.8)	3.1	(±1.8)
Hispanic	32.0	(±4.5)	30.8	(±4.3)	7.4	(±1.6)	5.7	(±2.3)
Female	27.4	(±5.9)	27.2	(±5.8)	5.5	(±2.4)	1.0	(±1.0)
Male	37.3	(±6.3)	34.7	(±6.1)	9.6	(±2.6)	10.9	(±4.6)
Grade								
9th	32.1	(±4.9)	29.5	(±4.4)	9.9	(±3.4)	7.8	(±3.0)
10th	33.9	(±4.5)	30.0	(±3.9)	10.8	(±2.4)	10.9	(±2.8)
11th	36.7	(±4.3)	32.8	(±4.6)	12.6	(±2.9)	9.5	(±2.2)
12th	41.2	(±5.6)	36.7	(±5.4)	17.7	(±4.3)	11.9	(±4.3)
Total	**36.0**	**(±3.7)**	**32.3**	**(±3.7)**	**12.8**	**(±2.7)**	**10.1**	**(±2.5)**

*Unweighted sample size = 11,631 students.
[†]Smoking cigarettes at any time during the 30 days preceding the survey.
[§]Smoking cigarettes on more than 25 of the 30 days preceding the survey.
[‡]Confidence interval.

Source: "Tobacco Use Among High School Students—United States, 1990," *1990 Youth Risk Behavior Surveillance System*, Centers for Disease Control, (Atlanta, GA, 1991)

and is considered a risk factor in Sudden Infant Death Syndrome (SIDS). The EPA estimates that one-half to one-third of all children under 5 years of age and millions of older children are exposed to tobacco smoke in the home.

CHILD ABUSE*

It is impossible to determine how many children suffer abuse. Observers can count the number of reported cases, which include only those known to public authorities, or they can survey families, in which case, parents may deny or downplay any abuse. For these reasons, most estimates of child abuse are generally considered low.

In 1963, 150,000 young victims of abuse or neglect came to the attention of authorities (1966, *Juvenile Court Statistics*, WDC: U.S. Children's Bureau); in 1990, an estimated 1.7 million reports on 2.1 million children were investigated (1992, *Working Paper 1: 1990 Summary Data Component*, WDC: National Center on Child Abuse and Neglect). Experts attribute the increased number of reported cases over the past decade to a greater recognition of the problem, not necessarily increased cases of abuse and neglect.

Drs. Richard Gelles and Murray A. Straus, in the *National Family Violence Survey* (1975) and the *National Family Violence Resurvey* (1985), found no statistically significant change in rates of violence to children from 1975 to 1985. However, the rate of severe violence declined from 140 to 107 per 1,000 children, and the rate of very severe violence declined from 36 to 19 per 1,000, a 47 percent decrease. They attributed the decrease to public awareness of abuse, better reporting, and better education.

TABLE 5.17

Comparison of students who were abused with students who were not abused on various risk items

(N = 406 and 21,300)

Item	At Risk	Not At Risk
Suspended from school	23.4	5.6
Attempted suicide	11.6	.6
Involved in pregnancy	4.2	.5
Student sold drugs	3.9	.5
Student used drugs	22.7	2.5
Family used drugs	30.8	2.9
Student used alcohol	24.1	4.2
Parent alcoholic	33.3	3.0
Student arrested	8.4	1.2
Student abused	100	0
Low grades in school	30.5	13.1
Failed courses	21.4	8.7
Overage in grade	30.0	15.9
Retained in grade	32.3	13.9
Excessive absences	17.2	6.7
Low self-esteem	47.5	11.7
Referred special education	21.9	9.6
Low reading scores	21.4	9.2
Parent sick last year	17.7	3.8
Parent died last year	1.7	.9
Parent lost job last year	15.8	3.8
Friend died last year	9.6	4.5
Student ill last year	12.3	3.0
Sibling died last year	2.5	.5
Father low-level job	30.5	16.6
Father not high school graduate	19.0	7.5
Mother low-level job	35.5	19.3
Mother not high school graduate	20.7	8.1
Parents' attitude negative	22.9	4.7
Language not English	5.9	4.9
Broken home	64.5	34.0
Moved frequently	33.5	15.5
Changed schools frequently	31.0	23.2
Parents divorced last year	23.4	6.5

Source: Jack Frymire, *Growing Up is Risky Business, and Schools Are Not to Blame*, Phi Delta Kappa, (Bloomington, IN, 1992)

Jack Frymier, in *Growing Up is Risky Business* (1992, Phi Delta Kappa), a project funded by the Ford Foundation, the John D. and Catherine T. MacArthur Foundation, and Phi Delta International, compared students who were abused with those who were not on a number of items. Those students who were abused were significantly higher on such measures as coming from a broken home, parents being alcoholics, and a variety of other crisis events (Table 5.17).

---

*For a complete discussion of Child Abuse, see *Domestic Violence—No Longer Behind the Curtain*, Information Plus (Wylie, TX 75098)

MISSING CHILDREN

During the 1980s, as a result of several prominent abductions and tragedies, the media focused public attention on the problem of missing children. Citizens became concerned and demanded action to address what appeared to be a national crisis. Congress, attempting to discover the nature and dimension of the problem, passed the 1984 Missing Children's Act (PL 98-473) that mandated the Office of Juvenile Justice and Delinquency (OJJDP) to conduct national incidence studies to determine the number of juveniles who were "victims of abduction by strangers" and those who were victims of "parental kidnappings." The resulting *National Incidence Studies of Missing, Abducted, Runaway, and Thrownaway Children* (NISMART) gave the first estimate based on comprehensive scientific investigation regarding children: 1) abducted by family members, 2) abducted by non-family members, 3) who ran away from home, 4) who were thrown out of home or abandoned, and 5) who were lost or missing because of an injury or other reasons. All estimates are for 1988.

Data Collection and Definitions

NISMART collected data from six separate sources: a randomly selected household survey; juvenile facilities, such as boarding schools and group homes; police records; reanalysis of FBI homicide data; and agencies that have contact with children.

Because of the difficulties in defining each of the problems, NISMART found it necessary to estimate the incidence of each problem according to at least two definitions. The first, "broad scope," generally defined the problem the way the families might define it, including not only serious episodes, but minor episodes that would be alarming to those involved. The second, "policy focal," defined the problem from the perspective of the police and other social agencies, restricting the episodes to those of a more serious nature in which children were at risk and in need of immediate intervention. Consequently, policy focal cases are a subdivision of broad scope cases. Tables 5.18 and 5.19 detail the NISMART definitions and criteria for family abduction, runaways, thrownaways, and non-family abduction.

Family Abductions

Family abductions are a side-effect of the growing number of divorces that involve children—divorce has tripled to a million a year over the past three

---

TABLE 5.18

NISMART Definitions—Criteria for Family Abduction, Runaways, and Thrownaways

	Broad Scope	**Policy Focal**
Family Abduction	An incident during which a family member in violation of a custody agreement or decree: ♦ Takes a child; or ♦ Fails to return or give a child over at the end of a legal agreed-upon visit, and the child is away at least overnight.	An incident that *in addition to meeting the broad scope criteria* involves the following: ♦ An attempt is made to conceal the taking or whereabouts of the child or to prevent contact with the child; or ♦ The child is transported out of State; or ♦ There is evidence that the abductor had the intent to keep the child indefinitely or permanently affect custodial privileges.
Runaways	Incidents during which children who leave: ♦ Are away from home at least 1 night; or ♦ Are under the age of 15 and stay away from home without permission for at least 1 night; or ♦ Are 15 or older and stay away at least 2 nights.	Incidents that *in addition to meeting the broad scope criteria* involve children who: ♦ Are without a familiar and secure place to stay; or ♦ Have run away from juvenile facilities.
Thrownaways	Incidents involving children who were away from home at least overnight, and: ♦ Were directly told to leave the household; or ♦ Were abandoned or deserted; or ♦ Wanted to come home but were denied permission; or ♦ Ran away, but whose parent(s) or caretaker(s) made no effort to recover them or did not care whether they returned.	Incidents that *in addition to meeting the broad scope criteria* involve children who: ♦ Were without a familiar and secure place to stay; or ♦ Were abandoned.

Source: Robert W. Street, "Missing Children: Found Facts," *NIJ Reports*, (WDC, 1990)

TABLE 5.19

NISMART Definitions—Criteria for Non-Family Abduction

	Policy Focal	
	Legal Definition	**Stereotypical**
Non-Family Abduction	An incident involving: ♦ The coerced and unauthorized taking of a child into a building or vehicle, or a distance of more than 20 feet; or ♦ The detention of a child for more than an hour; or ♦ The luring of a child for the purposes of committing another crime.	An incident that *in addition to meeting the legal definition criteria* involves abduction by a stranger whereby: ♦ The child is gone overnight; or ♦ The child is killed; or ♦ The child is transported a distance of 50 miles or more; or ♦ The child is ransomed; or ♦ The perpetrator evidences an intent to keep the child permanently.

Source: Robert W. Street, "Missing Children: Found Facts," *NIJ Reports*, (WDC, 1990)

decades. An estimated 10 million children live with separated or divorced parents. An estimated 15 percent of divorces produce battles over custody and visitation rights. Family abductions extend from cases in which the non-custodial parent kept the children overnight in violation of agreed upon terms (broad scope) to those in which they transport children across state lines with the intent of keeping them (policy focal).

Table 5.20 shows an estimated 354,100 broad scope family abductions in 1988. In contrast, an estimated 163,200 policy focal family abductions took place, or 46 percent of broad scope cases. Family abductions had the largest estimated incidence of any policy focal category.

Non-Family Abductions

Although far fewer children are abducted by strangers than by family members, the consequences are often far worse. As a result, all nonfamily abductions are counted in the more serious policy focal category. There is further distinction between the more inclusive legal definition abduction (3,200 to 4,600 children) which includes coerced taking, forcible detaining, or luring of a child, and the more exclusive stereotypical kidnapping (200 to 300), which may involve ransom demands and even murder.

Violence is prevalent in non-family abductions. Force was used against 87 percent of the victims, and a weapon was involved in 75 percent of the cases. About 2 percent of legal definition abductions ended in the murder of the child.

Runaways

Broad scope runaways (450,700) left or stayed away from home at least overnight or ran away from juvenile facilities (group foster homes, residential treatment centers, boarding school, juvenile detention centers). The criteria for being considered a runaway depends on age and amount of time away: two nights for those

TABLE 5.20

Estimates	Estimated Number of Children in 1988
Family Abductions	
Broad Scope	354,100
Policy Focal	163,200
Non-Family Abductions	
Legal Definition Abductions	3,200–4,600
Stereotypical Kidnappings	200–300
Runaways	
Broad Scope	450,700
Policy Focal	133,500
Thrownaways	
Broad Scope	127,100
Policy Focal	59,200
Lost, Injured, or Otherwise Missing	
Broad Scope	438,200
Policy Focal	139,100

Source: David Finkelhor, et al, *Missing, Abducted, Runaway and Thrownaway Children in America*, Office of Juvenile Justice and Delinquency Prevention, (WDC, 1990)

age 15 year or older, and one night for those 14 years or younger. Of the broad scope runaways, 133,500 were policy focal runaways who did not have a secure, familiar place to stay. Almost all runaways are teenagers, the majority of whom are girls (58 percent). A disproportionate number of runaway teens are from families with step-parents or live-in boyfriends or girlfriends.

Thrownaways

About 127,100 children fit the definitions for broad scope thrownaways in 1988. There were an estimated 59,200 policy focal thrownaways.

The label "throwaways" was given by researchers in the 1970s to juveniles who were made to leave home or were abandoned. The NISMART researchers revised the term on the rationale that "'(T)hrowaway'... connotes a quality of the child - uselessness or disposability. *Thrownaway,*' by contrast, unambiguously conveys what has been *done to the child.*" (Researcher's italics.)

The NISMART researchers also called into question the term "missing." They note:

A "missing" child . . . presumes that the parents want the child, and "miss" the child. In the case of the thrownaway, however, parents may not want the child back or may have themselves left and abandoned the child. If such parents do not know where the child is, it is out of choice.

Thrownaways are about 22 percent of the pooled group of runaways and thrownaways, which had simply been labeled runaways in the past. Fewer than 20 percent of children who were thrownaways lived with both parents. They were also twice as likely to have been the victims of domestic violence prior to their leaving than those who ran away (27 percent versus 11 percent).

TABLE 5.21

Deaths, by Age and Leading Cause: 1989

Excludes deaths of nonresidents of the United States. Deaths classified according to ninth revision of *International Classification of Diseases.*

AGE AND LEADING CAUSE OF DEATH	NUMBER OF DEATHS (1,000)			DEATH RATE PER 100,000 POPULATION		
	Total	Male	Female	Total	Male	Female
ALL AGES [1]						
All races [2]	2,150.5	1,114.2	1,036.3	866.3	921.0	814.3
White	1,853.8	950.9	903.0	887.2	930.2	846.0
Black	267.6	146.4	121.2	873.0	1,006.5	752.4
Leading causes of death:						
Heart disease	733.8	368.2	365.7	295.6	304.3	287.3
Malignant neoplasms (cancer)	496.2	263.3	232.8	199.9	217.6	183.0
Stroke (cerebrovascular disease)	145.5	57.3	88.2	58.6	47.4	69.3
Accidents	95.0	63.9	31.1	38.3	52.8	24.5
Chronic obstructive pulmonary disease	84.3	48.2	36.2	34.0	39.8	28.4
Pneumonia	76.6	35.7	40.8	30.8	29.5	32.1
Diabetes	46.8	19.7	27.1	18.9	16.3	21.3
Suicide	30.2	24.1	6.1	12.2	19.9	4.8
Chronic liver disease, cirrhosis	26.7	17.3	9.4	10.8	14.3	7.4
Homicide and legal intervention	22.9	17.7	5.2	9.2	14.6	4.1
1 TO 14 YEARS OLD						
All causes	16.2	9.5	6.7	32.4	37.3	27.4
Leading causes of death:						
Accidents	6.9	4.4	2.5	13.7	17.2	10.1
Malignant neoplasms (cancer)	1.7	0.9	0.7	3.3	3.6	3.0
Congenital anomalies	1.4	0.7	0.7	2.8	2.7	2.9
Homicide and legal intervention	0.9	0.5	0.4	1.8	2.0	1.6
Heart disease	0.6	0.3	0.3	1.2	1.2	1.1
Pneumonia and influenza	0.4	0.2	0.2	0.7	0.7	0.7
15 TO 24 YEARS OLD						
All causes	36.5	27.2	9.3	99.9	147.2	51.6
Leading causes of death:						
Accidents	16.7	12.6	4.1	45.8	68.5	22.7
Motor vehicle	12.9	9.4	3.5	35.4	51.1	19.5
Homicide and legal intervention	6.2	5.1	1.1	16.9	27.7	5.9
Suicide	4.9	4.1	0.8	13.3	22.2	4.2
Malignant neoplasms (cancer)	1.9	1.1	0.8	5.1	5.8	4.3
Heart disease	0.9	0.6	0.3	2.6	3.2	1.9
HIV infection [3]	0.6	0.5	0.1	1.7	2.7	0.6
25 TO 44 YEARS OLD						
All causes	141.4	99.5	42.0	176.1	248.9	103.9
Leading causes of death:						
Accidents	28.4	21.9	6.5	35.4	54.8	16.2
Motor vehicle	16.6	12.2	4.4	20.6	30.4	10.9
Malignant neoplasms (cancer)	21.1	9.5	11.5	26.2	23.8	28.6
HIV infection [3]	16.3	14.6	1.7	20.3	36.6	4.2
Heart disease	15.2	11.2	4.0	19.0	28.0	10.0
Suicide	11.9	9.4	2.4	14.8	23.6	6.1
Homicide and legal intervention	11.2	8.8	2.4	13.9	22.0	5.8
45 TO 64 YEARS OLD						
All causes	378.3	234.4	143.9	813.3	1,050.8	595.1
Leading causes of death:						
Malignant neoplasms (cancer)	135.2	73.3	62.0	290.9	328.5	256.2
Heart disease	112.3	79.3	33.0	241.5	355.4	136.4
Stroke (cerebrovascular disease)	15.1	8.1	7.0	32.5	36.4	28.9
Accidents	15.0	10.8	4.2	32.4	48.4	17.5
Chronic obstructive pulmonary disease	13.0	7.1	5.9	28.0	32.0	24.4
Chronic liver disease and cirrhosis	11.5	7.9	3.6	24.7	35.4	14.8
Diabetes	9.7	4.9	4.8	20.9	22.1	19.8
65 YEARS OLD AND OVER						
All causes	1,537.8	720.8	817.0	4,963.0	5,704.4	4,452.4
Leading causes of death:						
Heart disease	604.0	276.3	327.6	1,949.2	2,186.8	1,785.6
Malignant neoplasms (cancer)	336.2	178.4	157.8	1,065.1	1,412.1	859.9
Stroke (cerebrovascular disease)	126.7	47.2	79.5	408.8	373.6	433.0
Chronic obstructive pulmonary disease	70.0	40.3	29.7	225.8	319.0	161.8
Pneumonia and influenza	67.4	30.0	37.4	217.5	237.2	204.0
Diabetes	34.8	13.4	21.4	112.3	106.0	116.8
Accidents	26.8	13.5	13.3	86.6	107.0	72.5

[1] Includes those deaths with age not stated. [2] Includes other races, not shown separately. [3] Human immunodeficiency virus.

Source: U.S. National Center for Health Statistics, *Vital Statistics of the United States,* annual; and unpublished data.

Lost, Injured, or Otherwise Missing

Lost, injured, or otherwise missing is the catch-all category for children who are missing from their caretakers and do not fit into any other category. The broad scope defines these cases based on the child's age, disability, the amount of time missing, and whether the absence was due to an injury. An estimated 438,200 children fit this definition in 1988. A lost child is the classic missing child. However, children could also be missing because they lost track of the time or misunderstood when they should be home. Of these, 139,100 fit the focal policy definition because their caretakers contacted the police.

Even for lost children, being part of a two-parent family can make a difference. Only one out of three lost or injured children were from intact two-parent families. Almost half (47 percent) were under age 5.

MORTALITY AMONG CHILDREN

The National Center for Health Statistics, in *Trends and Current Status in Childhood Mortality: United States, 1900-85* (Hyattsville, MD, 1989), found large declines in childhood death rates during the last half of the 20th century. The majority of childhood deaths are from injuries and violence. There are also large racial and sex differences, especially regarding injury deaths. While death rates for all ages decreased, the largest declines were among children. Table 5.21 shows the leading causes of death, accidents being the leading cause of death among youths.

External Causes

Since 1968, the external-cause death rate for children has declined. External causes include motor vehicle injuries, drownings, homicide, and fire.

Motor Vehicle Injuries

In recent years, motor vehicle injury death rates have declined for each of the age groups. However, at ages 15-19, white males have had and continue to have the highest death rates. Black females have consistently had the lowest death rates for motor vehicle injuries.

Fires

Fires are responsible for the deaths of more young black children than any other cause of death. In 1968 and 1985, fires were the first and second leading causes of death among black children ages 1-4 and 5-9, respectively. Fire caused relatively few deaths among those ages 10-14 and 15-19 for any race. At this age, children are better able to escape from burning buildings.

TABLE 5.22

Death Rates From Accidents and Violence: 1970 to 1989

Rates are per 100,000 population. Excludes deaths of nonresidents of the United States. Beginning 1980, deaths classified according to the ninth revision of the *International Classification of Diseases.* ɹendix III]

CAUSE OF DEATH AND AGE	WHITE						BLACK					
	Male			Female			Male			Female		
	1970	1980	1989	1970	1980	1989	1970	1980	1989	1970	1980	1989
Total [1]	101.9	97.1	81.1	42.4	36.3	32.8	183.2	154.0	138.6	51.7	42.6	39.4
Motor vehicle accidents	39.1	35.9	27.0	14.8	12.8	12.1	44.3	31.1	28.3	13.4	8.3	9.3
All other accidents	38.2	30.4	24.5	18.3	14.4	12.7	63.3	46.0	37.0	22.5	18.6	15.0
Suicide	18.0	19.9	21.4	7.1	5.9	5.2	8.0	10.3	12.2	2.6	2.2	2.4
Homicide	6.8	10.9	8.2	2.1	3.2	2.8	67.6	66.6	61.1	13.3	13.5	12.9
15 to 24 years old	130.7	138.6	107.1	34.9	37.3	32.7	234.3	162.0	188.0	45.5	35.0	33.9
25 to 34 years old	96.6	118.4	96.0	23.8	29.0	26.6	384.4	256.9	205.9	76.0	49.4	47.4
35 to 44 years old	85.7	94.1	80.4	25.8	29.2	24.7	345.2	218.1	184.9	77.2	43.2	40.8
45 to 54 years old	87.5	90.8	73.8	30.4	31.8	25.5	303.3	207.3	144.0	65.5	40.2	30.8
55 to 64 years old	101.5	92.3	80.1	36.3	33.8	28.7	242.4	188.5	130.6	56.0	47.3	37.3
65 years old and over	216.9	163.9	151.9	122.4	87.2	81.4	220.0	215.8	187.1	107.9	102.9	87.8
65 to 74 years old	128.0	116.7	101.4	57.7	46.4	42.2	217.4	182.2	146.3	81.5	68.7	56.0
75 to 84 years old	229.3	209.2	197.5	149.0	101.5	92.0	236.0	261.4	230.2	140.1	137.5	101.5
85 years old and over	466.7	438.5	431.9	391.4	268.1	228.0	271.8	379.2	404.2	214.3	235.7	222.4

[1] Includes persons under 15 years old, not shown separately.

Source: Natinal Center for Health Statistics

TABLE 5.23

Percentage of high school students who reported carrying a weapon at least once during the 30 days preceding the survey, by race/ethnicity and gender — United States, Youth Risk Behavior Survey, 1990*

Race/ Ethnicity	Male		Female		Total	
	%	(95% CI[†])	%	(95% CI)	%	(95% CI)
White	28.6	(23.8–33.4)	5.3	(4.0– 6.6)	16.8	(13.9–19.7)
Black	39.4	(34.8–44.0)	16.7	(12.6–20.8)	27.2	(23.9–30.5)
Hispanic	41.1	(37.0–45.2)	12.2	(9.3–15.1)	25.8	(22.7–28.9)
Total	31.5	(27.6–35.4)	8.1	(6.5– 9.7)	19.6	(17.1–22.1)

*Unweighted sample size = 11,631 students.
†Confidence interval.

Source: "Weapon-Carrying Among High School Students—United States, 1990," *1990 Youth Risk Behavior Surveillance System*, Centers for Disease Control, (Atlanta, GA, 1991)

Homicide

Death rates from homicide have been increasing since 1968. Homicide has been and is the leading cause of death for black teenagers, both male and females. Since 1978, it has become the third leading cause of death for white male teenagers.

In 1989, young black males (15 to 24 years of age) died from homicide at an annual rate of 188 per 100,000. White males died from homicide at the rate of 107 per 100,000; black females, 34 per 100,000; and white females, 33 per 100,000. The overwhelming majority of deaths among young black males were firearm-associated (Table 5.22).

From 1980 through 1989, more than 11,000 persons died in the U.S. as a result of homicides committed by high-school aged youth using weapons. Firearms accounted for 65 percent of these homicides. The 1990 *Youth Risk Behavior Survey* reported that nearly 20 percent of all students in grades 9 through 12 claimed to have carried a weapon at least once within the previous 30 days. Males were significantly more likely to carry a weapon (32 percent) than females (8 percent). Hispanics (26 percent) and blacks (27 percent) were more likely to carry a weapon than whites (17 percent). (See Table 5.23.)

Suicide

Suicide rates for adolescents 15-19 years of age have quadrupled from 2.7 per 100,000 in 1950 to 11.3 in 1989. Suicide rates have always been considerably higher for white than black teenagers and higher for males than females. Since 1968, teenage suicide mortality has been increasing for all race-sex groups, except black females (for whom the rates are lowest). The highest rates continue to be among white males. (See Table 5.24.)

TABLE 5.24

Suicide Rates, by Sex, Race, and Age Group: 1970 to 1989
[See headnote, tables 117 and 122]

AGE	TOTAL [1]			MALE						FEMALE					
				White			Black			White			Black		
	1970	1980	1989	1970	1980	1989	1970	1980	1989	1970	1980	1989	1970	1980	1989
All ages [2]	11.6	11.9	12.2	18.0	19.9	21.4	8.0	10.3	12.2	7.1	5.9	5.2	2.6	2.2	2.4
10 to 14 years old	0.6	0.8	1.4	1.1	1.4	2.2	0.3	0.5	1.7	0.3	0.3	0.7	0.4	0.1	(B)
15 to 19 years old	5.9	8.5	11.3	9.4	15.0	19.4	4.7	5.6	10.3	2.9	3.3	4.5	2.9	1.6	2.3
20 to 24 years old	12.2	16.1	15.3	19.3	27.8	26.8	18.7	20.0	23.7	5.7	5.9	4.3	4.9	3.1	3.4
25 to 34 years old	14.1	16.0	15.0	19.9	25.6	24.9	19.2	21.8	22.0	9.0	7.5	5.9	5.7	4.1	3.7
35 to 44 years old	16.9	15.4	14.6	23.3	23.5	23.8	12.6	15.6	18.1	13.0	9.1	7.1	3.7	4.6	3.9
45 to 54 years old	20.0	15.9	14.6	29.5	24.2	24.2	13.8	12.0	10.9	13.5	10.2	8.0	3.7	2.8	3.0
55 to 64 years old	21.4	15.9	15.5	35.0	25.8	26.6	10.6	11.7	10.4	12.3	9.1	7.9	2.0	2.3	2.5
65 years and over	20.8	17.8	20.1	41.1	37.5	43.5	8.7	11.4	15.7	8.5	6.5	6.3	2.6	1.4	1.8
65 to 74 years over	20.8	16.9	18.0	38.7	32.5	35.1	8.7	11.1	15.4	9.6	7.0	6.4	2.9	1.7	(B)
75 to 84 years over	21.2	19.1	23.1	45.5	45.5	55.3	8.9	10.5	14.7	7.2	5.7	6.3	1.7	1.4	(B)
85 years and over	19.0	19.2	22.8	45.8	52.8	71.9	8.7	18.9	(B)	5.8	5.8	6.2	2.8	.	(B)

- Represents or rounds to zero. B Base figure too small to meet statistical standards for reliability of a derived figure.
[1] Includes other races, not shown separately. [2] Includes other age groups, not shown separately.

Source: National Center for Health Statistics

The 1990 *Youth Risk Behavior Survey* questioned students in grades 9 through 12 regarding their thoughts about suicide. During the year preceding the survey, 27.3 percent of all students in grades 9-12 reported that they had thought about attempting suicide. Sixteen percent had actually made a specific plan to attempt suicide. About half the students who made a plan actually made an attempt. Two percent of the students made an attempt that required medical attention. Blacks were less likely to consider or attempt suicide. (See Table 5.25.) The suicide rate

TABLE 5.25

Percentage of high school students reporting suicide ideation and suicidal behavior,* by gender and race/ethnicity — United States, Youth Risk Behavior Survey, 1990[†]

Category	Suicide ideation %	Suicide ideation (95% CI[c])	Made specific suicide plans %	Made specific suicide plans (95% CI)	≥1 Suicide attempt(s) %	≥1 Suicide attempt(s) (95% CI)	Suicide attempt requiring medical attention[§] %	Suicide attempt requiring medical attention[§] (95% CI)
Gender								
Female	33.9	(31.6–36.2)	20.2	(18.5–21.8)	10.3	(9.0–11.6)	2.5	(2.0–2.9)
Male	20.5	(18.2–22.7)	12.3	(10.3–14.3)	6.2	(4.8– 7.5)	1.6	(1.1–2.2)
Race/Ethnicity								
Hispanic	30.4	(27.4–33.3)	19.5	(17.0–22.0)	12.0	(10.3–13.6)	2.4	(1.6–3.1)
White	28.1	(25.6–30.6)	16.1	(14.4–17.7)	7.9	(6.6– 9.2)	2.1	(1.6–2.5)
Black	20.4	(17.1–23.7)	13.5	(10.0–16.9)	6.5	(5.4– 7.7)	1.4	(0.8–2.1)
Total	27.3	(25.2–29.4)	16.3	(14.8–17.8)	8.3	(7.2– 9.4)	2.1	(1.7–2.4)

*During the 12 months preceding the survey.
[†]Unweighted sample size = 11,631.
[§]Resulted in an injury or poisoning that had to be treated by a doctor or nurse.
[c]Confidence interval.

Source: "Attempted Suicide Among High School Students—United States, 1990," *1990 Youth Risk Behavior Surveillance System*, Centers for Disease Control,

---

TABLE 5.26

Comparison of students who attempted suicide with students who did not attempt suicide on various risk items

(N = 176 and 21,530)

Item	At Risk	Not At Risk
Suspended from school	29.5	5.8
Attempted suicide	100	0
Involved in pregnancy	6.3	.5
Student sold drugs	5.1	.5
Student used drugs	40.9	2.6
Family used drugs	22.7	3.3
Student used alcohol	46.0	4.3
Parent alcoholic	23.9	3.4
Student arrested	14.2	1.2
Student abused	26.7	1.7
Low grades in school	23.9	13.3
Failed courses	26.1	8.8
Overage in grade	21.6	16.2
Retained in grade	23.9	14.2
Excessive absences	26.1	6.7
Low self-esteem	38.6	12.2
Referred special education	15.3	9.8
Low reading scores	8.0	9.4
Parent sick last year	24.4	3.9
Parent died last year	4.0	.9
Parent lost job last year	18.8	3.9
Friend died last year	26.7	4.4
Student ill last year	27.3	3.0
Sibling died last year	2.8	.5
Father low-level job	13.6	16.9
Father not high school graduate	11.4	7.7
Mother low-level job	15.9	19.7
Mother not high school graduate	18.2	8.3
Parents' attitude negative	8.5	5.0
Language not English	7.4	4.9
Broken home	57.4	34.4
Moved frequently	27.3	15.7
Changed schools frequently	30.1	23.3
Parents divorced last year	18.8	6.4

Source: Jack Frymire, *Growing Up is Risky Business, and Schools Are Not to Blame*, Phi Delta Kappa, (Bloomington, IN, 1992)

---

among male homosexual teens is believed to be extremely high, although statistics are difficult to compile because sexual orientation is not part of public records or is often unknown to families.

Jack Frymier, in *Growing Up is Risky Business* (1992, Phi Delta Kappa), compared those students who attempted suicide with those who had not on a variety of risk items. Among the characteristics that were much higher for those who attempted suicide were drug and alcohol use, low self-esteem, and broken homes. Other crisis events were also more common to this group of students than to other students. (See Table 5.26.)

Dr. David Clark, a Chicago researcher, reports that the presence of a loaded handgun in the house is a potent risk factor for suicide among children. Sixty percent of the teenagers killed themselves with guns and, he reported, children of law enforcement officers, most of whom keep guns at home, account for a disproportionate number of suicides due to the access of guns.

The presence of a number of factors in a child's profile increases the likelihood of suicide. Among those factors are depression, substance abuse, behavioral disorders, the presence of a handgun, and a tendency toward perfectionism.

TABLE 5.27		
Firearm Death Rates Among Adolescents and Young Adults, by Race, Gender, and Age, 1988		
(Deaths per 100,000 Population in Specified Group)		
Gender, Age	White	Black
Male		
10-14	4.2	7.8
15-19	21.7	79.5
20-24	29.8	119.2
Female		
10-14	1.1	3.6
15-19	3.8	8.4
20-24	4.5	13.9

Source: National Center for Health Statistics.

Natural Causes

Since 1968, the leading natural causes of childhood death have been malignant neoplasms (cancers) and congenital anomalies (birth defects). In 1989, these two causes accounted for 37 percent of all childhood deaths from natural causes. The remaining deaths were spread across a variety of diseases, including heart disease, pneumonia, influenza, and HIV infection.

Firearm Deaths Among Children and Youth

The number of youths dying as a result of firearms has increased. The National Center for Health Statistics reports that since 1988, American teenage boys have been more likely to die from gunshot wounds than from all natural causes combined. From 1979 to 1984 the firearm death rate for teenagers ages 15 to 19 decreased 11 percent to 12.4 deaths per 100,000. After 1984, however, the rate increased 43 percent, rising to 17.7 deaths per 100,000 in 1988. The increases were largely concentrated among black males, who had a reate of death from firearms of 79.5 per 100,000 for 15 to 19 year olds and 119.2 per 100,000 among those 20 to 24 years. (See Table 5.27.)

With each age group, the causes of firearms deaths vary. Homicide and unintentional deaths each account for about half of the firearm deaths among children 1-9 years of age. At 10-14 years of age, suicide, homicide, and unintentional death each account for about one-third of the firearm deaths. Among teenagers, homicide accounts for 48 percent of the deaths, suicide for another 42 percent, and unintentional deaths for 8 percent.

If all homicide deaths are considered, the proportion of homicide deaths due to guns rose from 12 percent among 1 to 4 years olds to 39 percent of 5 to 9 years olds to 65 percent among 10 to 14 year olds to 71 percent of the homicide deaths among teenagers 15 to 19 years old. Among black males 15 to 19 years old, 82 percent of homicide deaths were caused by firearms. Similarly, 60 percent of suicide deaths among males 10 to 14 years of age and 15 to 19 years of age resulted from guns.*

---

* The National Center for Health Statistics points out that these data are based on <u>deaths</u> from firearms. It is likely that case-fatality rates have declined over the past two decades due to improvements in emergency medical treatment—today they can save the lives of more people who suffer from gunshot wounds than they could 20 years ago. Thus, the increase in firearm-related deaths among teenagers probably masks an even larger increase in the number of firearm-related incidents and injuries.

CHAPTER VI

GETTING AN EDUCATION

Amid the controversy surrounding the quality and direction of American education, the United States still remains one of the best educated nations in the world. In 1990, approximately 68 million Americans were involved, either directly or indirectly, in providing or receiving formal education. About 60.2 million people were enrolled in schools and colleges, while 3.5 million instructors were teaching at the elementary, secondary, or college level. Another 3.8 million were professional, administrative, and support staff at educational institutions (Table 6.1).

MOST CHILDREN ATTEND SCHOOL

Between 1965 (the earliest year for which data is available) and 1990, the percentage of 3- and 4-year-olds enrolled in school more than quadrupled, from about 11 percent to more than 44 percent. Similarly, the proportion of children 5 and 6 years old enrolled in school more than doubled from 1940 to 1990. Over 95 percent of all young people from 7 to 17 years old are attending school. The proportion of young people in school drops sharply to 57 percent among 18-and-19-year-olds, when

---

TABLE 6.1

Estimated number of participants in elementary and secondary education and in higher education: Fall 1990

[In millions]

Participants	All levels (elementary, secondary, and higher education)	Elementary and secondary schools			Institutions of higher education
		Total	Public	Private	
1	2	3	4	5	6
Total	67.5	51.2	45.5	5.7	16.3
Enrollment[1]	60.2	46.2	41.0	5.2	14.0
Teachers and faculty	3.5	2.7	2.4	0.4	[2]0.8
Other professional, administrative, and support staff	3.8	2.3	2.1	0.2	1.6

[1] Includes enrollments in local public school systems and in most private schools (religiously affiliated and nonsectarian). Excludes subcollegiate departments of institutions of higher education, residential schools for exceptional children, and Federal schools. Elementary and secondary includes most kindergarten and some nursery school enrollment. Excludes preprimary enrollment in schools that do not offer first grade or above. Higher education comprises full-time and part-time students enrolled in degree-credit and nondegree-credit programs in universities, other four-year colleges, and two-year colleges.

[2] Includes full-time and part-time faculty with the rank of instructor or above.

NOTE.—The enrollment figures include all students in elementary and secondary schools and colleges and universities. However, the data for teachers and other staff in public and private elementary and secondary schools are reported in terms of full-time equivalents. The staff data for institutions of higher education include all full-time and part-time professional, administrative, and support personnel. Because of rounding, details may not add to totals.

SOURCE: U.S. Department of Education, National Center for Education Statistics, unpublished projections and estimates. (This table was prepared April 1991.)

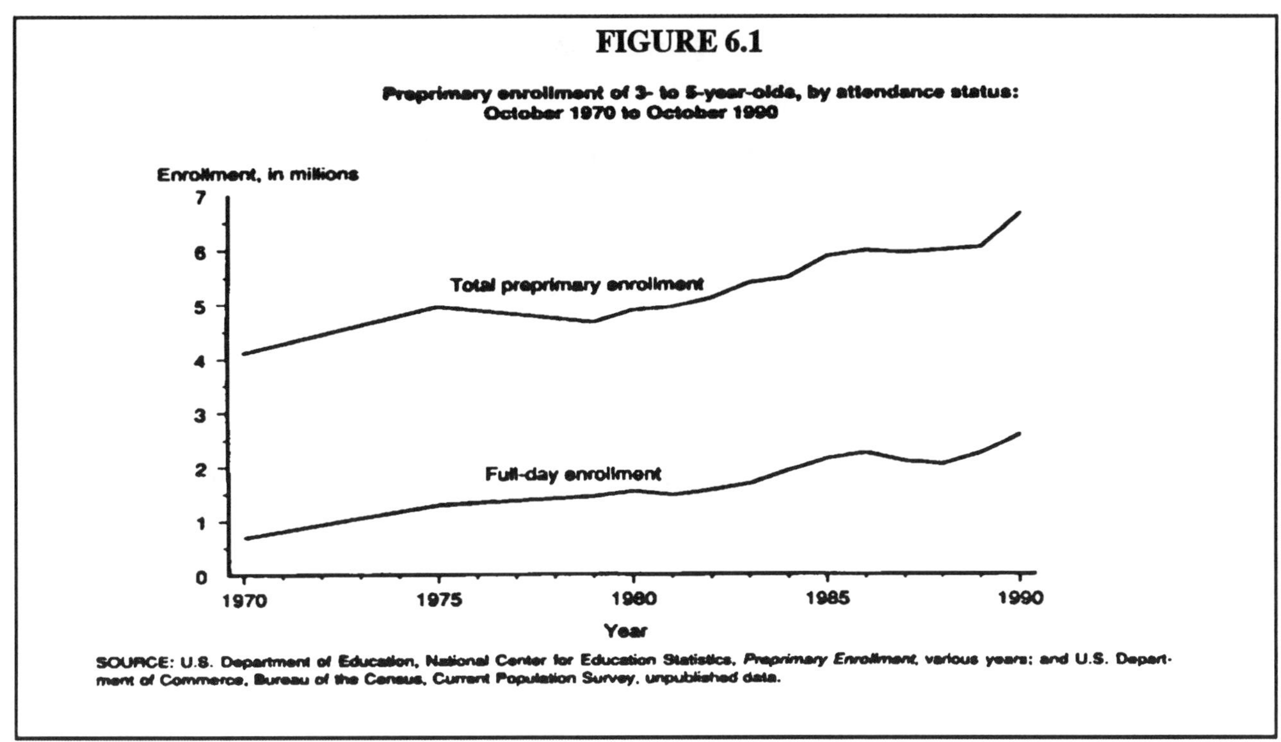

young people graduate from or leave high school and may not go on to any form of higher education.

PREPRIMARY, ELEMENTARY, AND SECONDARY ENROLLMENT

Preprimary, elementary, and secondary school enrollments reflect the number of births over a specified period. After World War II, the nation experienced a "baby boom" as returning soldiers settled down to start families. Consequently, school enrollment grew rapidly during the 1950s and 1960s when the "babies" matured to school age. Elementary enrollment reached a record high in 1969, and high school enrollment peaked in 1971. Since the late 1960s, however, the birth rate has declined, resulting in a steadily declining school enrollment. An "echo effect" occurred in the late 1970s and early 1980s when those born during the baby boom began their own families. This "echo effect" triggered a small increase in school enrollment in the early 1990s. In 1985, public and secondary school enrollment increased for the first time since 1971, and public enrollment has increased steadily since reaching 40.5 million in 1989.

Preprimary Growth

In contrast to the declining elementary and secondary school enrollment during the 1970s and early 1980s, preprimary enrollment showed substantial growth. Between 1970 and 1980, preprimary enrollment rose by 19 percent, from 4.1 million to 4.9 million. From 1980 to 1990, enrollment rose 37 percent to 6.7 million. This increase does not indicate growth in the number of young people ages 3 to 5, but rather the availability and interest in preschool education. In 1965, 12.5 million children were in this age group, but only 27 percent were enrolled in nursery school or kindergarten. By 1990, 59 percent of the 11.2 million preschool-aged children in this country were enrolled in preprimary programs.

An important factor in the increased participation of young children in preprimary programs is the high proportion in full-day programs. In 1990, almost two-fifths (39 percent) of young children attended school all day compared to 32 percent in 1980 and 17 percent in 1970, a direct consequence of increased labor force participation by mothers of young children (Figure 6.1).

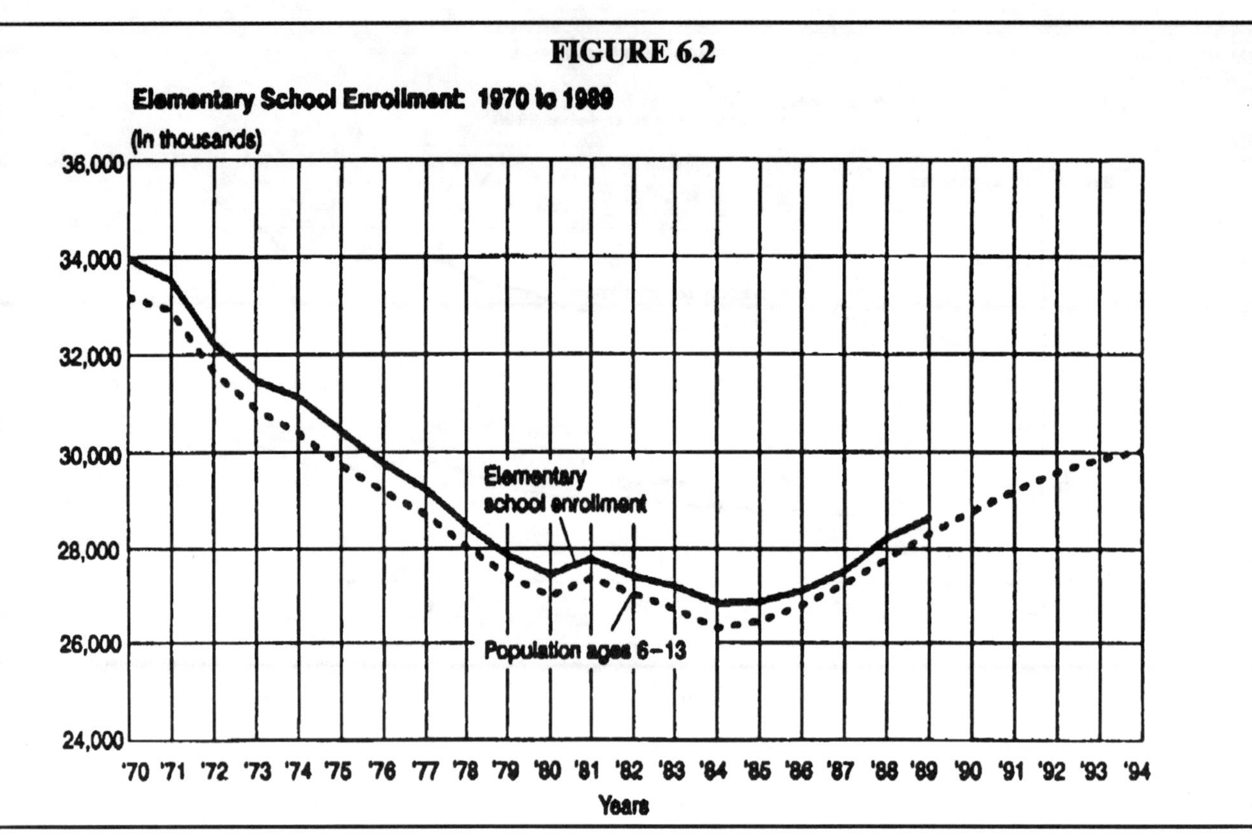

FIGURE 6.3

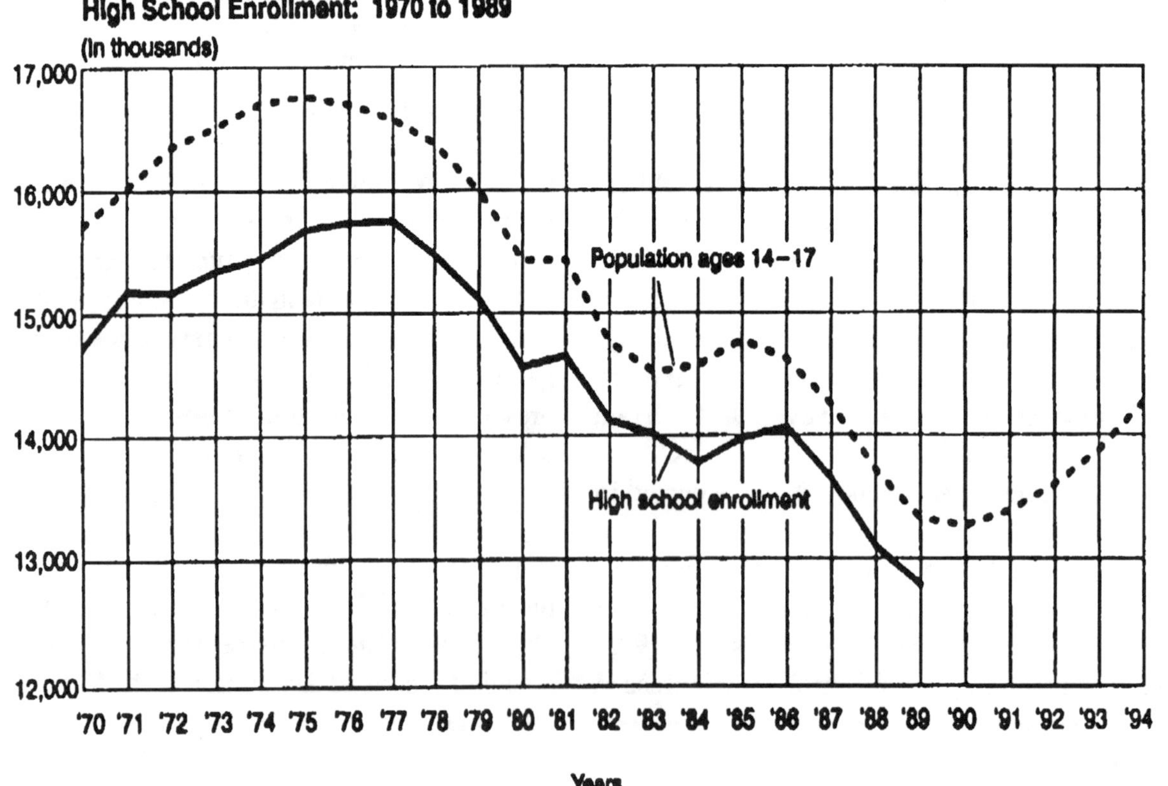

Source of both figures: National Center for Educational Statistics

TABLE 6.2

Private elementary and secondary enrollment and schools, by selected characteristics: 1987–88

Selected characteristics	Kindergarten through 12th grade enrollment[1]				Schools			
	Total	Catholic	Other religious	Non-sectarian	Total	Catholic	Other religious	Non-sectarian
1	2	3	4	5	6	7	8	9
Total	5,479,368	2,901,809	1,714,852	862,797	26,907	9,527	12,132	5,148
School enrollment								
Less than 150	841,262	177,719	449,991	213,552	13,122	1,820	8,058	3,245
150 to 299	1,744,413	938,072	559,389	246,952	8,125	4,225	2,697	1,203
300 to 499	1,291,757	837,426	318,467	135,864	3,454	2,211	868	374
500 to 749	784,027	467,333	189,650	127,044	1,319	801	315	203
750 or more	817,908	481,259	197,354	(²)	758	470	193	(²)
Percent minority students								
Less than 5%	2,432,130	1,258,384	873,632	300,114	12,435	4,309	6,766	1,360
5%, but less than 20%	1,573,610	766,996	503,369	303,245	7,436	2,306	3,275	1,855
20%, but less than 50%	671,945	380,109	152,504	139,333	3,239	1,177	1,045	1,017
50% or more	801,682	496,320	185,346	120,015	3,697	1,736	1,046	915
Community type[3]								
Rural/farming	523,494	186,451	216,070	120,973	5,181	1,108	3,359	715
Small city/town	989,361	525,604	317,135	146,621	6,210	2,340	2,916	954
Suburban	1,446,736	786,635	429,390	230,711	5,257	1,925	2,137	1,194
Urban	2,504,081	1,401,756	751,988	350,339	10,150	4,141	3,717	2.292

[1] Only includes prekindergarten and kindergarten students that attend schools which offer first grade or above.

[2] Too few sample cases (fewer than 30) for reliable estimates.

[3] Other types of communities are included in the totals but are not shown separately.

NOTE.—Data are based upon a sample survey and may not be strictly comparable with data reported elsewhere. Includes only schools which offer first grade or above. Because of rounding and missing values in cells with too few sample cases, details may not add to totals.

SOURCE: U.S. Department of Education, National Center for Education Statistics, "Schools and Staffing Survey, 1987–88." (This table was prepared July 1990.)

Enrollment Projections

During the 1990s, enrollment is expected to increase. The kindergarten through eighth grade enrollment, which grew to 29 million in 1989, is expected to rise to 30 million by 1994, an increase which reflects growth in the 6- to 13-year-old population (Figure 6.2).

Grades 9-12 show a different pattern. After secondary enrollment peaked at near 16 million in 1978, it dropped sharply to around 11.4 million in 1990. However, secondary enrollment is projected to exceed 14 million by 1994, reflecting growth in the 13- to 17-year-old population (Figure 6.3).

Expenditures Per Student

The national average per pupil expenditure for students in public elementary and secondary schools was $4,639 for the school year ending 1988-89. Per student expenditures varied significantly by state depending on the state's financial situation, the number of students, the cost of living, as well as the state's commitment to education. Alaska ($7,716), New York ($7,663), and New Jersey ($7,549) had the highest expenditure per student, while Mississippi ($2,874), Utah ($2,579), and Alabama ($3,197) had the lowest. While money spent is not the only indicator of a state's commitment to education or financial ability to offer an education, it is a significant indicator of the education students are receiving.

PRIVATE SCHOOLS

In 1987-88, about 5.5 million students attended about 27,000 private elementary and secondary schools throughout the country (Table 6.2). Private school students made up approximately 11 percent of all students.

Roman Catholic schools constitute almost 36 percent of all private schools. However, economic and social changes have caused a decline in Catho-

FIGURE 6.4

Percentage of 1988 eighth graders who lived with either both natural parents or a single mother, by school type

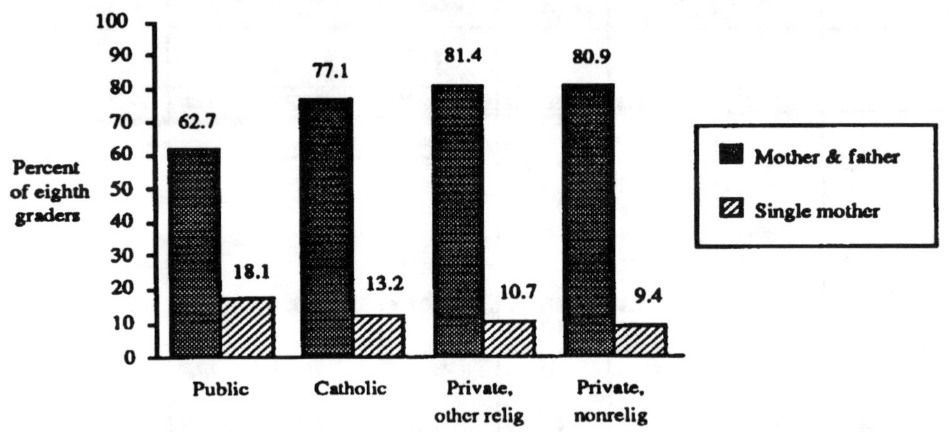

SOURCE: U.S. Department of Education, National Center for Education Statistics, National Education Longitudinal Survey of 1988: "Base-Year Parent Survey."

TABLE 6.3

Ages for compulsory school attendance and compulsory provision of services for special education students, by State: 1989–90

State	Compulsory attendance (November 1989)	Compulsory provision of services for special education (1989–90)	State	Compulsory attendance (November 1989)	Compulsory provision of services for special education (1989–90)
1	2	3	1	2	3
Alabama	7 to 16	5 to 20	Missouri	7 to 16	5 to 20
Alaska	[1]7 to 18	3 to 21	Montana	[6]7 to 16	6 to 18
Arizona	8 to 16	[2]5 to 21	Nebraska	7 to 16	Birth to 20
Arkansas	5 to 17	5 to 20	Nevada	7 to 17	5 to 21
California	6 to 16	[2]5 to 21	New Hampshire	6 to 16	3 to 20
Colorado	7 to 16	[2]5 to 20	New Jersey	6 to 16	3 to 21
Connecticut	7 to 16	3 to 21	New Mexico	6 to 18	3 to 21
Delaware	5 to 16	3 to 20	New York	[7]6 to 16	[3]3 to 21
District of Columbia	7 to 17	[3]3 to 21	North Carolina	7 to 16	5 to 20
Florida	6 to 16	5 to 18	North Dakota	7 to 16	3 to 20
Georgia	7 to 16	5 to 21	Ohio	6 to 18	5 to 21
Hawaii	6 to 18	3 to 20	Oklahoma	7 to 18	4 to 21
Idaho	7 to 16	3 to 20	Oregon	7 to 18	5 to 20
Illinois	7 to 16	3 to 21	Pennsylvania	8 to 17	[9]5 to 21
Indiana	7 to 16	5 to 17	Rhode Island	6 to 16	3 to 20
Iowa	7 to 16	Birth to 20	South Carolina	[8]5 to 17	5 to 20
Kansas	7 to 16	5 to 21	South Dakota	[6]7 to 16	3 to 20
Kentucky	[4]6 to 16	5 to 20	Tennessee	7 to 17	4 to 21
Louisiana	7 to 17	3 to 21	Texas	[9]7 to 17	3 to 21
Maine	7 to 17	5 to 19	Utah	6 to 18	[3]3 to 21
Maryland	6 to 16	Birth to 20	Vermont	7 to 16	[9]5 to 21
Massachusetts	6 to 16	3 to 21	Virginia	5 to 17	2 to 21
Michigan	6 to 16	Birth to 25	Washington	8 to 18	3 to 21
Minnesota	[5]7 to 18	Birth to 20	West Virginia	6 to 16	5 to 22
Mississippi	6 to 14	5 to 20	Wisconsin	6 to 18	3 to 20
			Wyoming	7 to 16	3 to 20

[1] Ages 7 to 16 or high school graduation.
[2] State or local discretion determines at what point in the year children become eligible for services.
[3] State has established two points in the program year by which children must be 3 years of age to be eligible for services.
[4] Must have parental signature for leaving school between ages of 16 and 18.
[5] Takes effect in the year 2000. Currently 7 to 16.
[6] May leave after completion of eighth grade
[7] The ages are 6 to 17 for New York City and Buffalo.
[8] Permits parental waiver of kindergarten at age 5.
[9] Must complete academic year in which 16th birthday occurs.

NOTE.—The Education of the Handicapped Act (EHA) Amendments of 1986 make it mandatory for all States receiving EHA funds to serve all 5- to 18-year-old handicapped children at present and all 3- to 5-year-old handicapped children by 1991.

SOURCE: U.S. Department of Education, Office of Special Education and Rehabilitative Services, *The Twelfth Annual Report to Congress on the Implementation of the Education of the Handicapped Act, 1990*; Education Commission of the States; "Compulsory School Age Requirements, March 1987," and unpublished revisions. (This table was prepared March 1991.)

lic school enrollment and in the number of Catholic schools. There were 9,911 Catholic schools in the U.S. in 1985; by 1990-91, there were only 8,587, according to the National Catholic Education Association. Many closures were in inner cities, where the racial makeup of the school has changed in recent years and financial difficulties made closure necessary. Between 1982 and 1989, Catholic school enrollment in preschool through grade 12 dropped from 3 million to 2.5 million. Despite this decline, Catholic school students still made up about half (48 percent) of all those in private schools.

Characteristics

The majority (58 percent) of private schools in 1988 were at the elementary level, while 26 percent were combined elementary and secondary levels. Less than 20 percent were nonsectarian schools, or those with no religious affiliation. Religiously-affiliated sectarian schools charged much lower tuition than nonsectarian schools. Figure 6.4 shows the percentage of eighth graders who attended public, private, and religious-affiliated schools by their family situations.

SCHOOL ATTENDANCE

Days in Attendance

American students spend an average of 178 days a year in school, with 5.14 hours of class per day. Students in larger school districts, in metropolitan areas, and in the North Atlantic states attend slightly more days, on the average, than others. Among other west-

ern nations, only Belgian students attend fewer school days. In Japan, 8th graders attend 243 days of school per year, high school seniors, 216 days.

Compulsory Attendance

Most industrialized western nations require children to attend school for about 10 years. In the U.S., all states require that students attend school through at least age 16, with the exception of Mississippi, which has a compulsory age of 14 years (Table 6.3). Montana and South Dakota permit students to leave school after completion of the 8th grade, if they wish.

Parental Involvement

The National Center for Education Statistics, in its *National Education Longitudinal Survey of 1988* (1992, WDC), reported student-parent interaction regarding school issues. Table 6.4 and Fig-

---

TABLE 6.4

Comparison of NELS:88 parent and student responses to related questions regarding parental involvement: percent of parents or students

Parents		Students	
(percent)			
Parent restrictions on TV viewing		*Parent limits TV viewing*	
Limit hours	61.7	Never	36.9
Monitor programs	47.2	Rarely	25.9
Restrict early/late viewing	84.4	Sometimes	23.1
		Often	14.2
Parent regularly discusses experiences		*Student discusses high school activities with parents three or more times during school year*	
79.4		56.9	
Parent regularly discusses high school plans		*Student discusses high school plans with mother three or more times during school year*	
47.2		52.1	
Parent helps with homework		*Parent checks on homework*	
Seldom/never	29.4	Never/rarely	25.8
Once or twice/month	27.1	Sometimes	29.5
Once or twice/week to almost every day	42.8	Often	44.5
Parent attends PTA meetings		*Parent attends school meetings*	
34.9		49.5	

SOURCE: U.S. Department of Education, National Center for Education Statistics, National Education Longitudinal Survey of 1988: "Base-Year Parent and Student Survey."

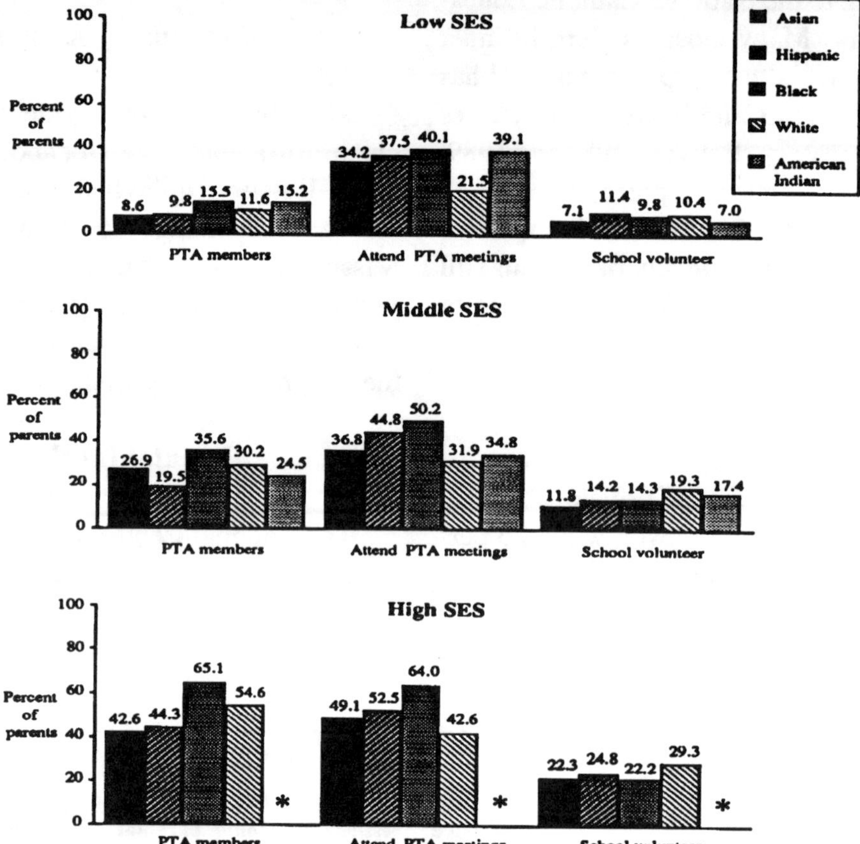

FIGURE 6.5

Percentage of 1988 eighth graders' parents who participated in PTA activities or volunteered in the school, by race–ethnicity and SES

* Sample of American Indians too small (less than 30) for a reliable estimate.

SOURCE: U.S. Department of Education, National Center for Education Statistics, National Education Longitudinal Survey of 1988: "Base-Year Parent Survey."

FIGURE 6.6

Percentage of 1988 eighth graders' parents who regularly discussed current school experiences, by race–ethnicity among middle-SES parents[15]

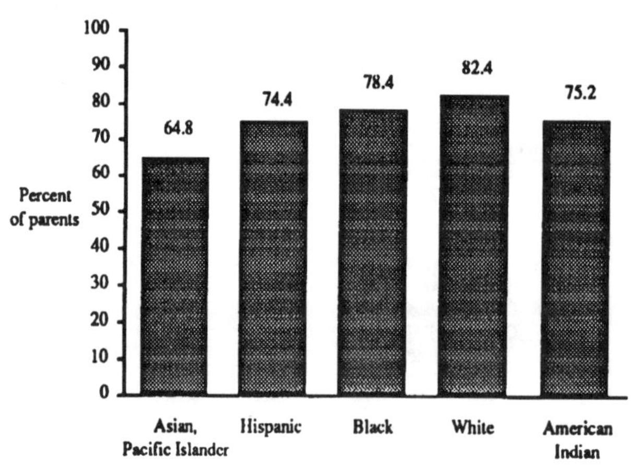

SOURCE: U.S. Department of Education, National Center for Education Statistics, National Education Longitudinal Survey of 1988: "Base-Year Parent Survey."

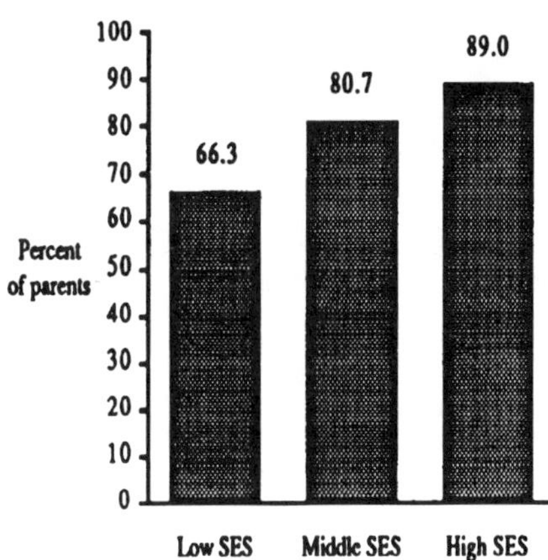

SOURCE: U.S. Department of Education, National Center for Education Statistics, National Education Longitudinal Survey of 1988: "Base-Year Parent Survey."

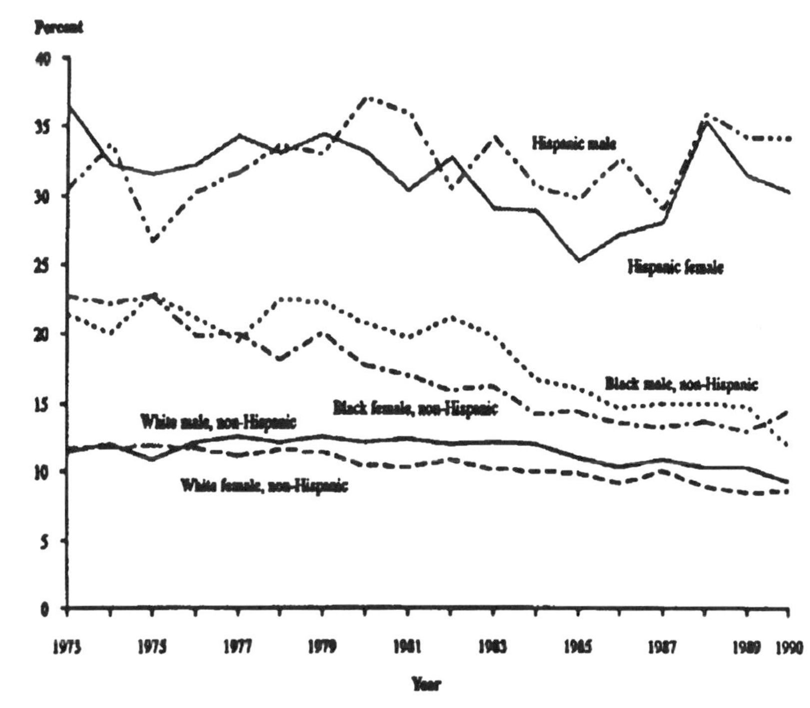

SOURCE: U.S. Department of Commerce, Bureau of the Census, Current Population Survey, October (various years), unpublished data.

ures 6.5 to 6.7 show the relationship of parent expectations and involvement with their children and various characteristics.

DROPPING OUT

Dropout Rates

The U.S. Department of Education uses three types of dropout rates to measure different facets of dropping out: 1) the *event rate* measures the proportion of students who drop out in a single year; 2) the *status rate* measures the proportion of the population that has not completed high school at any given point in time, regardless of when they dropped out; 3) the *cohort rate* measures what happens to a single group (or cohort) of students over a period of time.

In 1990, the average event rate was 4.1 percent of all students in grades 10-12. The status rate was almost 12 percent of all 16- to 24-year-olds. The cohort rate for the class of 1980 was 17.3 percent for those who failed to graduate by June 1982 (Figure 6.8).

Trends in Dropout Rates

Despite the public perception that dropout rates are increasing, the U.S. Education Department reports that they actually declined about 2 percentage points over the past 10 years. The failing rates for both blacks and whites, with a sharper decline for blacks. The decline of both event and status rates for blacks resulted in a narrowing of the difference between black and white dropout rates—from 13 percent in 1968 to 2 percent in 1990 among 16- to 24-year-olds. Hispanic rates remained high throughout the period. Between 9 and 11 percent of Hispanic students dropped out of high school each year.

SCHOOL PERFORMANCE

While students perform academically in varied ways according to their natural abilities, they also are affected by a number of social, economic, and emotional events. Table 6.5 compares the academic performance of students who are "at risk" (for certain behaviors, such as not finishing school, getting into trouble, for experiencing an early pregnancy), with students who have low risk factors. For example, 35 percent of those with poor grades experience low self-esteem as opposed to 9 percent of those who were not at risk for certain behvaiors.

Collectively, American students perform less well academically than students from many other countries. In 1990, U.S. 13-year-olds placed 13th and 12th behind other nations in both mathematics and science, respectively (Table 6.6).

HANDICAPPED CHILDREN

In 1976, Congress passed the Education of the Handicapped Act (PL 94-142, superseded by PL 98-199), that required schools to develop programs for handicapped children. Formerly, most handicapped students had few options other than institutionalization or nursing care. This legislation requires that handicapped children be put in the "least restrictive environment," which has led to increased efforts to educate them in regular classrooms (often referred to as mainstreaming).

The act defines handicapped children as those who are mentally retarded, hard of hearing, deaf, orthopedically impaired, other health impaired,

TABLE 6.5

Comparison of students with low grades in school with students whose grades were not low on various risk items

(N = 2,906 and 18,800)

Item	At Risk	Not At Risk
Suspended from school	19.6	3.8
Attempted suicide	1.4	.7
Involved in pregnancy	1.4	.4
Student sold drugs	2.4	.3
Student used drugs	9.6	1.9
Family used drugs	7.5	2.8
Student used alcohol	11.0	3.6
Parent alcoholic	7.5	3.0
Student arrested	4.9	.7
Student abused	4.3	1.5
Low grades in school	100	0
Failed courses	50.4	2.5
Overage in grade	38.9	12.7
Retained in grade	38.6	10.5
Excessive absences	24.1	4.2
Low self-esteem	35.4	8.8
Referred special education	20.4	8.2
Low reading scores	26.2	6.8
Parent sick last year	4.9	3.9
Parent died last year	1.0	.9
Parent lost job last year	6.0	3.7
Friend died last year	6.0	4.4
Student ill last year	4.6	3.0
Sibling died last year	.5	.5
Father low-level job	25.6	15.5
Father not high school graduate	13.7	6.8
Mother low-level job	27.7	18.4
Mother not high school graduate	15.8	7.2
Parents' attitude negative	14.5	3.6
Language not English	7.2	4.6
Broken home	47.7	32.5
Moved frequently	22.3	14.8
Changed schools frequently	28.4	22.6
Parents divorced last year	8.2	6.6

Source: Jack Frymier, *Growing Up is Risky Business, and Schools are Not to Blame*, Phi Delta Kappa, (Bloomington, IN, 1992)

TABLE 6.6

Science and Mathematics Achievement of U.S. 13-Year-Olds, 1990

Rank	Country	Average Percent Correct
Science:		
1	Korea	78
2	Taiwan	76
3	Switzerland	74
4	Hungary	73
5	Soviet Union	71'
6	Slovenia	70
7	Israel	70
8	Canada	69
9	France	69
10	Scotland	68
11	Spain	68
12	**United States**	**67**
13	Ireland	63
14	Jordan	57
Math:		
1	Korea	73
2	Taiwan	73
3	Switzerland	71
4	Soviet Union	70
5	Hungary	68
6	France	64
7	Israel	63
8	Canada	62
9	Scotland	61
10	Ireland	61
11	Slovenia	57
12	Spain	55
13	**United States**	**55**
14	Jordan	40

Source: Educational Testing Service, *Learning Science* and *Learning Mathematics*, The International Assessment of Educational Progress (February 1992). Ranks calculated by the Children's Defense Fund are based on unrounded percentages; there are no ties.

speech and language impaired, visually impaired, seriously emotionally disturbed, and children with specific learning disabilities who require special education and related services.

Special Education Programs

As a result of the Education of the Handicapped Act, increasing numbers of children have been served in programs for the handicapped. In 1988-89, 11 percent of children were in these programs, compared to 8.6 percent in 1977-78. Most of the increase occurred among those identified as learning disabled—2 percent of all children in 1977-78 to 5 percent in 1988-89. In 1988-89, more than 4.5 million students were enrolled in special education classes (Table 6.7).

What About Homeless Children?

It is impossible to determine how many children are homeless. Several studies have attempted to make estimates. Families with children make up one-third of all homeless people. The National Academy of Sciences estimates that 100,000 children go to sleep homeless each night.

The General Accounting Office, in *Children and Youths: About 68,000 Homeless and 186,000 in Shared Housing At Any Given Time* (1989, WDC), estimated a total of 68,067 homeless youth. The Children's Defense Fund, in *Homeless Families: Failed Policies and Young Victims* (1991, WDC), compared estimates of the numbers of homeless by a variety of sources. (See Table 6.8.)

Homelessness harms children's educational achievement. Those who are homeless have difficulty with transportation to school, maintaining necessary documents, and privacy for homework, sleep, and interaction with parents. Table 6.9 shows the difficulty experienced by homeless children as opposed to those children who are low income but housed.

COLLEGE ENTRANCE EXAMINATIONS

SAT and ACT

Students wishing to enter most colleges and universities in the United States must take either the Scholastic Aptitude Test (SAT) or the American College Test (ACT) as part of their admission requirements. The SAT is the primary admissions test for 22 states, mostly in the East and on the West Coast. The ACT is more popular in 28 states

TABLE 6.7

Children 0 to 21 years old served in federally-supported special education programs, by type of handicap: 1976-77 to 1988-89

Type of handicap	1976–77	1977–78	1978–79	1979–80	1980–81	1981–82	1982–83	1983–84	1984–85	1985–86	1986–87	1987–88	1988–89
1	2	3	4	5	6	7	8	9	10	11	12	13	14

Number served,[1] in thousands

Type of handicap	1976–77	1977–78	1978–79	1979–80	1980–81	1981–82	1982–83	1983–84	1984–85	1985–86	1986–87	1987–88	1988–89
All conditions	3,692	3,751	3,889	4,005	4,142	4,198	4,255	4,298	4,315	4,317	4,374	4,447	4,544
Learning disabled	796	964	1,130	1,276	1,462	1,622	1,741	1,806	1,832	1,862	1,914	1,928	1,987
Speech impaired	1,302	1,223	1,214	1,186	1,168	1,135	1,131	1,128	1,126	1,125	1,136	953	967
Mentally retarded	959	933	901	859	829	786	757	727	694	660	643	582	564
Seriously emotionally disturbed	283	288	300	329	346	339	352	361	372	375	383	373	376
Hard of hearing and deaf	87	85	85	80	79	75	73	72	69	66	65	56	56
Orthopedically handicapped	87	87	70	66	58	58	57	56	56	57	57	47	47
Other health impaired	141	135	105	106	98	79	50	53	68	57	52	45	43
Visually handicapped	38	35	32	31	31	29	28	29	28	27	26	22	23
Multihandicapped	—	—	50	60	68	71	63	65	69	86	97	77	85
Deaf-blind	—	—	2	2	3	2	2	2	2	2	2	1	2
Preschool handicapped[2]	(3)	(3)	(3)	(3)	(3)	(3)	(3)	(3)	(3)	(3)	(3)	363	394

Percentage distribution of children served

Type of handicap	1976–77	1977–78	1978–79	1979–80	1980–81	1981–82	1982–83	1983–84	1984–85	1985–86	1986–87	1987–88	1988–89
All conditions	100.0	100.0	100.0	100.0	100.0	100.0	100.0	100.0	100.0	100.0	100.0	100.0	100.0
Learning disabled	21.6	25.7	29.1	31.9	35.3	38.5	40.9	42.0	42.4	43.1	43.8	43.4	43.8
Speech impaired	35.3	32.6	31.2	29.6	28.2	27.0	26.6	26.2	26.1	26.1	26.0	21.4	21.1
Mentally retarded	26.0	24.9	23.2	21.7	20.0	18.7	17.8	16.9	16.1	15.3	14.7	13.1	12.7
Seriously emotionally disturbed	7.7	7.7	7.7	8.2	8.4	8.1	8.3	8.4	8.6	8.7	8.8	8.4	8.3
Hard of hearing and deaf	2.4	2.3	2.2	2.0	1.9	1.8	1.7	1.7	1.6	1.5	1.5	1.3	1.3
Orthopedically handicapped	2.4	2.3	1.8	1.6	1.4	1.4	1.3	1.3	1.3	1.3	1.3	1.1	1.1
Other health impaired	3.8	3.6	2.7	2.6	2.4	1.9	1.2	1.2	1.6	1.3	1.2	1.0	1.0
Visually handicapped	1.0	0.9	0.8	0.8	(4)	0.7	0.7	0.7	0.7	0.6	0.6	0.5	0.5
Multihandicapped	—	—	1.3	1.5	1.6	1.7	1.5	1.5	1.6	2.0	2.2	1.7	1.8
Deaf-blind	—	—	0.1	(4)	0.1	(4)	(4)	0.1	(4)	(4)	(4)	(4)	(4)
Preschool handicapped[2]	(3)	(3)	(3)	(3)	(3)	(3)	(3)	(3)	(3)	(3)	(3)	8.2	8.7

Number served as a percent of total enrollment[5]

Type of handicap	1976–77	1977–78	1978–79	1979–80	1980–81	1981–82	1982–83	1983–84	1984–85	1985–86	1986–87	1987–88	1988–89
All conditions	8.33	8.61	9.14	9.62	10.12	10.48	10.75	10.95	11.00	10.95	11.00	11.11	11.30
Learning disabled	1.80	2.21	2.66	3.06	3.57	4.05	4.40	4.60	4.67	4.72	4.81	4.82	4.94
Speech impaired	2.94	2.81	2.85	2.85	2.85	2.84	2.86	2.87	2.87	2.85	2.86	2.38	2.41
Mentally retarded	2.16	2.14	2.12	2.09	2.03	1.96	1.91	1.85	1.77	1.68	1.62	1.45	1.40
Seriously emotionally disturbed	0.64	0.66	0.71	0.79	0.85	0.85	0.89	0.92	0.95	0.95	0.96	0.93	0.94
Hard of hearing and deaf	0.20	0.20	0.20	0.19	0.19	0.19	0.18	0.18	0.18	0.17	0.16	0.14	0.14
Orthopedically handicapped	0.20	0.20	0.16	0.16	0.14	0.14	0.14	0.14	0.14	0.14	0.14	0.12	0.12
Other health impaired	0.32	0.31	0.25	0.25	0.24	0.20	0.13	0.13	0.17	0.14	0.13	0.11	0.11
Visually handicapped	0.09	0.08	0.08	0.08	0.08	0.07	0.07	0.07	0.07	0.07	0.07	0.05	0.06
Multihandicapped	—	—	0.12	0.14	0.17	0.18	0.16	0.17	0.17	0.22	0.24	0.19	0.21
Deaf-blind	—	—	0.01	0.01	0.01	(6)	0.01	0.01	(6)	0.01	(6)	(6)	(6)
Preschool handicapped[2]	(3)	(3)	(3)	(3)	(3)	(3)	(3)	(3)	(3)	(3)	(3)	0.91	0.98

[1] Includes students served under Chapter I and Education of the Handicapped Act (EHA).

[2] Includes preschool children 3-5 years served under the EHA and 0-5 years served under Chapter I.

[3] Prior to 1987-88, these students were included in the counts by handicapping condition. Beginning in 1987-88, States are no longer required to report preschool handicapped students (0-5 years) by handicapping condition.

[4] Less than .05.

[5] Based on the enrollment in public schools, kindergarten through 12th grade, including a relatively small number of prekindergarten students.

[6] Less than .005.

— Data not available.

NOTE.—Counts are based on reports from the 50 States and District of Columbia only (i.e., figures from U.S. territories are not included). Increases since 1987-88 are due in part to new legislation enacted Fall 1986, which mandates public school special education services for all handicapped children ages 3 through 5 by the 1990-91 school year. Some data have been revised from previously published figures. Because of rounding, details may not add to totals.

SOURCE: U.S. Department of Education, Office of Special Education and Rehabilitative Services, *Annual Report to Congress on the Implementation of The Education of the Handicapped Act*, various years; National Center for Education Statistics, Common Core of Data survey. (This table was prepared March 1990.)

TABLE 6.8

Estimates of the Number of Homeless Children

National Academy of Sciences (1988)	100,000 children nightly
U.S. Department of Education (1989)	273,000 school-age children annually
General Accounting Office (1989)	68,000 children nightly and 310,000 annually
Urban Institute (1988)	61,500 nightly
National Coalition for the Homeless (1990)	500,000 children annually
California Department of Social Services (1989)	156,000 children annually in California alone
Western Center on Law and Poverty (1989)	200,000 children annually in California alone

If the same proportion of children are homeless throughout the nation as were homeless in California in 1989, there were between 1.6 million and 2 million homeless children in America that year.

Source: *Homeless Families: Failed Policies and Young Victims*, Children's Defense Fund, (WDC, 1991)

TABLE 6.9

Percentage of Homeless and Housed Children With Grade Failure, Special Class Placements, and Excessive School Absenteeism

	Homeless children	Housed low-income children
Repeated a grade	30%	18%
Placed in special classes	28%	24%
Missed more than one week of school in past three months	42%	22%
Missed more than three weeks of school in past three months	17%	4%

Source: David L. Wood, MD, MPH; R. Burciaga Valdez, PhD, MHSA; Toshi Hayashi, PhD; and Albert Shen, MPH, "Health of Homeless Children and Housed, Poor Children," *Pediatrics*, Vol. 86, No.6, December 1990

TABLE 6.10

SAT and TSWE Scores

For 1991, the mean SAT verbal score is 422 and the mean mathematical score is 474 (below and page 9). This

Table A. Mean SAT scores for College-Bound Seniors 1967-1991*

	Verbal			Math		
	Males	Females	Total	Males	Females	Total
1967	463	468	466	514	467	492
1968	464	466	466	512	470	492
1969	459	466	463	513	470	493
1970	459	461	460	509	465	488
1971	454	457	455	507	466	488
1972	454	452	453	505	461	484
1973	446	443	445	502	460	481
1974	447	442	444	501	459	480
1975	437	431	434	495	449	472
1976	433	430	431	497	446	472
1977	431	427	429	497	445	470
1978	433	425	429	494	444	468
1979	431	423	427	493	443	467
1980	428	420	424	491	443	466
1981	430	418	424	492	443	466
1982	431	421	426	493	443	467
1983	430	420	425	493	445	468
1984	433	420	426	495	449	471
1985	437	425	431	499	452	475
1986	437	426	431	501	451	475
1987	435	425	430	500	453	476
1988	435	422	428	498	455	476
1989	434	421	427	500	454	476
1990	429	419	424	499	455	476
1991	426	418	422	497	453	474

*The averages for 1967 through 1971 are estimates. College-Bound Seniors reports were not prepared in those years.

Source: Printed with permission from *1991 Profiles of SAT and Achievement Test Takers.* © College Entrance Examination Board

on a scale of one to 26. The mean SAT scores for 1992 were 423 for the verbal section (the all-time low verbal score) and 476 for the mathematical section. The average composite ACT score was 20.6 in 1992.

More Takers, Lower Scores

In 1992, 1,034,131 students took the SAT, a little more than one-third of high school seniors and about two-thirds of those going directly to college. The number of students taking both SAT and ACT has grown steadily, especially over the past few years. College admission officers report significant increases in applicants despite the declining number of high school graduates since 1980. This may be because students are applying to a larger number of schools, or it may be that a higher percentage of high school graduates are

in the Midwest, South, and West, where a large percentage of students attend public colleges and universities. These national, standardized, two and one-half-hour tests measure a student's mathematical and verbal reasoning ability in a way intended to assess a student's readiness for college. Students who take these tests usually plan to continue their education beyond high school; therefore, these tests do not profile all high school students.

Performance on the SAT is measured on a scale of 200 to 800. The ACT results are measured pursuing a college education. The larger the pool of those taking the test, the lower the scores will be because the increase in the number of students will likely come from those least academically qualified to attend college. The College Board estimated that if all three million high school seniors took the test, the average verbal score would be 376 (instead of 427), and the average math score would be 411 (instead of 476).

As seen in Table 6.10, test scores have dropped since the 1960s. The College Board Advisory Panel on the Scholastic Aptitude Test Decline has attributed the decline in college entrance examination scores from 1963 to 1970, "in large part from that fact that proportionately more students with demonstrated lower scoring records began taking it." While that may explain the initial drop, a major part of the post-1970 drop resulted from a decline in performance of students who had previously done well in these tests. SAT scores were at their lowest point in 1980-81 and began to rise in 1982, continuing to rise through most of the 1980s. Recent scores, however, are still well below the 1967 highs of 466 (verbal) and 492 (math).

Characteristics of Test Takers

The small majority of those taking the SAT in 1991 were women (52 percent). About 72 percent were white, although the proportion of minority test takers has been steadily rising, from 13 percent in 1973 to 27 percent in 1991. Ten percent of students taking the SAT were black; 8 percent, Asian American; 7 percent, Hispanics; and 1 percent, American Indian. Among all groups, Asian Americans were the only group in which equal numbers of men and women took the test.

TABLE 6.11

HIGHEST LEVEL OF PARENTAL EDUCATION	NUMBER OF SAT TAKERS	PERCENT	% MALE/FEMALE	SAT-V MEAN	SAT-M MEAN
No High School Diploma	46,206	5	42/58	339	409
High School Diploma	354,151	38	45/55	395	443
Associate Degree	71,239	8	47/53	407	454
Bachelor's Degree	251,386	27	49/51	442	497
Graduate Degree	221,408	23	50/50	476	528
INTENDED COLLEGE MAJOR					
Agriculture/Natural Resources	12,781	1	58/42	408	445
Architecture/Environ. Design	28,613	3	65/35	409	484
Arts:Visual & Performing	56,560	6	42/58	430	452
Biological Sciences	39,402	4	43/57	467	512
Business & Commerce	176,687	19	50/50	398	463
Communications	41,676	4	37/63	443	460
Computer/Information Sciences	27,135	3	63/37	398	467
Education	73,940	8	22/78	406	441
Engineering	97,939	10	82/18	446	548
Foreign/Classical Languages	6,143	1	23/77	476	502
General/Interdisciplinary	3,869	0	43/57	492	515
Health & Allied Services	127,812	14	32/68	418	471
Home Economics	3,408	0	13/87	367	403
Language & Literature	12,010	1	33/67	534	517
Library & Archival Sciences	255	0	22/78	485	473
Mathematics	6,318	1	53/47	469	605
Military Sciences	6,053	1	84/16	420	471
Philosophy/Religion/Theology	3,369	0	64/36	471	499
Physical Sciences	13,287	1	67/33	497	572
Public Affairs & Services	23,612	3	53/47	376	409
Social Sciences & History	115,698	12	34/66	451	477
Technical & Vocational	10,766	1	63/37	354	402
Undecided	48,754	5	55/45	422	476
DEGREE-LEVEL GOAL					
Certificate Program	15,328	2	49/51	353	399
Associate Degree	20,075	2	41/59	365	376
Bachelor's Degree	251,233	27	50/50	395	444
Master's Degree	266,180	28	47/53	436	493
Doctoral/Related Degree	189,753	20	44/56	472	527
Other	8,035	1	45/55	350	403
Undecided	184,796	20	46/54	418	468

Source: Printed with permission from *1991 Profiles of SAT and Achievement Test Takers.* © College Entrance Examination Board

Fifty-eight percent of students taking the test in 1991 came from homes in which the highest level of education achieved by their parents was an associate degree or higher. The higher the education of the parents, the higher the student tended to score (Table 6.11). Rural and urban students scored lower than students from the suburbs, medium-sized cities, and small towns and cities. Private school students averaged the highest scores, followed by students in religious schools and, lastly, students from public schools.

Racial, Ethnic Differences

The gap between the SAT total mean scores of black and white students has been narrowing over the past 15 years. The scores of blacks increased a total of 50 points, while those of whites increased a total of 14 points.

Despite the increases in minority scores, the scores still lag far behind white scores. College Board officials believe that the pace of change is so "alarmingly slow," that at this rate, it will take more than 44 years to achieve parity.

HOME SCHOOLING

A number of parents, unhappy with public schools, have begun teaching their children at home. The Home School Legal Defense Association estimates that between 250,000 and 750,000 families are home-schooling their children. Most are Christians who are offended by what they feel is an increasingly humanistic curriculum in public schools. They are also disturbed by what they consider growing violence, decaying morals, and the decline in academics. Some critics believe that many parents do not have the qualifications to adequately teach children.

CHAPTER VII

SEXUALITY AND PREGNANCY

EARLY SEXUAL ACTIVITY

The Center for Disease Control's 1990 national school-based *Youth Risk Behavior Survey* measured the prevalence of behaviors among young people. The survey found that 54 percent of youth in grades 9 through 12 had had sexual intercourse. The proportion of those who had intercourse rose from 40 percent of those in the ninth grade to 72 percent of those in grade 12. More than half of all teenagers in the United States admitted to being sexually active by the time they were 17 (grade 11). Male students were more likely than female students to ever have had sexual intercourse (61 percent and 48 percent, respectively) (Table 7.1).

Most Likely At Risk

American Teens Speak: Sex, Myth, TV, and Birth Control (1986, New York), a Louis Harris and Associates survey prepared for the Planned Parenthood Federation of America, found that those teenagers with the least resources were those most likely to have begun sexual activity at a younger age. Teens with parents who were not college graduates, those with grades averaging C or below, and blacks were more likely to have been involved in early sexual activity.

TABLE 7.1

Percentage of high school students reporting having had sexual intercourse,* by sex, race/ethnicity, and grade – United States, Youth Risk Behavior Survey, 1990[†]

| | Ever had sexual intercourse | | | | | |
| | Female | | Male | | Total | |
Category	%	(95% CI[§])	%	(95% CI)	%	(95% CI)
Race/Ethnicity						
White	47.0	(±2.4)	56.4	(±4.5)	51.6	(±2.9)
Black	60.0	(±5.4)	87.8	(±2.4)	72.3	(±3.7)
Hispanic	45.0	(±5.5)	63.0	(±5.5)	53.4	(±4.7)
Grade						
9th	31.9	(±4.1)	48.7	(±5.7)	39.6	(±4.5)
10th	42.9	(±5.5)	52.5	(±6.9)	47.6	(±4.9)
11th	52.7	(±5.7)	62.6	(±6.3)	57.3	(±5.5)
12th	66.6	(±3.9)	76.3	(±4.1)	71.9	(±3.1)
Total	48.0	(±2.7)	60.8	(±4.3)	54.2	(±2.9)

*Ever and during the 3 months preceding the survey.
[†]Unweighted sample size = 11,631 students.
[§]Confidence interval.

Source: "Sexual Behavior Among High School Students—United States, 1990," *Morbidity and Mortality Weekly Report*, Massachusetts Medical Socierty, (Waltham, MA, 1992)

Reasons for Not Delaying Sex

Both sexes listed social pressure as the major factor in not waiting to have sex until they were older. Girls mentioned "peer pressure" most often (34 percent), followed by "boys pressure girls into it" (17 percent), and "everyone is doing it" (14 percent). Another 14 percent mentioned "curiosity." Only a small proportion mentioned being in love with their partner or wanting to feel grown up. Boys were less likely than girls to mention social pressure as an important factor in not delaying sex (26 percent); they were more likely to mention "sexual feeling/desire." (See Table 7.2.)

TABLE 7.2

REASONS WHY TEENAGERS DON'T DELAY SEX

Q.: From what you've heard or seen, what are some of the reasons why many teenagers don't wait to have sexual intercourse until they are older?

		Gender		Those Who Have	
				Had Sexual	Not Had Sexual
Base	Total Teenagers	Boys	Girls	Intercourse	Intercourse
	1000	513	486	350	600
	%	%	%	%	%
Social Pressure (61)					
Peer pressure	30	26	34	37	27
Everyone is doing it	12	10	14	14	11
Boys talk girls/pressure into it	9	2	17	10	10
Friends talk about it	5	7	3	7	5
Want to be popular	3	2	3	2	3
So can boast to friends	2	3	2	2	2
Sexual Feelings/Desires (30)					
In love with partner	8	6	11	10	7
Want sexual gratification	8	10	5	12	6
Like sex/it's fun	5	6	3	4	5
Long time to wait	5	6	4	6	5
Makes you feel cool	4	7	2	2	5
Curiosity (25)					
Curiosity	15	16	14	20	13
Don't want to miss something	3	4	2	4	3
Want to feel grown up	7	7	7	8	7
Other					
Influenced by media	3	4	2	4	3
Don't understand consequences	3	2	3	2	3
Problems at home	2	1	3	1	2
Want to have baby	1	1	1	1	1
Nothing to wait for	1	1	1	*	1
All other reasons	15	11	18	16	14

*Less than 0.5%.

Source: *American Teens Speak: Sex, Myth, TV, and Birth Control*, Louis Harris and Associates, Inc., conducted for the Planned Parenthood Federation of America, Inc., (NY, 1986)

CONTRACEPTIVE USE

The 1990 *Youth Risk Behavior Survey* found considerable indifference to the use of contraception, prompting researchers to observe that the questions should not be, "Why are there so many teenage pregnancies?" but rather, "Why are there not many more?" Among sexually active students, 78 percent used some form of contraception (Table 7.3). White females (81 percent) were more likely than black (71 percent) and Hispanic (63 percent) females to have used contraception. Approximately 45 percent of students reported that they or their partners used condoms (Table 7.4). Males who used alcohol or cocaine were less likely to use condoms.

Reasons for Non-Use

Less than half (41 percent) of sexually active teenagers used contraceptives during their first intercourse, according to the *American Teens Speak* survey. Two-thirds of this group said that they did not use birth control because they had not planned to have intercourse—"It just happened." Unexpected sexual activity seemingly continued to limit the use of contraceptives even after the first sexual encounter since it was the most frequently given response for not using birth control.

When teenagers were asked why their peers did not use birth control, they offered a variety of answers, some of which were considered more valid than unexpected sex. Almost two out of five teens thought their peers did not use contraception simply because they preferred not to use it. They also cited lack of access to birth control and fear that the teens' parents would find out. About 14 percent said their peers believed that pregnancy would not happen to them.

The researchers noted that lack of birth control use by sexually active youth was caused by "ignorance, naivete, embarrassment, fear of disapproval, recklessness, thoughtlessness, or stupidity." They maintain that the reason most often given for non-use—"unexpected sex" may be a rationalization for the students' failure to plan for something that could be anticipated. This may be the result of

TABLE 7.3

Percentage of high school students* reporting contraceptive[†] use at last sexual intercourse, by sex and race/ethnicity – United States, Youth Risk Behavior Survey, 1990[§]

Race/Ethnicity	Female		Male		Total	
	%	(95% CI[¶])	%	(95% CI)	%	(95% CI)
White	81.1	(±2.7)	80.1	(±4.9)	80.6	(±3.1)
Black	71.4	(±6.7)	76.3	(±4.7)	74.3	(±4.3)
Hispanic	62.6	(±6.9)	69.1	(±5.9)	66.2	(±4.9)
Total	77.7	(±2.5)	77.8	(±3.7)	77.7	(±2.5)

*Among students reporting sexual intercourse during the 3 months preceding the survey.
[†]Contraceptive methods include birth control pills, condoms, withdrawal, or another method.
[§]Unweighted sample size = 11,631 students.
[¶]Confidence interval.

TABLE 7.4

Percentage of high school students* reporting use of condoms during last sexual intercourse, by sex and race/ethnicity – United States, Youth Risk Behavior Survey, 1990[†]

Race/Ethnicity	Female		Male		Total	
	%	(95% CI[§])	%	(95% CI)	%	(95% CI)
White	41.7	(±3.3)	50.0	(±4.5)	45.9	(±3.1)
Black	36.7	(±7.8)	54.5	(±3.8)	47.1	(±4.9)
Hispanic	28.1	(±7.8)	46.8	(±6.5)	38.4	(±5.1)
Total	40.0	(±3.0)	49.4	(±3.3)	44.9	(±2.5)

*Among students reporting sexual intercourse during the 3 months preceding the survey.
[†]Unweighted sample size = 11,631 students.
[§]Confidence interval.

Source of both tables: "Sexual Behavior Among High School Students—United States, 1990," *Morbidity and Mortality Weekly Report*, Massachusetts Medical Socierty, (Waltham, MA, 1992)

personal failings, a tendency toward risk-taking, or a culture that suggests through the media that "planning" and "romance" are mutually exclusive terms.

Sexually Transmitted Diseases - STDs

The *Youth Risk Behavior Survey* concluded that 4 percent of all students reported having had a sexually transmitted disease. Black students (8 percent) were more likely to report having had an STD than white (3 percent) or Hispanic (4 percent) students.

PREGNANCY AND ABORTION TRENDS

Births and Birth Rates

For the past decade, overall birth rates among U.S. teenagers have remained fairly stable, although they remain far higher than those of other comparable, industrialized Western nations. Data from 1989 show small, yet significant, increases in births among teens aged 15 to 19. 517,989 babies were born to teenagers in 1989, up from 488,961 the year before. This represents not only an increase in the number of births to teens, but also an 8 percent increase in the teen birth <u>rate</u> (the number per 1,000 females).

Marital and Non-Marital Births

The number of marital births, (babies born to parents who are married to each other) dropped dramatically during the 1980s, while the number of non-marital births rose steadily. In 1988, two-thirds (65 percent) of births to teenagers occurred outside of marriage (Figure 7.1).

Nationwide, white mothers (54 percent) are far less likely than black mothers (91 percent) to be unmarried at the time of birth. Although only 30 states and the District of Columbia report data for Hispanics, in those states, they are more likely than whites, but less likely than blacks, to have non-marital births.

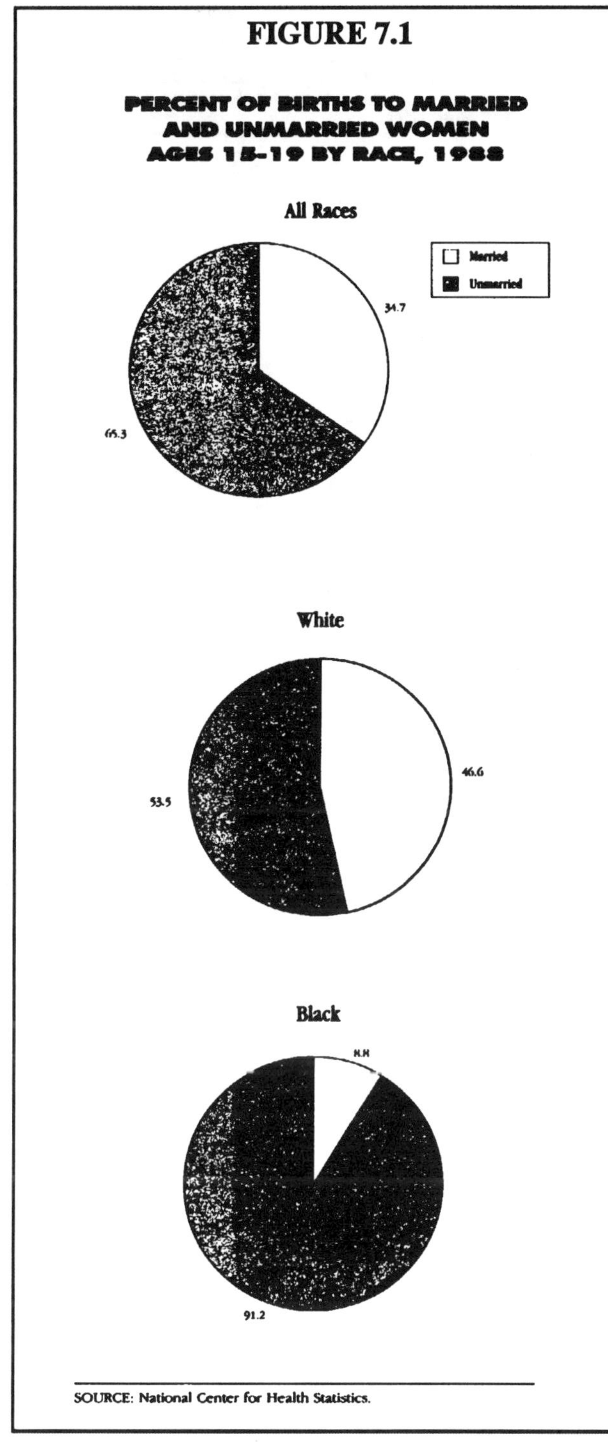

Abortion

The Alan Guttmacher Institute (AGI) reports that the abortion rate for teens in the U.S. has changed little in the past decade, despite the increase in pregnancies among teens. Currently, teens have an abortion rate of 43.8 per 1,000 females. Abortions among females under 20 accounted for one-quarter of the abortions performed in the U.S. Forty-one percent of pregnant teens ages 15 through 19 have had abortions. The AGI reports that women having abortions are predominantly young, single, and poor (Figure 7.2).

A 1991 study by the Robert Sterling Clark Foundation, the David and Lucile Packard Foundation, and the Planned Parenthood Federation of America interviewed unmarried minors seeking an abortion. Table 7.5 shows the percentage of those teens by background characteristics. The likelihood of abortion increased with each year of age. White teens accounted for 55 percent of the abortions; blacks, 30 percent; Hispanics, 12 percent; and Asians or others, 4 percent. Teens living with their biological mothers only represented 46 percent of abortions, followed by those who lived with both parents (38 percent). By religion, 44 percent of those seeking an abortion were Protestant, 30 percent were Roman Catholic, and only 1 percent were Jewish. Twenty-two percent reported no religious affiliation.

The study questioned girls about family relationships (Tables 7.6 and 7.7). Teens reported, in general, having more contact, closeness, and conversation with mothers than fathers regarding sexual issues. Forty-eight percent of mothers knew that their daughters were sexually active and, of those mothers, 58 percent encouraged the use of birth-control.

Teens reported that 61 percent of parents knew about the abortions. Mothers were more likely to know (59 percent) than were fathers (26 percent).

Among minors who did not tell their parents about the abortions (Table 7.8), the most common reasons given were fear of disappointing the parent and fear of parental anger and punishment, including physical harm (76 percent combined). Other reasons cited included shame regarding the sexual activity, concern for parental "stress," and the possibility that the parent might force a particular decision regarding the pregnancy or the relationship with the boyfriend.

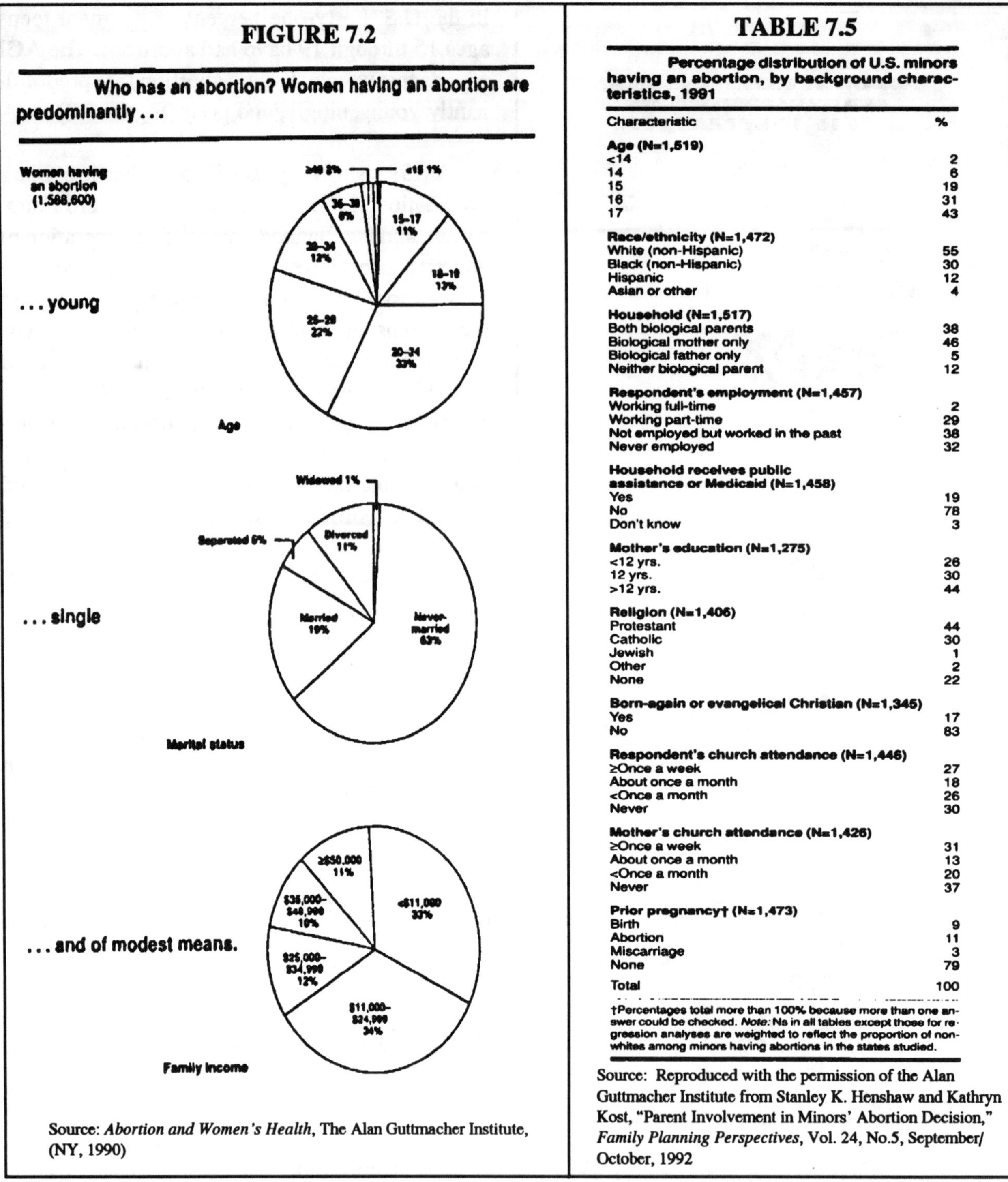

Source: *Abortion and Women's Health*, The Alan Guttmacher Institute, (NY, 1990)

TABLE 7.5

Percentage distribution of U.S. minors having an abortion, by background characteristics, 1991

Characteristic	%
Age (N=1,519)	
<14	2
14	6
15	19
16	31
17	43
Race/ethnicity (N=1,472)	
White (non-Hispanic)	55
Black (non-Hispanic)	30
Hispanic	12
Asian or other	4
Household (N=1,517)	
Both biological parents	38
Biological mother only	46
Biological father only	5
Neither biological parent	12
Respondent's employment (N=1,457)	
Working full-time	2
Working part-time	29
Not employed but worked in the past	38
Never employed	32
Household receives public assistance or Medicaid (N=1,458)	
Yes	19
No	78
Don't know	3
Mother's education (N=1,275)	
<12 yrs.	26
12 yrs.	30
>12 yrs.	44
Religion (N=1,406)	
Protestant	44
Catholic	30
Jewish	1
Other	2
None	22
Born-again or evangelical Christian (N=1,345)	
Yes	17
No	83
Respondent's church attendance (N=1,446)	
≥Once a week	27
About once a month	18
<Once a month	26
Never	30
Mother's church attendance (N=1,426)	
≥Once a week	31
About once a month	13
<Once a month	20
Never	37
Prior pregnancy† (N=1,473)	
Birth	9
Abortion	11
Miscarriage	3
None	79
Total	100

†Percentages total more than 100% because more than one answer could be checked. *Note:* Ns in all tables except those for regression analyses are weighted to reflect the proportion of nonwhites among minors having abortions in the states studied.

Source: Reproduced with the permission of the Alan Guttmacher Institute from Stanley K. Henshaw and Kathryn Kost, "Parent Involvement in Minors' Abortion Decision," *Family Planning Perspectives*, Vol. 24, No.5, September/October, 1992

Parental involvement laws are gaining favor with legislators around the nation. Thirty-five states have them, although they are enforced in only 18, with the others blocked by court orders. The constitutional issue of parental notification remains one of the most hotly debated issues in abortion law. Table 7.9 displays the legal requirements in the various states. For more information on abortion, see *Abortion* (1992, Information Plus, Wylie, Texas).

Consequences of Early Motherhood

Almost six of 10 (59 percent) women who received payments from Aid to Families with Dependent Children (AFDC) in 1988 (the last year

TABLE 7.6

Percentage distribution of U.S. minors having an abortion and of those who live with a parent, by indicators of relationship with parent, according to parent

Indicator	All minors		Those who lived with parent	
	Mother	Father	Mother	Father
Closeness to parent	(N=1,512)	(N=1,454)	(N=1,267)	(N=631)
Very close	49	20	52	31
Somewhat close	37	35	38	48
Not close	11	23	11	21
Little or no contact†	2	23	na	na
Talked to parent about feelings, problems and fears	(N=1,505)	(N=1,452)	(N=1,262)	(N=630)
Very freely	24	5	25	7
Somewhat freely	44	20	46	30
Not freely	29	52	29	63
Little or no contact†	2	23	na	na
Talked to parent about sexual issues	(N=1,506)	(N=1,434)	(N=1,262)	(N=628)
Very freely	21	4	21	4
Somewhat freely	29	11	30	14
Not freely	48	63	49	82
Little or no contact†	2	23	na	na
Parent knew before pregnancy that daughter had had sex	(N=1,510)	(N=1,495)	(N=1,258)	(N=642)
Yes	48	19	47	25
Not sure	16	11	16	14
No	31	46	33	58
Got pregnant the first time	4	2	5	3
Little or no contact†	2	23	na	na
Parent's attitude about daughter having sex‡	(N=1,508)	(N=1,473)	(N=1,256)	(N=634)
Disapproved	34	29	38	47
Left it up to daughter	25	8	23	10
Unknown	19	37	19	40
Encouraged use of birth control	42	10	42	14
Little or no contact†	2	23	na	na
Parent's attitude if he or she knew daughter was having sex‡	(N=718)	(N=285)	(N=592)	(N=158)
Disapproved	29	36	31	42
Left it up to daughter	33	24	31	22
Unknown	10	26	11	23
Encouraged use of birth control	58	31	57	32
Total	100	100	100	100

†Communicates with parent less than once a year. ‡Percentages total more than 100% because more than one answer could be checked. *Note:* na=not applicable.

TABLE 7.7

Percentage distribution of minors, by parental knowledge of their abortion and source of parental knowledge, according to minor's age

Parental knowledge and source	All	≤14	15	16	17
ONE OR BOTH PARENTS	(N=1,519)	(N=122)	(N=284)	(N=467)	(N=647)
Knew	61	90	74	59	51
Told by respondent	45	55	52	43	42
Found out†	15	35	22	16	8
Neither knew‡	39	10	26	41	49
MOTHER	(N=1,519)	(N=122)	(N=284)	(N=467)	(N=647)
Knew	59	88	73	58	49
Told by respondent	43	55	49	41	40
Told by someone else	10	20	14	11	6
Found out	6	13	11	6	3
Did not know‡	41	12	27	42	52
Not told	38	9	25	39	48
Mother deceased or could not be contacted	2	2	1	2	3
Respondent not sure	1	2	§	1	1
FATHER	(N=1,480)	(N=116)	(N=278)	(N=454)	(N=632)
Knew	26	45	28	26	21
Told by respondent	12	14	13	12	12
Told by someone	12	29	12	13	9
Found out	1	2	3	1	1
Did not know‡	74	55	72	74	79
Not told	53	27	48	53	60
Father deceased or could not be contacted	20	26	23	20	18
Respondent not sure	1	2	1	1	1
Total	100	100	100	100	100

†Neither was told, but one or both found out. ‡Includes cases in which the respondent did not know if the parent had been told. §<0.5% of respondents.

Source of both tables: Reproduced with the permission of the Alan Guttmacher Institute from Stanley K. Henshaw and Kathryn Kost, "Parent Involvement in Minors' Abortion Decision," *Family Planning Perspectives*, Vol. 24, No.5, September/October, 1992

for which figures are available) were teenagers when they gave birth to their first child. Having children too young often cuts the mother's education short, as well as limiting her ability to support herself. Eighty percent of teen mothers dropped out of school, and only 56 percent ever graduated from high school. A female who begins parenting in her teens makes half the lifetime earnings of a woman who waits until she is 20 to have her first child. Unfortunately, the cycle is difficult to break since her children are often born into poverty that can drastically limit their futures as well.

Long-term welfare dependency is defined by the Family Support Act as being on welfare for three out of five years. Among women still in their twenties, 21 percent of the mothers who were 17 years or younger when they had their first child received AFDC during three of the previous five years. Eleven percent of those who had their first child between 18 and 19 years of age were also welfare-dependent.

Thirty percent of teen mothers are married and living with their husbands. About half live with relatives, and another 5 percent live with both their husbands and other relatives. Fewer than 10 percent of black teen mothers live with their mothers, but half of white teen mothers do. Among both races, only about one in seven teen mothers lives alone with her child or children.

YOUNG UNWED FATHERS

Young, unwed fathers come from all racial and ethnic backgrounds, all socioeconomic strata, and from both urban and rural communities. However, as a group, they tend to be educationally disadvantaged, have poor employment prospects, and be more likely to be unemployed. Black youth who father children outside of marriage are not very different from their white counterparts, although white fathers are more likely to have histories of deviant behavior, such as criminal records or drug use.

Rates

The most current data on unwed fatherhood (1984) found that 7 percent (1.1 million) of white, black, and Hispanic males between the ages of 19 and 26 reported ever being unwed fathers. Twenty-five percent of black males in their age group, 10 percent of Hispanics, and 3 percent of white males reported being unmarried fathers. About one-third of these unwed fathers had married by 1984 (not necessarily to the mothers of their children), but white and Hispanic (49 percent and 44 percent, respectively) unwed fathers were far more likely than black unwed fathers (24 percent) to be married.

Socioeconomic Background

The 1984 data indicated that young black men or those from low-income families were disproportionately represented among unwed fathers. Only 4 percent of all men ages 19-26 years who were never-married fathers were white, compared with 20 percent of black men in this age group. A young man who was raised in a family that received welfare (AFDC) was also more likely to become a never-married father.

Parental Involvement

Based on the 1984 study, more than half of unwed fathers lived within 10 miles of their children and visited them weekly. Of those who made regular visits, about 50 percent reported making child support payments. White and Hispanic males were more likely than black men to marry the mother of at least one of their children.

TABLE 7.9

RESTRICTIONS ON MINORS' ACCESS TO ABORTION

	ONE-PARENT	TWO-PARENT	CONSENT	NOTICE	MANDATORY COUNSELING[1]	JUDICIAL BYPASS	ENJOINED/ NOT ENFORCED	ENFORCED
ALABAMA	X		X			X		X
ALASKA	X		X				X[2]	
ARIZONA	X		X			X	X[2]	
ARKANSAS		X		X		X		X
CALIFORNIA	X		X			X	X[2]	
COLORADO	X		X				X[2]	
CONNECTICUT					X			X
DELAWARE		X	X				X[2]	
DISTRICT OF COLUMBIA								
FLORIDA								
GEORGIA	X			X		X		X
HAWAII								
IDAHO		X		X			X	
ILLINOIS		X		X		X	X[2]	
ILLINOIS[3]		X	X				X[2]	
INDIANA	X		X			X		X
IOWA								
KANSAS	X			X		X		X
KENTUCKY		X	X			X	X[2]	
LOUISIANA	X		X			X		X
LOUISIANA[3]		X	X				X[2]	
MAINE					X[4]			X
MARYLAND	X			X[5]				X
MASSACHUSETTS		X	X			X		X
MICHIGAN	X		X			X		X[6]
MINNESOTA		X		X		X		X
MISSISSIPPI		X	X			X	X[2]	
MISSOURI	X		X			X		X
MONTANA	X			X			X	
NEBRASKA	X			X		X		X
NEVADA	X			X		X	X[2]	
NEW HAMPSHIRE								
NEW JERSEY								
NEW MEXICO	X		X				X[2]	
NEW YORK								
NORTH CAROLINA								
NORTH DAKOTA		X	X			X		X
NORTH DAKOTA[3]	X	X	X[7]	X			X[2]	
OHIO	X			X		X		X
OKLAHOMA								
OREGON								
PENNSYLVANIA	X		X			X	X[8]	
RHODE ISLAND	X		X			X		X
SOUTH CAROLINA	X[9]		X			X		X
SOUTH DAKOTA	X		X				X	
TENNESSEE	X[10]			X[5]			X	
TEXAS								
UTAH	X[10]			X				X
VERMONT								
VIRGINIA								
WASHINGTON								
WEST VIRGINIA	X			X[5]		X		X
WISCONSIN	X[11]		X			X		X
WYOMING	X		X			X		X
TOTAL (NO. OF STATES & DC)	27	10	22	15	2	25	17	22

1. These statutes require a minor to receive counseling in which the possibility of consulting her parents is discussed.
2. This statute has been declared unenforceable by a court or attorney general.
3. This state has two different provisions.
4. This statute offers mandatory counseling as an alternative to one-parent consent with a judicial bypass.
5. The notice requirement may be waived by a physician under certain circumstances.
6. This statute will be enforceable 90 days after the 1992 legislature adjourns.
7. An unenforced statute requires one-parent consent for a minor's post-viability abortion.
8. Upheld by the U.S. Supreme Court in *Planned Parenthood v. Casey* but currently unenforced pending further litigation.
9. This statute also allows consent of a grandparent.
10. This statute is a two-parent notice law interpreted as requiring notice to one parent.
11. This statute allows consent of an adult family member.

VULNERABILITY TO OUT-OF
WEDLOCK BIRTHS

While many teens who become pregnant come from economically disadvantaged backgrounds, poverty is not the only factor in teenage pregnancy. Andrew Sum, in his analyses of basic skill levels of teens from the *National Longitudinal Survey of Young Adults* (unpublished papers, 1986, Boston, MA: Center for Labor Market Studies, Northeastern University), reported that teenagers whose families lived in poverty were three and one-half times more likely to become teenage mothers than those not living in poverty. Poor teenagers were about five times as likely to become young mothers as their counterparts whose family incomes were over $30,000. A teen was more likely to become a teenage mother if her mother, grandmother, or sister had done so.

The Children's Defense Fund found that, in addition to poor economic conditions, both male and female teens with low basic math and reading skills were also more likely to become teen parents. Because of their poor academic progress, they are less likely to advance beyond high school into further education or successful employment. Twenty percent of teens who lived below the poverty level, in addition to possessing below average reading and math skills, were parents of a child. These teens have limited options. Their opportunities, skills, and hopes for the future are less than those of more advantaged teens.

Charles F. Westoff, professor of sociology and demographic studies at Princeton University, in "Unintended Pregnancy in America and Abroad," *Family Planning Perspectives* (November/December 1988, Vol. 20, No. 6), observed that America has the most diverse ethnic and socioeconomic culture in the Western world. Dr. Westoff believes that an underclass has developed, primarily in the inner-city minority ghetto where middle class values are rejected. The typical middle-class values of education, hard work, thrift, and other issues associated with delayed gratification have not worked in that environment, so they are shunned by many young people. Dr. Westoff points out that, in addition, there is a tendency toward risk-taking among American youth, which is not limited to poor, minority youths from single-parent homes.

Elise Jones et al., in *Teenage Pregnancy in Industrialized Countries* (1986, Yale University Press: New Haven, CT), blames the ambivalence among policy makers in the U.S. The media implies that sex is romantic and exciting and neglects issues of responsibility and hardship. Advertisements use sex and sexual symbols to sell products ranging from cars to soft drinks. However, at the same time, sex education in public schools is still a controversial subject. In other words, teens are encouraged, however subtly, to engage in sex, without the knowledge to behave responsibly. Also, despite the use of sex in the media, society still says, "Good girls don't." Many teens are understandably confused by such mixed messages.

AIDS AWARENESS AND
SEXUAL BEHAVIOR

By 1992, the Center for Disease Control (CDC) reported 7,000 to 10,000 cases of AIDS in children in the United States. Countless more are infected with HIV, the virus that causes AIDS. A portion of those infected were young adults who engaged in sex without the proper precautions during their adolescent years. In 1989, researchers from the CDC and the Department of Education conducted the *Secondary School Student Health Risk Survey* (SSSHRS). They found that 54 percent of all high school students had had some form of HIV/AIDS education in school. A higher proportion of 10th grade students reported having had HIV/AIDS education than students in other secondary grades. Blacks (55 percent) and whites (54 percent) were slightly more likely than Hispanics (51 percent) to have had instruction.

When the students were questioned about their knowledge or belief about AIDS, virtually all (98 to 99 percent) knew that sharing IV needles and sexual contact with an infected person were the two most frequent methods of transmitting the AIDS virus. More than nine out of 10 knew a pregnant woman could transmit the virus to her baby.

Other responses indicated their incomplete knowledge. About 12 percent believed birth control pills offered protection against HIV infection, and almost one-quarter (23 percent) thought you could tell if a person had AIDS by looking at them.

For additional information on AIDS among youth, see Chapter V—Health and Safety.

CHAPTER VIII

JUVENILE CRIME AND VICTIMIZATION

For some young people, growing up is a turbulent time. While their peers are playing football, going to proms, and making plans for their adulthood, a growing numbers of juveniles are, for whatever reason, having brushes with the law.

JUVENILE CRIME

The FBI *Uniform Crime Reports* (UCR) reported that 1,749,343 juveniles were arrested in 1991. While each state has its own definition of

TABLE 8.1

Total Arrests of Persons under 15, 18, 21, and 25 Years of Age, 1991

[10,148 agencies; 1991 estimated population 189,961,000]

Offense charged	Total all ages	Number of persons arrested				Percent of total all ages			
		Under 15	Under 18	Under 21	Under 25	Under 15	Under 18	Under 21	Under 25
TOTAL	10,743,755	614,063	1,749,343	3,244,997	4,908,560	5.7	16.3	30.2	45.7
Murder and nonnegligent manslaughter	18,654	302	2,626	6,722	10,192	1.6	14.1	36.0	54.6
Forcible rape	30,350	1,742	4,766	8,745	13,468	5.7	15.7	28.8	44.4
Robbery	139,182	9,979	35,632	61,981	86,098	7.2	25.6	44.5	61.9
Aggravated assault	368,483	16,029	52,653	100,001	158,203	4.3	14.3	27.1	42.9
Burglary	328,790	44,320	109,965	168,084	213,484	13.5	33.4	51.1	64.9
Larceny–theft	1,215,303	168,007	369,227	533,450	677,244	13.8	30.4	43.9	55.7
Motor vehicle theft	161,628	20,076	70,659	100,181	120,607	12.4	43.7	62.0	74.6
Arson	14,916	4,756	6,940	8,391	9,699	31.9	46.5	56.3	65.0
Violent crime[1]	556,669	28,052	95,677	177,449	267,961	5.0	17.2	31.9	48.1
Property crime[2]	1,720,637	237,159	556,791	810,106	1,021,034	13.8	32.4	47.1	59.3
Crime Index total[3]	2,277,306	265,211	652,468	987,555	1,288,995	11.6	28.7	43.4	56.6
Other assaults	789,144	50,026	122,624	211,150	335,600	6.3	15.5	26.8	42.5
Forgery and counterfeiting	77,066	1,221	6,866	19,272	33,297	1.6	8.9	25.0	43.2
Fraud	292,597	2,870	10,943	40,627	93,629	1.0	3.7	13.9	32.0
Embezzlement	10,602	158	784	2,505	4,441	1.5	7.4	23.6	41.9
Stolen property; buying, receiving, possessing	130,579	10,107	35,220	61,822	82,201	7.7	27.0	47.3	63.0
Vandalism	252,469	53,730	107,890	144,351	175,427	21.3	42.7	57.2	69.5
Weapons; carrying, possessing, etc.	178,955	10,693	37,575	70,785	102,070	6.0	21.0	39.6	57.0
Prostitution and commercialized vice	81,536	148	1,075	7,875	24,250	.2	1.3	9.7	29.7
Sex offenses (except forcible rape and prostitution)	82,228	7,406	14,417	21,565	31,052	9.0	17.5	26.2	37.8
Drug abuse violations	781,250	8,582	60,428	174,608	317,541	1.1	7.7	22.3	40.6
Gambling	12,913	143	912	2,243	3,550	1.1	7.1	17.4	27.5
Offenses against family and children	72,527	996	2,944	9,185	20,007	1.4	4.1	12.7	27.6
Driving under the influence	1,288,876	402	13,437	112,991	329,755	[4]	1.0	8.8	25.6
Liquor laws	453,807	9,320	104,210	311,161	357,216	2.1	23.0	68.6	78.7
Drunkenness	657,119	1,994	16,372	74,446	169,357	.3	2.5	11.3	25.8
Disorderly conduct	569,314	32,346	99,322	187,133	289,980	5.7	17.4	32.9	50.9
Vagrancy	31,262	596	2,257	5,186	8,276	1.9	7.2	16.6	26.5
All other offenses (except traffic)	2,480,902	74,706	247,853	586,947	1,026,278	3.0	10.0	23.7	41.4
Suspicion	14,707	1,253	3,150	4,994	7,042	8.5	21.4	34.0	47.9
Curfew and loitering law violations	73,125	21,859	73,125	73,125	73,125	29.9	100.0	100.0	100.0
Runaways	135,471	60,296	135,471	135,471	135,471	44.5	100.0	100.0	100.0

[1]Violent crimes are offenses of murder, forcible rape, robbery, and aggravated assault.
[2]Property crimes are offenses of burglary, larceny–theft, motor vehicle theft, and arson.
[3]Includes arson.
[4]Less than one-tenth of 1 percent.

Source: *Crime in the United States 1991*, Federal Bureau of Investigation, (WDC, 1992)

TABLE 8.2

Male Arrests, Distribution by Age, 1991

[10,148 agencies; 1991 estimated population 189,961,000]

Offense charged	Total all ages	Ages under 15	Ages under 18	Ages 18 and over
TOTAL	8,729,684	468,371	1,351,758	7,377,926
Percent distribution[1]	100.0	5.3	15.5	84.5
Murder and nonnegligent manslaughter	16,733	283	2,504	14,229
Forcible rape	29,964	1,706	4,679	25,285
Robbery	127,280	8,786	32,525	94,755
Aggravated assault	318,180	13,104	44,678	273,502
Burglary	299,541	39,841	100,688	198,853
Larceny–theft	825,976	121,094	263,323	562,653
Motor vehicle theft	145,446	16,992	62,669	82,777
Arson	12,965	4,306	6,319	6,646
Violent crime[2]	492,157	23,879	84,386	407,771
Percent distribution[1]	100.0	4.9	17.1	82.9
Property crime[3]	1,283,928	182,233	432,999	850,929
Percent distribution[1]	100.0	14.2	33.7	66.3
Crime Index total[4]	1,776,085	206,112	517,385	1,258,700
Percent distribution[1]	100.0	11.6	29.1	70.9
Other assaults	659,120	37,087	93,778	565,342
Forgery and counterfeiting	50,116	820	4,567	45,549
Fraud	167,066	1,961	7,933	159,133
Embezzlement	6,474	113	508	5,966
Stolen property; buying, receiving, possessing	114,964	8,915	31,645	83,319
Vandalism	224,934	49,093	98,890	126,044
Weapons; carrying, possessing, etc.	166,133	9,744	35,193	130,940
Prostitution and commercialized vice	27,786	80	510	27,276
Sex offenses (except forcible rape and prostitution)	76,440	6,793	13,407	63,033
Drug abuse violations	652,168	7,200	53,899	598,269
Gambling	11,270	139	888	10,382
Offenses against family and children	59,406	591	1,932	57,474
Driving under the influence	1,117,678	318	11,591	1,106,087
Liquor laws	366,496	5,189	75,189	291,307
Drunkenness	588,569	1,414	13,837	574,732
Disorderly conduct	455,189	24,552	78,531	376,658
Vagrancy	27,898	501	1,956	25,942
All other offenses (except traffic)	2,057,464	56,206	195,497	1,861,967
Suspicion	12,287	980	2,481	9,806
Curfew and loitering law violations	53,511	15,122	53,511	....
Runaways	58,630	25,441	58,630	....

TABLE 8.3

Female Arrests, Distribution by Age, 1991

[10,148 agencies; 1991 estimated population 189,961,000]

Offense charged	Total all ages	Ages under 15	Ages under 18	Ages 18 and over
TOTAL	2,014,871	155,692	397,585	1,616,486
Percent distribution[1]	100.0	7.7	19.7	80.3
Murder and nonnegligent manslaughter	1,921	19	122	1,799
Forcible rape	386	36	87	299
Robbery	11,902	1,193	3,107	8,795
Aggravated assault	50,303	2,925	7,975	42,328
Burglary	29,249	4,479	9,277	19,972
Larceny–theft	389,327	46,913	105,904	283,423
Motor vehicle theft	16,182	3,084	7,990	8,192
Arson	1,951	450	621	1,330
Violent crime[2]	64,512	4,173	11,291	53,221
Percent distribution[1]	100.0	6.5	17.5	82.5
Property crime[3]	436,709	54,926	123,792	312,917
Percent distribution[1]	100.0	12.6	28.3	71.7
Crime Index total[4]	501,221	59,099	135,083	366,138
Percent distribution[1]	100.0	11.8	27.0	73.0
Other assaults	130,024	12,939	28,846	101,178
Forgery and counterfeiting	26,950	401	2,299	24,651
Fraud	125,531	909	3,010	122,521
Embezzlement	4,128	45	276	3,852
Stolen property; buying, receiving, possessing	15,615	1,192	3,575	12,040
Vandalism	27,535	4,637	9,000	18,535
Weapons; carrying, possessing, etc.	12,822	949	2,382	10,440
Prostitution and commercialized vice	53,750	68	565	53,185
Sex offenses (except forcible rape and prostitution)	5,788	613	1,010	4,778
Drug abuse violations	129,082	1,382	6,529	122,553
Gambling	1,643	4	24	1,619
Offenses against family and children	13,121	405	1,012	12,109
Driving under the influence	171,198	84	1,846	169,352
Liquor laws	87,311	4,131	29,021	58,290
Drunkenness	68,550	580	2,535	66,015
Disorderly conduct	114,125	7,794	20,791	93,334
Vagrancy	3,364	95	301	3,063
All other offenses (except traffic)	423,438	18,500	52,356	371,082
Suspicion	2,420	273	669	1,751
Curfew and loitering law violations	19,614	6,737	19,614	....
Runaways	76,841	34,855	76,841	....

Source of both tables: *Crime in the United States 1990*, Federal Bureau of Investigation, (WDC, 1992)

juvenile, most states put the upper age limit at 17 years old, although some states set it as low as 15 years of age. The UCR, in its breakdown of arrest records by age, uses "under 18 years" as one category. Five percent of all arrests were for violent crimes (murder, forcible rape, robbery, aggravated assault, burglary, larceny-theft, and motor vehicle theft), 32 percent for property crimes, and the rest were for a wide variety of offenses including fraud, vandalism, prostitution, offenses against family and children, vagrancy, etc. About 11 percent of arrests involved drug or liquor law offenses. (See Table 8.1.)

Males were arrested far more frequently than females; 77 percent of those arrested were males versus 23 percent for women. Males were arrested more than four times more often for the more serious crimes listed by the FBI Crime Index. Female juveniles were arrested more often than male juveniles only for running away and prostitution. (See Tables 8.2 and 8.3.) It is important to remember that while the juvenile population declined by 14 percent over the past decade, juvenile arrests increased.

THE CRIMES

The Office of Juvenile Justice and Delinquency Prevention (OJJDP), a branch of the United States Department of Justice, keeps two sets of statistics on juvenile crime—juveniles who go to court and juveniles who are put in custody (1991, "Children in Custody," *Juvenile Justice Bulletin*, WDC). The OJJDP has divided juvenile crimes into general categories for statistical purposes. The two main categories are **delinquency offenses** (acts which are illegal regardless of the age of the perpetrator) and **status offenses**. Status offenses include those acts which are illegal only for minors, such as running away, truancy, curfew violations, ungovernablility, and liquor law violations.

Processing

There is no uniform procedure for processing juvenile cases, but cases do follow a similar path. They are first screened by an intake department which may be the court itself, a state department of social services, or a prosecutor's office. The intake officer may decide that the case will be dismissed for lack of evidence or be resolved informally by referring it to a social service agency, by imposing a fine or other form of restitution, or through informal probation. A petition is filed with the court requesting an adjudicatory (meaning that it will be judged) or waiver hearing when a case is to be handled formally. At an adjudicatory hearing the case can be dismissed or recommendations can be made for sentencing, but in cases where a youth is judged to be delinquent or a

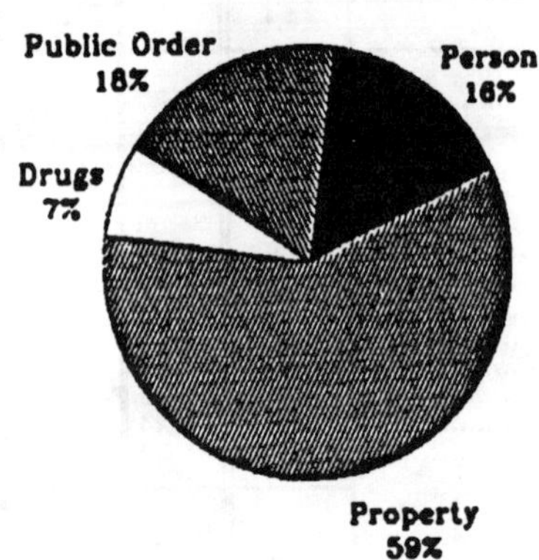

FIGURE 8.1
Offense Characteristics of
Delinquency Cases, 1988

Source: Juvenile *Court Statistics, 1988*, National Center for Juvenile Justice (WDC, December 1990)

TABLE 8.4

Delinquency Case Trends, 1987-1988

	Number of Cases (in thousands)				Number of Cases (in thousands)		
	1987	1988	Percent Change		1987	1988	Percent Change
Delinquency	1,150	1,156	0.5	Race			
Person	184	190	3.0	White	810	790	-2.4
Property	683	681	-0.3	Person	106	107	0.5
Drugs	73	81	10.1	Property	499	487	-2.4
Public Order	209	204	-2.5	Drugs	49	50	0.6
				Public Order	156	147	-5.5
Age				Nonwhite	340	366	7.5
15 or Less	644	652	1.3	Person	78	83	6.5
Person	107	113	5.3	Property	184	194	5.4
Property	412	413	0.2	Drugs	24	31	29.8
Drugs	25	29	14.7	Public Order	54	57	6.3
Public Order	99	98	-1.7				
16 or More	506	503	-0.5	Secure Detention	229	237	3.7
Person	77	77	0.0	Person	43	46	7.5
Property	27	27	-1.1	Property	112	113	0.9
Drugs	48	52	7.6	Drugs	22	26	22.3
Public Order	110	107	-3.1	Public Order	53	52	-1.0
Sex				White	139	136	-2.2
Male	932	941	0.9	Person	20	21	5.0
Person	148	152	2.7	Property	72	69	-4.1
Property	557	557	0.1	Drugs	10	11	4.5
Drugs	62	69	11.6	Public Order	37	35	-4.1
Public Order	166	163	-1.7				
Female	218	215	-1.4	Nonwhite	89	101	12.8
Person	37	38	4.3	Person	22	24	9.9
Property	126	124	-1.9	Property	40	43	9.9
Drugs	12	12	1.8	Drugs	11	16	38.3
Public Order	43	41	-5.4	Public Order	16	17	6.0

Note: Detail may not add to total because of rounding

Source: *Juvenile Court Statistics 1988*, National Center for Juvenile Justice (WDC, December 1990)

status offender, the case then goes to a disposition hearing where the judge decides the most appropriate sentence. Options may include commitment to an institution for delinquents, referral to an agency, community service, or restitution. If a waiver hearing is requested, the juvenile court judge is asked to decide if the case should be waived to a criminal court for prosecution where the youth will be tried as an adult.

Court Statistics

Juvenile courts disposed of an estimated 559,000 delinquency cases in 1988 (the most recent year for which these statistics are available). A case may include more than one charge, i.e. a youth who is brought in on three different robbery charges at the same time is counted as one case. Disposal refers to a court taking definite action.

The Offenses

The number of juvenile delinquency cases increased only 0.5 percent from 1987 to 1988 (the latest year for which complete statistics are available). Property offenses made up 59 percent of the cases, 16 percent involved an offense against persons, and 7 percent were drug law violations (Figure 8.1). Between 1987 and 1988, drug cases increased 10 percent, person offense cases increased 13 percent, while property offense cases declined 0.3 percent (Table 8.4).

The delinquency rate (per 1,000 youth) increases with age. Fifty-six percent of petitioned delinquency cases involved youth who were 15 years or younger (Figure 8.2). Delinquency case rates per 1,000 youth averaged 70 cases for 15 year olds, increased to 83 per 1,000 for 16-year-olds, and was 90 per 1,000 for 17-year-olds (Figure 8.3). Status offenses declined sharply after 17 years of age except for liquor law violations (Figure 8.4). Offenses such as truancy and ungovernability dropped between 15 and 17 years of age while liquor law violations continued to increase with age (Figure 8.5). Almost half of delinquent crimes were nonindex crimes (crimes not counted by the

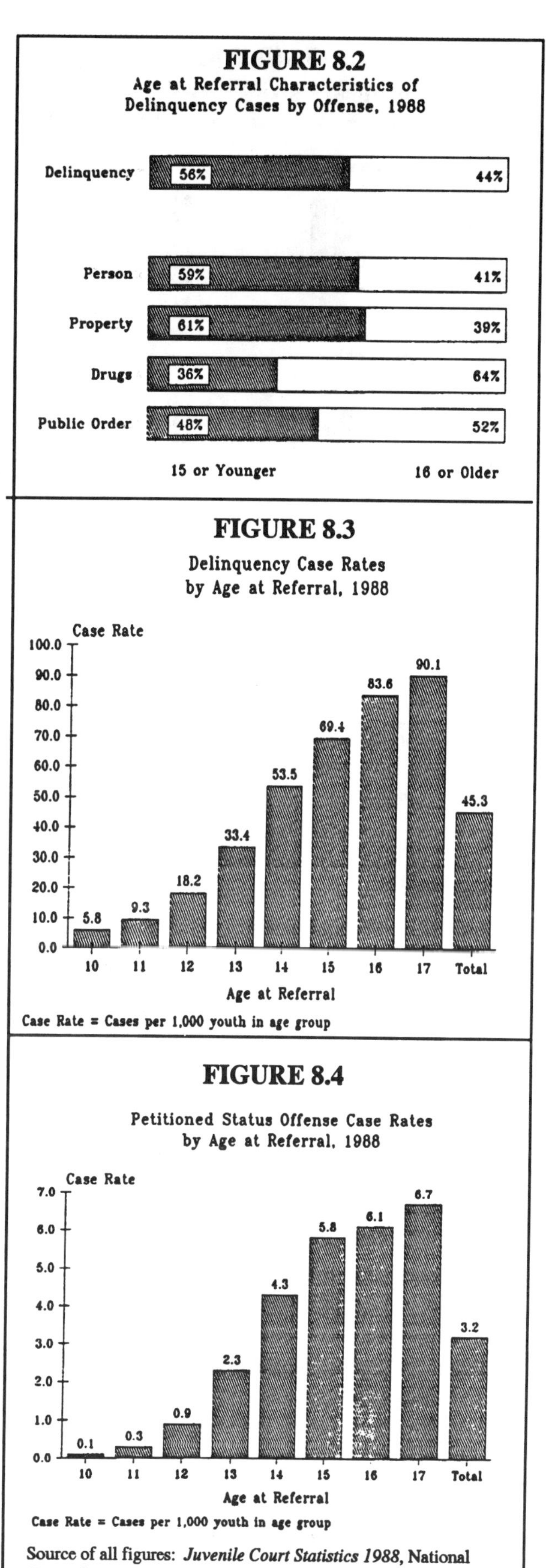

Source of all figures: *Juvenile Court Statistics 1988*, National Center for Juvenile Justice (WDC, December 1990)

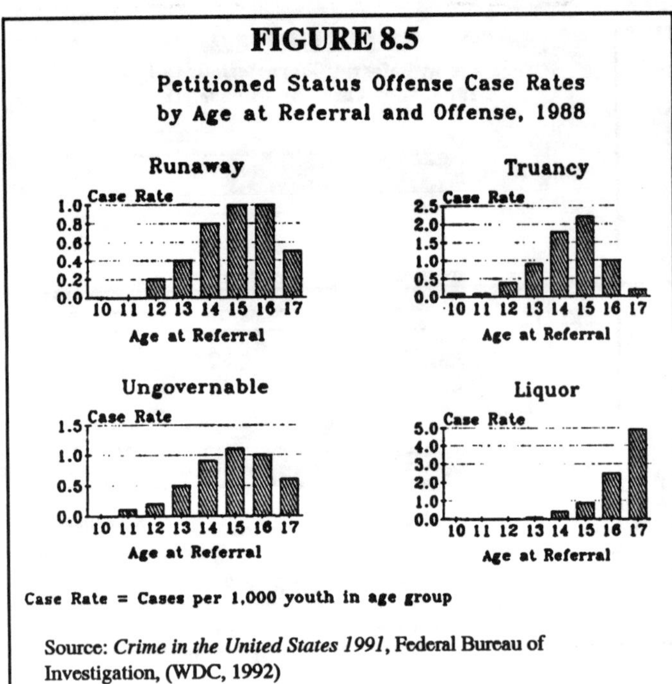

Source: *Crime in the United States 1991*, Federal Bureau of Investigation, (WDC, 1992)

TABLE 8.5

Reasons for Referral of Delinquency Cases, 1988

Reason for Referral	Number of Cases	Percent
Index Violent	**68,400**	**5.9**
Criminal Homicide	1,700	0.1
Forcible Rape	4,000	0.3
Robbery	21,300	1.8
Aggravated Assault	41,400	3.6
Index Property	**503,000**	**43.5**
Burglary	130,500	11.3
Larceny-Theft	311,100	26.9
Motor Vehicle Theft	54,700	4.7
Arson	6,700	0.6
Nonindex Delinquency	**584,500**	**50.6**
Simple Assault	102,300	8.9
Stolen Property Offenses	30,000	2.6
Trespassing	48,100	4.2
Vandalism	82,300	7.1
Weapons Offenses	22,000	1.9
Other Sex Offenses	17,000	1.5
Drug Law Violations	80,200	6.9
Obstruction of Justice	78,500	6.8
Liquor Law Violations	14,000	1.2
Disorderly Conduct	46,300	4.0
Other Delinquent Acts	63,800	5.5
Total Delinquency	**1,156,000**	**100.0**

Note: Detail may not add to total because of rounding.

Source: *Juvenile Court Statistics 1988*, National Center for Juvenile Justice (WDC, December 1990)

FBI statistics), while 6 percent were violent crimes, and 44 percent were index property crimes. (See Table 8.5.)

In 1988, 82,000 status offense cases were formally handled by the courts, a decrease of 2 percent between 1987 and 1988. Fifty-six percent of all formally processed status offenders were below the age of 16. These youth were involved in 65 percent of all runaway cases, 84 percent of truancy cases, 69 percent of ungovernable cases, but only 19 percent of all status liquor law violations (Figure 8.6). This pattern reverses with age. Status liquor law violations made up 57 percent of the offenses of youths 16 years or older and only 11 percent of those who were younger, while truancy represented 40 percent of the younger youth's offenses, dropping to 9 percent of those 16 or older (Figure 8.7). Liquor law violations, unlike other offenses which decrease with age, more than quadrupled between the ages of 15 and 17 (Figure 8.5).

Characteristics

While relatively few females are involved in violent crimes, females are involved in a much greater proportion of status offenses (41 percent). They represent nearly two-thirds of the runaway offenses and nearly half of the ungovernability cases. Liquor law violations are the only area in which the males dominate (76 percent) (Figure 8.8). Between 1987 and 1988, white status cases declined by 3 percent, while nonwhite cases increased by 2 percent. The most striking difference between whites and non-whites is that 94 percent of the liquor law violations are committed by whites, while the other offenses are divided, on average, 80 percent white, 20 percent nonwhite (Figure 8.9). The rate, however, of delinquent youths per 1,000 is approximately twice as high for nonwhites at every age (Figure 8.10). In status offense cases, the reverse is true. The nonwhite rate is somewhat higher among the younger juveniles, nearly the same at 15-years-old and less than half at 17-years-old. This is due to the higher white rate of liquor law violations, more than 5 per 1,000 whites versus 1 per 1,000 nonwhites. (See Figure 8.11.)

Drug and Alcohol Offenses

In 1989, drug and alcohol offenses accounted for 12 percent of juveniles detained, up from 8

FIGURE 8.6

Age at Referral Characteristics of Petitioned Status Offense Cases by Offense, 1988

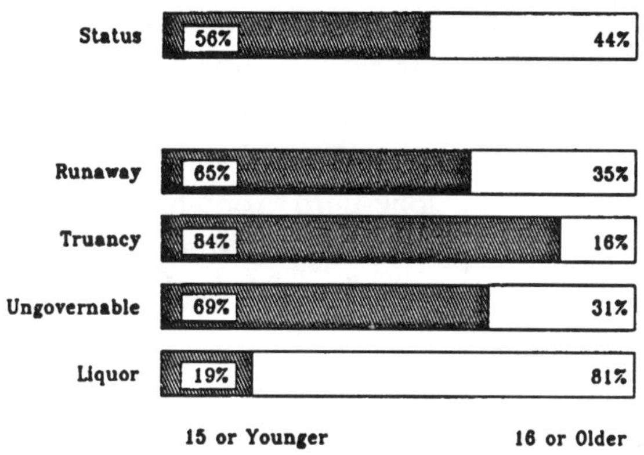

FIGURE 8.9

Race Characteristics of Petitioned Status Offense Cases by Offense, 1988

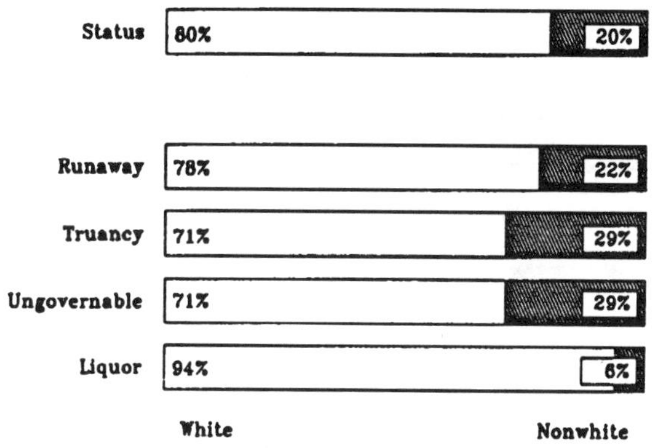

FIGURE 8.7

Offense Characteristics of Petitioned Status Offense Cases by Age at Referral, 1988

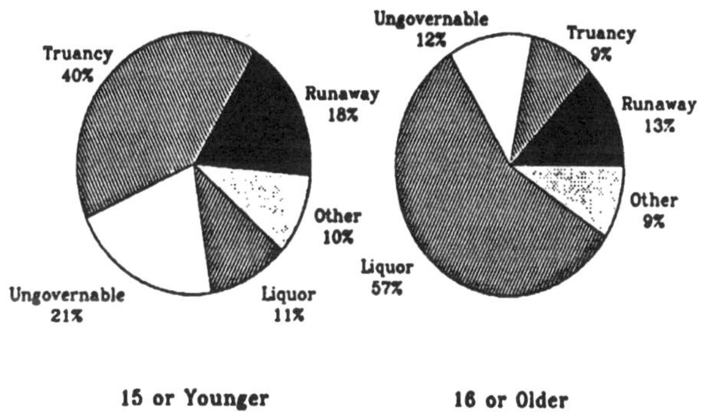

FIGURE 8.10

Delinquency Case Rates, by Race and Age at Referral, 1988

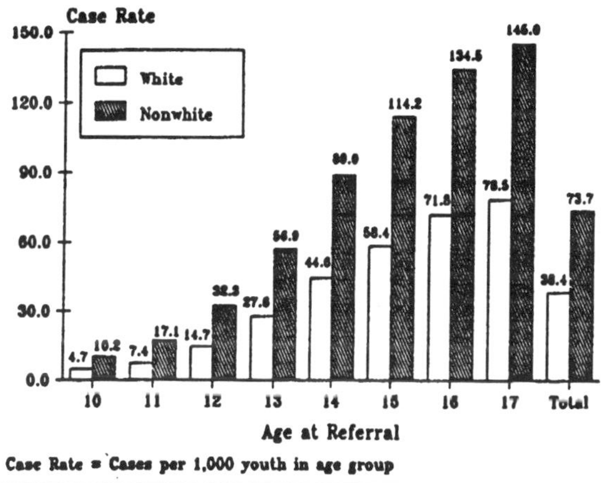

FIGURE 8.8

Sex Characteristics of Petitioned Status Offense Cases by Offense, 1988

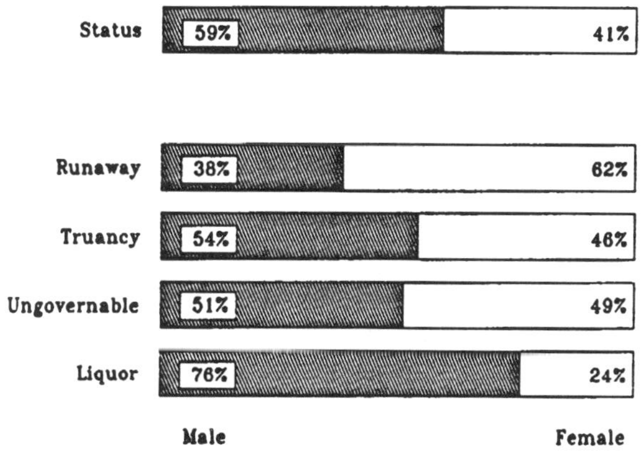

FIGURE 8.11

Petitioned Status Offense Case Rates by Race and Age at Referral, 1988

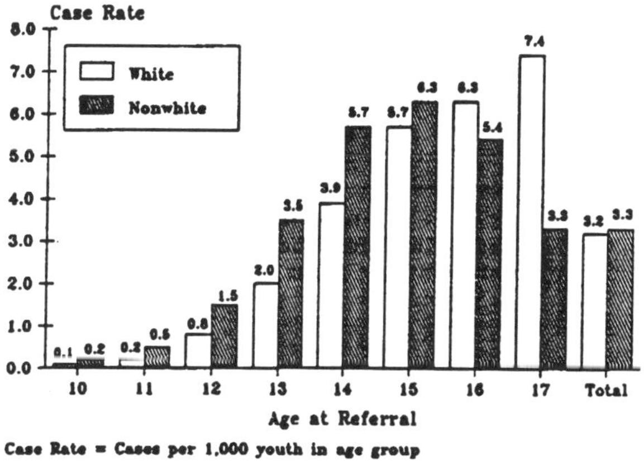

Source of all figures: *Juvenile Court Statistics 1988*, National Center for Juvenile Justice (WDC, December 1990)

estingly, victims report that offenders younger than 20 years of age appeared to be under the influence in 29 percent of the situations, but in only 18 percent of the offenses committed by persons 21 or older. It is important to note that in an additional one-third to one-half of the situations, the victims could not determine whether the victim was or was not under the influence of a substance, but the victim could not rule out the possibility.

CHANGING PHILOSOPHIES

Traditionally, the philosophical difference between juvenile delinquency proceedings and adult criminal proceedings has been that juvenile offenders were viewed as misguided and correctable rather than as a criminal. Juveniles were "delinquent," not guilty; they received treatment, not punishment; juvenile proceedings took place in a closed court to protect the offender and his or her family; there were wide discretionary powers for probation officers, the court and correction agencies, depending on a youth's past history; long-term incarceration was rare; and cases were disposed of quickly with a broad range of disposition alternatives.

percent in 1987 (Table 8.6). The Bureau of Justice Statistics (BJS) suggests that growth in the prison population before 1984 may have been linked to increases in incarceration for serious offenses. Much of the growth since 1984, however, has resulted from the increase in drug violations and the even greater increase in the probability of going to jail or prison for drug offenders.

Furthermore, the Bureau of Justice Statistics reports that victims believe their offenders were under the influence of drugs or alcohol in 38 percent of the offenses if the offenders were male, and 17 percent if the offenders were female. Inter-

The current trend in juvenile justice is to treat juveniles more like adults. If they are treated like adults, chronic offenders may receive adult sentences, removing them from society, and getting away from the notion of rehabilitation and replacing it with punishment for a crime committed. On the other hand, in adult court, juveniles will be entitled to open court-room proceedings and jury trials.

YOUTH GANGS

Although gangs have been a part of American life since the early 18th century, today's gangs pose a greater threat to public safety and order than ever before. Youth gangs originated as social clubs, but are now motivated by violence, intimidation, and the illegal trafficking of drugs and weapons.

A gang can be defined as a group of persons with a unique name, identifiable marks or symbols, who claim a territory or turf, who associate on a regular basis, and who engage in criminal or anti-social behavior.

The increasing violence of youth today is leading more and more juveniles into criminal court. "Today we are arresting more gang members than ever before; we are getting more convictions than ever before; and we are getting longer sentences than ever before, but ironically, we have more gangs than ever before," Frank Radke, the Commanding Officer of the Gang Crimes Section of the Chicago Police Department declared recently in a conference on gang crime. When we think of juvenile crime today, we often think of street gangs.

Drugs and Gangs

Some gang activity occurs because of turf wars, and some is drug related. Schools are often extensions of the street for juvenile gang and drug activity. Law enforcement experts report growing evidence that drugs are contributors to increases in gang violence. The extremely high profits and the abundance of cocaine have contributed to the spread of gangs all across the nation.

The Jamaican Posse is an example of an organized drug gang (not necessarily made up of juveniles). These gangs are not only well established in the drug trade, they are extremely violent. The Drug Enforcement Administration estimates that posses are responsible for 40 percent of the crack cocaine business in the United States.

Young Juveniles

One of the most disturbing aspects of the gang problem is the number of young children involved. Older gang members recruit 8,9, and 10 year-olds to sell drugs and be lookouts because the penalties are very minimal for juveniles that young. Ironically, the change in the status offense laws discouraging detention for juveniles has given older gang members a persuasive argument in recruiting young children. It is hard for many underprivileged 9 and 10 year-olds to turn away from the lure of earning $200 a week for being a lookout for a crack house, especially if there are no negative consequences. The gangs also serve as a family for children whose own families may be dysfunctional. "We don't have to intimidate youngsters to recruit them. They want to be with us now. We know what they need," a gang member told officials. Gangs provide emotional support, shelter, and clothing—in essence, what the child's family may not be providing. Nonetheless, some children are intimidated into joining gangs either out of fear or for protection from other gangs.

CHILDREN IN CUSTODY

What are the courts doing with the growing population of juvenile offenders? In about one third of the formally and informally petitioned cases of delinquency and status offenses, the court orders a youth placed outside the home. There are many different types of facilities for youth including juvenile detention centers, shelters, reception and diagnostic centers, training schools, camps, ranches, and group homes. Not all of the placed youths are accused delinquent and status offenders. Some are placed for treatment or as a result of abuse, dependency, or neglect. Some are held temporarily while other arrangements are being made.

Characteristics of Youth in Custody

The Bureau of Justice Statistics, in *Survey of Youth in Custody, 1987* (WDC, 1988), reported

TABLE 8.7

Selected demographic characteristics of juveniles held in public juvenile facilities on census days: 1987 and 1989.

	1987	1989	Percent change
Total juveniles	**53,503**	**56,123**	**+5%**
Sex			
Male	46,272	49,443	+7%
Female	7,231	6,680	−8%
Minority status			
Nonminority[a]	23,375	22,201	−5%
Minority	30,128	33,922	+13%
Black[b]	20,898	23,836	+14%
Hispanic[c]	7,887	8,671	+10%
Other	1,343	1,415	+5%
Age on date of census			
9 years and under	73	45	−38%
10–13 years	2,811	3,276	+17%
14–17 years	43,898	44,894	+2%
18 years and over	6,721	7,908	+18%

[a] Includes whites not of Hispanic origin.
[b] Includes blacks not of Hispanic origin.
[c] Includes both whites and blacks of Hispanic origin.

Source: *Children in Custody, 1989*, Office of Juvenile Justice and Delinquency Prevention, (WDC, 1991)

that only about 42 percent of juveniles and young adults in juvenile detention, correctional, and shelter facilities have completed more than eight years of school, compared to 76 percent of the general population in this age group. Among those 18-24 years old in these facilities, fewer than 10 percent were high school graduates, compared to 79 percent of this age group in the general population.

There were more than seven times as many male offenders (88 percent) in custody as females (12 percent) in public institutions at the time of the 1989 census. (See Table 8.6.) Females were more often placed in private facilities. In public facilities, whites made up 40 percent of the population, blacks, 42 percent, Hispanics, 15 percent, and other races, 2 percent. Juveniles under 9 years old represented 0.1 percent of those in custody, 6 percent were 10 to 13 years-olds, 80 percent were 14 to 17 years old, and 14 percent were 18 years or older (Table 8.7).

Nineteen out of 20 (94 percent) juveniles were held for delinquent offenses, nearly 5 percent were in custody for status offenses, and approximately 1 percent were detained or committed because they were abused, neglected, or were other nonoffenders or voluntary admissions. Although the number of juveniles in custody increased by 5 percent between 1987 and 1989, the number held for serious, violent offenses including murder, non-negligent manslaughter, robbery and aggravated assault increased 8 percent. The number of juveniles held for drug and alcohol violations increased by 58 percent. (See Table 8.6.)

Characteristics of Institutions

More than half (55 percent) of the public institutions were long-term and the rest (45 percent) were short-term. Long-term facilities held two-thirds of the juveniles in custody, primarily those who had been committed for a criminal offense or had been placed for treatment. Short-term facilities housed mainly young people awaiting judgment, commitment, or placement. There are two different types of facilities within the private/public sector—institutional environments which impose restrictions on residents' movement and limit access to the community and open environments which allow greater movement and more access to the community. These include shelters, ranches, forestry camps or farms, halfway homes and group homes. About 59 percent of youth were in an institutional environment, while the remaining 41 percent were held in open environment facilities.

Chronic Offenders are Responsible for Most Juvenile Crime

A 1988 study, "Court Careers of Juvenile Offenders," conducted by Howard Snyder for the

Office of Juvenile Justice and Delinquency Prevention (results published in "Study Sheds New Light on Court Careers of Juvenile Offenders," 1988, WDC), found that a youth's second appearance in court under the age of 16 is a good predictor of future delinquency. Those youths who committed a serious crime were not the only ones to become repeat offenders. The younger the offender, however, the more likely it was that the youth would later be referred to the court for a violent offense.

JUVENILE VICTIMS

The BJS, in "Criminal Victimization 1991," (1992, WDC), reported that young people (those under age 25) are disproportionately greater victims of violent crime and theft than older persons. Younger teens (12-15 years) had an overall victimization rate of 163.9 per 1,000 persons; older teens (16-19 years) had a victimization rate of 185.1 per 1,000; and young adults (20-24 years) had the highest rate of 189.4 per 1,000 (Table 8.8).

TABLE 8.8

Victimization rates for persons age 12 and over, by type of crime and age of victims

Type of crime	Rate per 1,000 persons in each age group						
	12–15	16–19	20–24	25–34	35–49	50–64	65 and over
All personal crimes	163.9	185.1	189.4	106.3	75.5	45.0	23.2
Crimes of violence	62.7	91.1	74.6	34.9	20.0	9.6	3.8
Completed	23.6	32.4	27.9	15.3	6.9	3.3	1.6
Attempted	39.1	58.7	46.7	19.6	13.1	6.3	2.2
Rape	1.1 *	3.5	1.7	1.0	0.6	0.2 *	0.0 *
Robbery	10.0	8.3	13.9	7.2	4.0	1.8	1.9
Completed	5.9	4.9	8.7	5.4	2.6	1.4	1.1
With injury	1.5 *	2.6	3.1	1.8	0.9	0.3 *	0.3 *
From serious assault	0.3 *	1.0 *	2.3	0.9	0.5 *	0.1 *	0.3 *
From minor assault	1.2 *	1.6 *	0.8 *	0.9	0.5 *	0.2 *	0.0 *
Without injury	4.4	2.4	5.6	3.6	1.6	1.1	0.8 *
Attempted	4.1	3.4	5.2	1.8	1.5	0.5 *	0.8 *
With injury	1.3 *	0.9 *	1.5	0.5 *	0.7	0.1 *	0.1 *
From serious assault	0.4 *	0.3 *	0.8 *	0.3 *	0.5 *	0.0 *	0.0 *
From minor assault	0.9 *	0.6 *	0.8 *	0.2 *	0.3 *	0.1 *	0.1 *
Without injury	2.8	2.5	3.7	1.3	0.7	0.4 *	0.7 *
Assault	51.6	79.2	59.0	26.6	15.4	7.6	1.8
Aggravated	12.9	25.5	23.0	8.3	3.9	2.4	0.9
Completed with injury	5.5	7.8	8.9	3.4	1.5	0.5 *	0.3 *
Attempted with weapon	7.5	17.6	14.1	4.9	2.4	1.9	0.6 *
Simple	38.7	53.8	36.0	18.3	11.4	5.2	0.9
Completed with injury	12.0	17.7	9.3	6.1	2.7	1.4	0.2 *
Attempted without weapon	26.7	36.0	26.7	12.2	8.7	3.7	0.7 *
Crimes of theft	101.2	94.1	114.8	71.4	55.6	35.4	19.5
Completed	98.8	89.0	105.0	65.5	51.8	32.8	18.8
Attempted	2.4	5.1	9.8	5.9	3.8	2.6	0.6 *
Personal larceny with contact	2.5	3.1	3.5	2.8	1.5	1.8	2.6
Purse snatching	0.2 *	0.7 *	0.5 *	0.8	0.5	0.8	0.9
Pocket picking	2.4	2.4	3.0	2.0	1.0	1.0	1.8
Personal larceny without contact	98.7	90.9	111.3	68.7	54.0	33.6	16.8
Completed	96.3	86.0	101.5	62.9	50.4	31.2	16.3
Less than $50	63.4	38.8	29.4	22.5	17.4	10.3	6.6
$50 or more	29.3	43.2	67.8	37.3	30.8	18.2	8.3
Amount not available	3.6	4.0	4.3	3.1	2.3	2.7	1.4
Attempted	2.4	5.0	9.8	5.8	3.6	2.4	0.5 *
Population in each age group	13,783,200	13,364,290	17,989,660	42,829,550	53,833,490	33,103,780	30,440,910

Note: Detail may not add to total shown because of rounding.

* Estimate is based on about 10 or fewer sample cases.

Source: *Criminal Victimization in the United States, 1991*, Bureau of Justice Statistics, (WDC, 1992)

TABLE 8.9

Students reporting at least one victimization at school, by personal and family characteristics

Student characteristic	Total number of students	Percent of students reporting victimization at school		
		Total	Violent	Property
Sex				
Male	11,166,316	8%	2%	7%
Female	10,367,776	8	2	8
Race				
White	17,306,626	8%	2%	7%
Black	3,449,488	8	2	7
Other	797,978	10	2 *	8
Hispanic origin				
Yes	2,026,968	7%	3%	5%
No	19,452,697	9	2	8
Not ascertained	74,428	3*	--	3*
Age				
12	3,220,891	9%	2%	7%
13	3,318,714	10	2	8
14	3,264,574	11	2	9
15	3,214,109	9	3	7
16	3,275,002	9	2	7
17	3,273,628	8	1	7
18	1,755,675	5	1*	4
19	231,348	2*	--	2*
Number of times family moved in last 5 years				
None	18,905,538	8%	2%	7%
Once	845,345	9	2*	7
Twice	610,312	13	3*	11
3 or more	1,141,555	15	6	8
Not ascertained	51,343	5*	5*	--
Family income				
Less than $7,500	2,041,418	8%	2%	8%
$7,500 - $9,999	791,086	4	1*	3
$10,000 - $14,999	1,823,150	9	3	7
$15,000 - $24,999	3,772,445	8	1	8
$25,000 - $29,999	1,845,313	8	2	7
$30,000 - $49,999	5,796,448	10	2	8
$50,000 and over	3,498,382	11	2	8
Not ascertained	1,983,840	7	3	5
Place of residence				
Central city	5,816,321	10%	2%	8%
Suburbs	10,089,207	9	2	7
Nonmetropolitan area	5,648,564	8	1	7

*Estimate is based on 10 or fewer sample cases
--Less than .5%.

Source: *School Crime*, Bureau of Justice Statistics, (WDC, 1992)

School Crime

The National Crime Victimization Survey (NCVS) studied crime in the nation's schools during the first half of 1989. The report (Bastian and Taylor, 1991, "School Crime," WDC: Bureau of Justice Statistics) found that 9 percent of students ages 12 to 19 were crime victims in or around their schools. Two percent reported one or more violent crimes, mainly simple assault, and 7 percent reported property crime.

A nearly equal number of male and female, black and white, and city and suburban students reported being victimized. Hispanic students, however, were less likely than non-Hispanics to experience a property crime. Income did not greatly influence the rate of violent crime—slightly more students with household incomes of $10,000 to $14,999 were victims of violent crime, while those in the income range of $7,500 to $9,999 were victimized less often. Wealthier students suffered more property crimes than poorer students. (See Table 8.9.)

Hispanics and blacks were more fearful of being victimized going to and from school although equal percentages of all races were afraid of attack while in school (22 percent.) Younger students and central city students were more afraid in school and out. (See Table 8.10).

From Fistfights to Gunfights

According to the Bureau of Justice, 3 percent of males report having brought a weapon to school for protection compared to 1 percent of females (Table 8.11). Equal percentages of black, white, and Hispanic students carried weapons and they did so more frequently in the center city than in the

Older teens had an extraordinarily high assault rate (79.2 per 1,000), while younger teens also had a high rate of 51.6 per 1,000. Older teens are more likely than the general public to be attacked by strangers; younger teens are more likely to be attacked by non-strangers. Crimes of theft accounted for the overwhelming portion of crimes against persons of all ages, especially teens. Younger teens suffered 101.2 thefts per 1,000 persons, while older teens had 94.7 thefts per 1,000 persons. Young adults (20 to 24 years of age) also had high victimization rates (114.8 per 1,000 persons).

TABLE 8.10

Students avoiding places at school out of fear, or ever fearing an attack, by selected student characteristics

Student characteristic	Total number of students	Avoiding places at school	Ever fearing an attack — At school	Ever fearing an attack — Going to and from school
Sex				
Male	11,166,316	6%	22%	14%
Female	10,387,776	6	21	16
Race				
White	17,306,626	6%	22%	13%
Black	3,449,488	7	22	21
Other	797,978	6	22	16
Hispanic origin				
Yes	2,026,968	8%	26%	22%
No	19,452,697	6	21	14
Not ascertained	74,428	14°	23°	16°
Age				
12	3,220,891	8%	27%	18%
13	3,318,714	7	27	17
14	3,264,574	7	24	15
15	3,214,109	6	21	13
16	3,275,002	5	20	14
17	3,273,628	4	17	12
18	1,755,825	4	13	10
19	231,346	8°	20	15
Number of times family moved in last 5 years				
None	18,905,538	6%	21%	15%
Once	845,345	5	18	11
Twice	610,312	6	27	16
3 or more	1,141,555	6	26	16
Not ascertained	51,343	7	24°	14°
Family income				
Less than $7,500	2,041,418	8%	24%	18%
$7,500-$9,999	791,086	8	25	18
$10,000-$14,999	1,823,150	8	25	18
$15,000-$24,999	3,772,445	6	23	15
$25,000-$29,999	1,845,313	6	21	15
$30,000-$49,999	5,798,448	5	21	13
$50,000 or more	3,406,382	4	18	11
Not ascertained	1,983,848	5	18	16
Place of residence				
Central city	5,816,321	8%	24%	16%
Suburbs	10,089,207	5	20	12
Nonmetropolitan area	5,648,564	6	22	13

°Estimate is based on 10 or fewer sample cases

Source: *School Crime*, Bureau of Justice Statistics, (WDC, 1992)

suburbs or nonmetropolitan areas. However, the 1990 national school-based *Youth Risk Behavior Survey* (YRBS) found figures much higher. The YRBS reported that 20 percent of all students (grades 9-12) had carried a weapon during the previous 30 days. (Students were not asked if the behavior was at school.)

A bill introduced into the U.S. Congress (HR 4538, "Classroom Safety Act of 1992") portrayed the rising incidence of violence in America's schools:

• Nearly 3 million crimes occur on or near school campuses every year;

• One-fourth of major school districts use metal detectors to screen for weapons;

• Twenty percent of teachers report having been threatened with violence by a student.

A CONGRESSIONAL HEARING

On May 16, 1989, the Select Committee on Children, Youth, and Families held a hearing titled, "Down These Mean Streets: Violence By and Against America's Children." Numerous officials submitted testimony and prepared statements on the nature and effects of violence and crime among juveniles and young adults. Summaries of several statements follow.

Carl Bell, M.D., Executive Director of the Community Mental Health Council, Chicago, Illinois, testified that higher poverty rates result in an especially high level of violence in inner city black communities. He noted the Centers for Disease Control (CDC) statistic that murder is the leading cause of death among black males ages 15-44 and black females ages 15-34. Although blacks are only 12 percent of the population, they are 44 percent of murder victims. He cited surveys conducted by his Council that show that black children are exposed to excessive levels of violence—39 percent had witnessed a shooting, 34 percent had seen a stabbing, and 23 percent had witnessed a murder. Similar findings have been made in Milwaukee and Detroit. Exposure to violence has been linked to poor school performance, behavioral problems, and "post traumatic stress disorders" similar to those suffered by Vietnam veterans.

Deborah Meier, principal of Central Park East Secondary School, New York, NY, testified that continued exposure to violence (even if only on television and in the movies) causes children to perceive it as normal and to equate it with power. Their heroes are tough-minded men who get the job done regardless of laws and social morals. At the same time, they view teachers and parents as less powerful people who struggle in situations that offer no stature, glamour, or money. The streets, not the schools, offer excitement and powerful adult figures, and potentially more rewards.

The Honorable Reggis B. Walton, Associate Judge, Superior Court of the District of Columbia, observed that the steady escalation and severity of crimes committed by juveniles in Washington, D.C. is related to the fact that many teenagers and even pre-teens are involved in the sale of illicit drugs. He advocated that juveniles who commit particularly violent crimes be prosecuted as adults. He argued that many young people become part of the illegal drug trade because the risk of punishment is not harsh enough. He attributed delinquency and violence to family breakdown and the number of boys growing up without fathers. He added that youth do not have access to an adequate number of services and activities, such as athletic and youth facilities that would help keep them out of trouble.

Delbert Elliott, Ph.D., Professor of Sociology, Institute for Behavioral Science, University of Colorado, Boulder, Colorado, noted that research suggests that the increase in adolescent violence is not a result of an increased number of youth commit-ting violent crimes, but rather an increase in the number and severity of crimes committed by youth who are violent offenders. Dr. Elliott also cited the relationship of high crime rates with drug use and the availability of lethal weapons. He noted that drugs do not cause violence in youth, but aggravate the tendencies of violence-oriented youth. He listed four risk factors for those who become involved with violence: 1. weak bonding to the family; 2. weak ties at school; 3. personal beliefs that justify violence; 4. involvement in groups that condone violence. He said that the strongest predictor of violence is a young person's peer group.

TABLE 8.11

Students reporting that they had taken something to school to protect themselves

Student characteristic	Total number of students	Percent of students who had taken a weapon or object to school for protection
Sex		
Male	11,166,316	3 %
Female	10,387,776	1
Race		
White	17,306,626	2 %
Black	3,449,488	2
Other	797,978	2
Hispanic origin		
Yes	2,026,968	2 %
No	19,452,897	2
Not ascertained	74,428	--
Place of residence		
Central city	5,816,321	3 %
Suburbs	10,089,207	2
Nonmetroplitan area	5,648,564	1

Source: *School Crime*, Bureau of Justice Statistics, (WDC, 1992)

CHAPTER IX

RECREATION AND THE USE OF TIME

At one time, when the economy was primarily agricultural, young people were treated as if they were already adult. Their labor was needed on farms, and they generally began work at a very young age. All activities, including schooling, occupied less time in a young person's life than the very important contribution they made to the economic welfare of the family. There was no "adolescence" as we know it today.

Today's young people are usually not expected to contribute to the economic welfare of the family. Although many hold part-time, or even full-time jobs, greater importance is now attached to their education as more young people are expected to attend and complete, high school and, often, even college. The transition into adulthood lasts longer, and the teen years known as adolescence, bridges the period between childhood and adulthood.

Teen Time

What do teens do with their time? Some parents claim they watch too much television; certain experts believe teens do not get enough physical exercise; teachers complain they spend too little time on schoolwork or reading.

University of Maryland researcher, John Robinson, in his 1985 *Americans' Use of Time Project,* found that teens average less than three hours a week in work-related activity, including travel to and from work. Teens spent about 24 hours per week in school-related activities. Adolescents aged 12 through 15 spent more time

TABLE 9.1

Teen Time

(time use among adolescents aged 12 to 17 and unmarried adults aged 18 to 29, in hours per week, 1985)

NON-FREE TIME	12 to 17	unmarried 18 to 29	FREE TIME	12 to 17	unmarried 18 to 29
Classes	18.1	4.1	Organizations, meetings	1.2	0.5
Homework	3.1	3.4	Church, synagogue	1.0	0.5
Travel, school	2.7	0.8	Travel, organizations	0.4	0.3
Work-related	2.8	29.0	Sports events	0.8	0.3
Cooking	0.9	2.2	Cultural events	0.3	0.4
Cleaning, laundry	2.2	3.2	Movies	0.6	0.7
Yardwork, repairs	1.9	1.2	Visiting, social	4.4	7.8
Garden, pets	0.5	0.2	Travel, social	2.1	2.5
Child care	1.2	1.8	Sports	3.3	1.8
Shopping	2.4	2.4	Walk, outdoors	2.0	1.9
Services	0.5	0.7	Hobbies, arts	1.1	0.7
Adult care	0.6	0.6	Games	2.8	0.9
Travel, shop	1.5	1.9	Other recreation	1.0	0.5
Wash, dress	6.4	6.8	Radio, records	0.9	0.7
Eat at home	5.6	4.2	TV	17.7	14.2
Eat out	2.5	2.7	Reading	1.3	1.9
Sleep	62.6	55.9	Conversation	2.6	3.1
Naps	1.3	1.7	Correspondence	0.4	0.4
Private, other*	3.5	1.9	Relax, think	0.8	1.1
Travel, personal	0.7	1.6			

* Not ascertained.

Source: Americans' Use of Time Project

TABLE 9.2
High School Seniors' Activities

Daily leisure activities of high school seniors, by type of activity and sex: 1976 to 1990

Activity and sex	Percent participating in activity each day								
	1976	1980	1984	1985	1986	1987	1988	1989	1990
Watch television	71	72	73	72	74	71	73	71	72
Males	71	72	76	74	77	74	74	77	74
Females	71	73	69	69	71	69	71	66	70
Read books, magazines, or newspapers	59	59	53	51	50	48	46	47	47
Males	58	59	52	50	50	49	47	48	50
Females	62	59	54	52	51	48	46	46	46
Get together with friends	52	51	48	47	49	47	50	51	49
Males	55	55	51	52	52	49	54	56	52
Females	48	47	43	43	46	45	48	46	45
Participate in sports and exercise	44	47	44	43	44	44	44	44	46
Males	52	57	54	53	54	55	57	55	56
Females	36	38	33	34	36	34	31	33	34
Spend at least one hour of leisure time alone	40	42	44	42	42	43	42	42	41
Males	39	40	42	40	40	44	41	44	40
Females	41	44	45	45	43	44	42	41	42
Work around house, yard, or car	41	40	41	35	34	33	32	29	28
Males	33	30	35	28	27	27	25	24	22
Females	49	49	47	42	41	38	37	34	35
Ride around in a car for fun	—	33	34	35	36	36	37	36	34
Males	—	38	40	39	41	40	41	42	36
Females	—	28	27	31	31	32	33	31	32
Play a musical instrument or sing	28	29	30	29	27	28	27	27	28
Males	22	25	24	24	22	24	23	23	26
Females	35	34	37	35	32	32	31	30	31
Do art or craft work	12	13	12	11	14	14	13	13	15
Males	10	12	14	12	14	15	12	13	15
Females	13	14	10	10	13	13	12	13	14
Do creative writing	6	5	6	6	7	6	6	6	7
Males	4	4	6	4	6	6	6	5	6
Females	6	6	6	7	7	7	6	7	8

—Data not available.

SOURCE: U.S. House of Representatives, Select Committee on Children, Youth, and Families, *U.S. Children and Their Families: Current Conditions and Recent Trends*, 1987. University of Michigan, Institute for Social Research, *Monitoring the Future*, various years.

TABLE 9.3

TIME ALLOCATION AMONG SCHOOL-AGE CHILDREN, U.S. AND JAPAN (HOURS PER WEEK)

Activity	U.S. (1981–82)			Japan (1986)			
	Primary School	Junior H.S.	Senior H.S.	Primary School	Junior H.S.	Senior H.S.	College & Univ.
Household work	2.7	4.6	4.8	3.0	3.3	4.1	5.8
Market work	1.2	2.1	3.9	0.1	0.2	2.4	10.3
School work	27.0	31.9	30.0	46.5	62.8	60.4	41.2
In school	25.2	28.7	26.2	38.2	46.6	41.5	32.4
Studying	1.8	3.2	3.8	8.3	16.2	19.0	8.8
Playing games and sports	15.0	8.3	7.0	11.4	3.4	0.7	1.1
Reading	0.9	1.2	1.6	2.8	2.6	3.3	6.4
TV	15.6	17.5	14.2	15.0	15.4	17.7	14.9
Sleep	68.2	59.6	60.3	64.4	56.5	53.0	47.6
Eating	9.0	8.0	7.8	10.6	9.8	9.6	10.0
Personal care	5.2	6.7	6.7	7.1	7.6	8.1	8.4
Subtotal	144.8	150.4	136.3	160.9	161.6	159.3	145.7
Not allocated	23.2	27.6	31.7	7.1	6.4	8.7	22.3
Total	168.0	168.0	168.0	168.0	168.0	168.0	168.0

Source: *Journal of Economic Literature*, Vol. xxxix, (June 1991)

sleeping, watching television, and playing games than did older teens or adults. Table 9.1 shows how teens use their time in a variety of activities. Table 9.2 shows the percentage of high school seniors participating in various leisure activities.

In a comparison of how U.S. and Japanese children used their time, the most significant finding was that Japanese children spent twice the time doing school work and reading than did American children and, subsequently, had less "non-allocated" (spare) time than American youth (Table 9.3).

Sports

According to the *Americans' Use of Time Project*, adolescents participated in sports 3.3 hours per week. Table 9.4 and Figure 9.1 show the sports chosen by many teens. Among those under the age of 18, the largest numbers participated in swimming, bicycling, camping, and the team sports, basketball and volleyball. Swimming, bicycling, and running/jogging were the most popular sports among persons 18 to 24 years of age. Sports participation decreased after the age of 18, gener-

TABLE 9.4
Sports Participation

Percentage of population 7 years old and over participating in sports activities in the past year, by age: 1986 to 1988

Activity	1986			1987			1988		
	7 years old and over	12- to 17-year-olds	18- to 24-year-olds	7 years old and over	12- to 17-year-olds	18- to 24-year-olds	7 years old and over	12- to 17-year-olds	18- to 24-year-olds
Aerobic exercising*	10.2	11.5	16.4	10.7	12.3	18.6	11.2	9.5	18.3
Backpacking	3.7	7.6	5.8	4.1	8.4	7.0	4.2	6.3	7.9
Baseball	6.5	23.8	9.4	7.0	23.2	9.4	6.2	21.2	8.2
Basketball	9.9	35.4	16.8	11.6	40.2	18.7	10.7	36.8	18.3
Bicycle riding*	23.1	47.5	23.9	24.5	48.4	26.5	24.8	45.4	27.3
Calisthenics*	6.7	14.1	8.8	7.9	17.3	11.3	6.3	10.4	9.6
Camping	19.2	26.0	20.9	20.4	28.9	22.8	19.5	27.5	21.6
Exercise walking*	24.9	13.4	22.4	26.8	14.1	22.2	28.7	15.4	9.1
Exercising with equipment*	14.9	20.8	26.8	16.0	21.5	27.5	13.3	16.0	23.9
Fishing—fresh water	19.0	24.2	20.7	18.5	22.8	21.5	18.3	22.3	13.4
Fishing—salt water	5.7	5.8	5.5	5.8	6.0	5.8	6.0	6.2	8.1
Football	5.6	23.4	10.8	6.9	26.2	14.3	5.7	22.5	12.4
Golf	9.3	8.8	11.8	9.3	8.4	13.5	10.5	9.2	10.3
Hiking	7.9	10.7	9.9	8.0	9.3	10.7	9.2	10.5	10.4
Hunting/shooting firearms	9.6	12.4	13.4	9.5	10.2	14.3	7.9	8.5	10.4
Racquetball	3.6	5.0	8.3	3.6	6.0	9.7	4.3	5.3	7.0
Running/jogging*	10.8	23.2	18.8	11.4	26.5	20.4	10.6	20.4	24.3
Skiing-alpine/downhill	4.5	9.0	9.8	4.7	9.6	10.6	5.7	10.2	11.0
Skiing-cross country	2.2	2.9	1.9	2.3	3.4	2.4	2.7	3.2	1.9
Soccer	3.8	16.3	2.9	4.5	19.9	3.4	4.0	16.8	3.2
Softball	9.7	22.1	15.9	9.9	22.5	16.8	9.5	21.3	16.2
Swimming*	33.8	56.0	41.8	30.5	53.3	38.9	32.8	55.1	41.2
Tennis	8.4	19.1	16.9	7.8	16.7	14.4	8.0	15.5	15.3
Volleyball	9.7	24.5	18.5	10.9	31.8	17.1	10.1	25.5	17.2

* Participant engaged in activity at least six times in the year.

SOURCE: U.S. Department of Commerce, Bureau of the Census, *Statistical Abstract of the United States, 1990.* National Sporting Goods Association, *Sports Participation in 1986*, Series I; *Sports Participation in 1987*, Series I.

FIGURE 9.1

Sports Participation

Participation in sports activities, by age: 1988

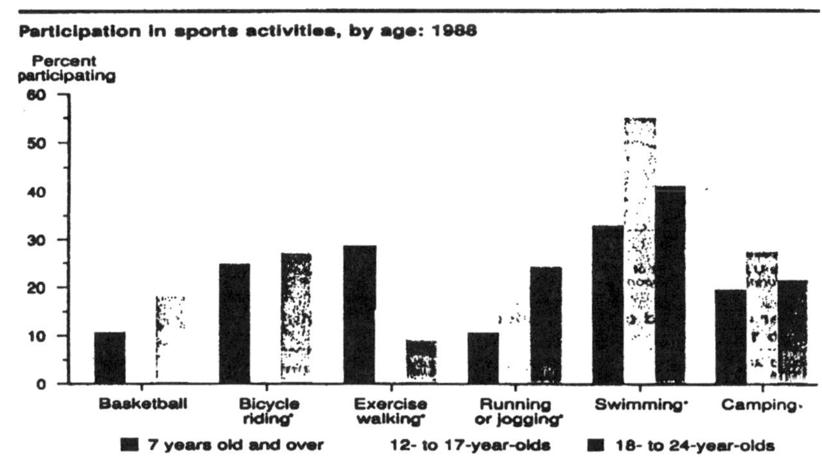

ally at about the time of graduation from secondary school.

Computer Time

Today's children will likely be the first truly computer-literate generation. In 1984, 30 percent of children aged 3 to 17 had used a computer. By 1989, that level had risen to 46 percent. Undoubtedly, the rate is even higher today as schools widely include computer training in the curriculum.

Children have greater access to computers than the typical adult. More than half of all elementary school children used computers at school, compared to 40 percent of high school and college students (Figure 9.2). U.S. Department of Education figures indicate that twenty-four percent of children live in homes with computers. Computer ownership peaks for households headed by 35-to-44 year olds. Children are also more likely than adults to take advantage of computers when they're available. Seventy-one percent of children with computers at home use them, compared with 58 percent of adults who have home access. Both children and adults who live in households with higher incomes and education levels are more likely to use com-

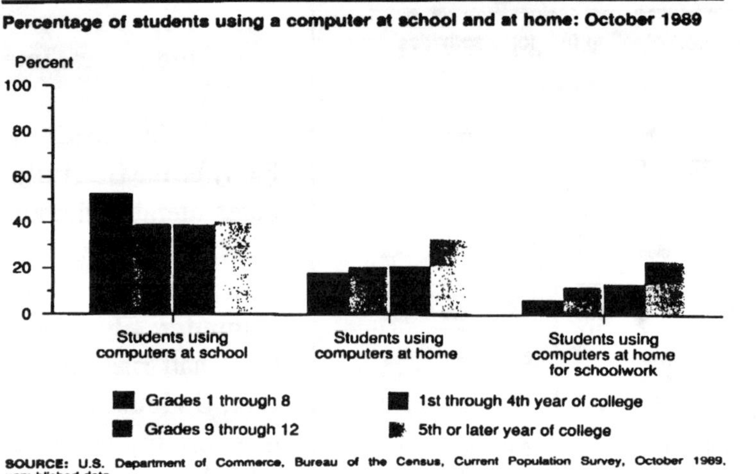

TABLE 9.5

Computer Use by Students

Student use of computers, by level of instruction and household income: October 1989

Household income	Student level				
	Total*	Grades 1 through 8	Grades 9 through 12	1st through 4th year of college	5th or later year of college
Percentage of students using computers at school					
Total	42.7	52.3	39.2	39.2	40.7
Less than $5,000	36.7	40.4	35.6	40.1	53.5
$5,000 to $9,999	36.1	40.3	32.7	40.5	60.2
$10,000 to $14,999	38.4	44.4	39.1	30.8	55.2
$15,000 to $19,999	41.5	50.9	34.8	39.6	44.0
$20,000 to $24,999	42.4	51.8	40.1	32.5	44.4
$25,000 to $29,999	46.1	56.4	43.8	40.4	42.1
$30,000 to $34,999	44.2	56.8	37.8	37.1	33.3
$35,000 to $39,999	45.2	58.3	41.5	34.5	45.3
$40,000 to $49,999	44.7	59.7	36.7	38.1	35.4
$50,000 to $74,999	47.0	61.2	44.6	43.4	31.8
More than $74,999	51.2	67.0	45.8	49.6	31.0
Percentage of students using computers at home for any purpose					
Total	18.8	17.8	20.7	21.3	33.4
Less than $5,000	8.4	4.1	6.6	17.7	29.4
$5,000 to $9,999	5.4	2.7	4.4	14.2	28.4
$10,000 to $14,999	7.2	6.2	6.5	11.8	26.5
$15,000 to $19,999	11.3	9.2	13.6	15.8	33.6
$20,000 to $24,999	12.9	11.6	13.6	16.9	32.2
$25,000 to $29,999	17.0	16.5	17.1	19.2	29.6
$30,000 to $34,999	17.7	17.6	20.2	19.4	30.7
$35,000 to $39,999	21.4	22.2	25.1	22.1	26.5
$40,000 to $49,999	25.7	27.5	27.7	21.7	40.7
$50,000 to $74,999	31.6	33.8	34.3	27.6	41.1
More than $74,999	43.8	50.9	53.4	33.9	41.4
Percentage of students using computers at home for school work					
Total	8.9	6.3	12.2	13.7	23.9
Less than $5,000	5.0	1.5	4.1	12.6	23.8
$5,000 to $9,999	3.2	0.6	2.6	10.3	26.5
$10,000 to $14,999	3.5	1.8	3.6	8.1	19.3
$15,000 to $19,999	4.5	2.1	5.2	9.3	30.2
$20,000 to $24,999	5.7	3.8	7.6	10.5	23.8
$25,000 to $29,999	6.4	4.1	8.2	12.3	19.7
$30,000 to $34,999	8.0	5.7	12.0	12.8	19.8
$35,000 to $39,999	10.5	7.9	15.0	15.9	18.7
$40,000 to $49,999	11.9	9.7	17.1	14.3	29.4
$50,000 to $74,999	15.2	12.7	21.2	17.5	28.5
More than $74,999	22.0	21.9	34.2	21.2	22.2

* Includes data for nursery school and kindergarten students.
SOURCE: U.S. Department of Commerce, Bureau of the Census, Current Population Survey, October 1989, unpublished data.

puters (Table 9.5). The primary reason children use computers is to play games, cited by 84 percent of those who use computers at home. Forty percent use computers at home to do schoolwork, and 25 percent do word processing.

Household Tasks

Changes in family and social structures have resulted in shifts in the division of labor within families. Family maintenance has traditionally been determined by the gender roles of the family members. The husband has primarily used his time in income-producing activities, while the wife devoted her time to household chores. Children modeled their behavior after their parents, girls performing female-typical tasks, and boys assuming the chores traditionally associated with adult males.

Studies have found that such sex-specific roles have eroded slightly. Factors contributing to the change are the increasing numbers of women in the labor force and the rise in the number of single-parent households. These changes in the role of the female parent have altered traditional family time-use patterns.

Hilton and Haldeman (1991, "Gender Differences in the Performance of Household Tasks by Adults and Children in Single-Parent and Two-Parent, Two-Earner Families"), in their study of family members and household tasks, reveal that

• In single-parent families, male and female children spent approximately equal time on household tasks: girls spent more time in dishwashing; boys spent more time on physical care of family members.

• In two-parent families, the primary difference between male and female task performance was in time spent on housecleaning, with females exceeding males in time spent on that chore.

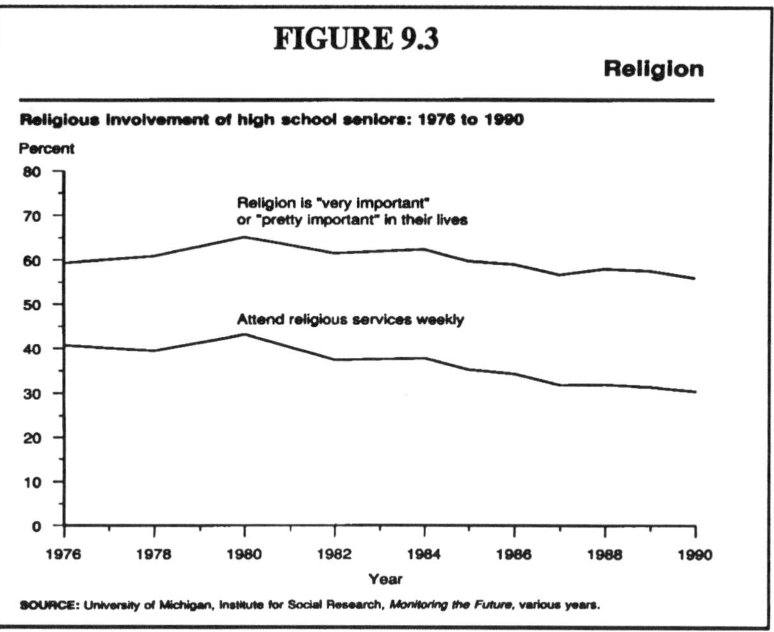

• Children were considerably less sex-specific (doing tasks traditionally associated with primarily the male or female roles) in their household task behavior than were parents. Boys in two-parent families were the least sex-segregated of the males in the study. Girls in single-parent families were the least sex-segregated in their household task performance of all adults and children.

Religion

Religion plays a smaller role in the lives of teenagers than it did a decade ago. The *Use of Time Project* reported that adolescents spent one hour per week in church-related activity. In 1990, fewer teens (56 percent) reported that religion was "very important" or "pretty important" in their lives than in 1980 (65 percent) (Figure 9.3). The number of teens who attended religious services dropped from 43 percent in 1980 to 30 percent in 1990.

For information on the time spent by youths in employment, see Chapter IV.

CHAPTER X

THE WORLD'S CHILDREN

Childhood should be a time of nurturing, growing, learning, playing, and preparing for adulthood. For many children, childhood is, essentially, a carefree, positive experience. For many other children, however, it is a time for little more than survival.

A UNITED NATIONS SUMMIT

In 1990, children from all over the world met with more than 70 world leaders at the United Nations (UN) in New York to ask for a better future for all the children of the world. Four of the main problems that face children throughout the world are death, disease, hunger, and illiteracy. UNICEF (United Nations International Children's Emergency Fund) has set goals it hopes to achieve by the year 2000.

Death

Nearly 1.5 million children die before they are 5 years old. Countries that are torn by war and/or are experiencing famine have the highest mortality rates for children. In 1988, the death rate for children under 5 years old in Afghanistan was 300 per 1,000 live births, compared with 13 per 1,000 in the United States and 7 per 1,000 in Finland. Other countries with high death rates were Bangladesh (188 per 1,000), Nigeria (174 per 1,000), and India (149 per 1,000).

UNICEF goals for the year 2000 include reducing the death rates for children under age 5 years by one-third, providing access to prenatal care to all women, making family planning educa-

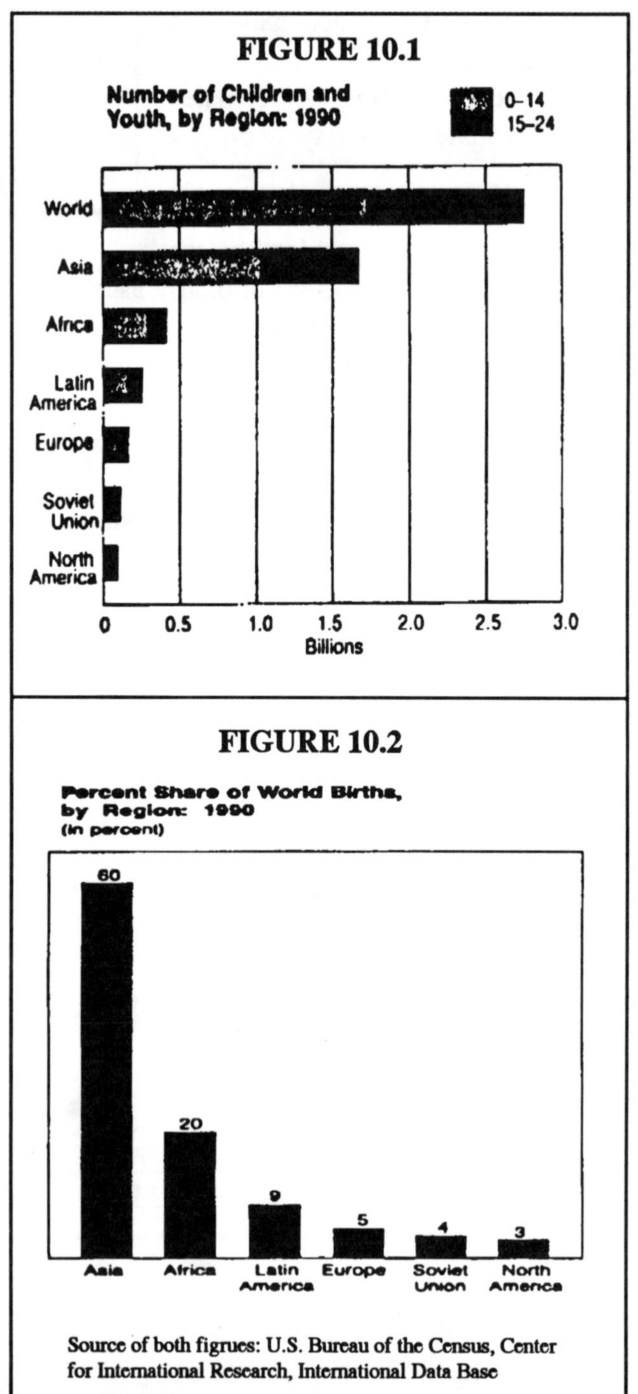

Source of both figures: U.S. Bureau of the Census, Center for International Research, International Data Base

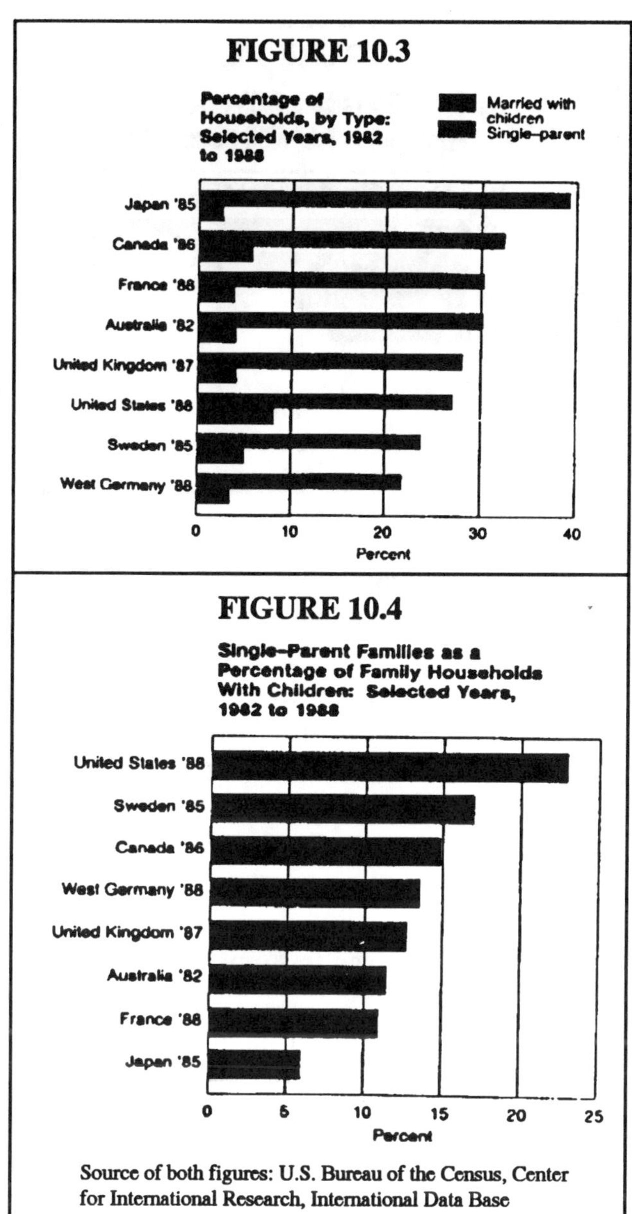

Source of both figures: U.S. Bureau of the Census, Center for International Research, International Data Base

tion and services available to all couples, and increasing recognition of special health and nutritional needs of women at all life stages.

Recent political upheaval around the world (Bosnia, Somalia, the fall of Communism in Eastern Europe and the U.S.S.R.) have subjected untold numbers of children to war, hunger, injury, and death.

Disease

Almost two-thirds of the deaths among young children are from diseases or conditions that can be remedied: diarrhea, respiratory infections, measles, and newborn tetanus. The latest threat, HIV (human immunodeficiency virus), which causes AIDS (acquired immune deficiency syndrome), is believed to infect an estimated 1.5 million women who could potentially pass it on to their unborn children.

UNICEF hopes to eradicate polio within the next 10 years, eliminate tetanus in newborns, reduce measles by 90 percent, cut deaths from diarrhea in half, and make safe water and sanitation available to every family.

Hunger

About 40 percent of the world's children under 5 years of age suffer from the effects of malnutrition themselves or as a result of being born to a mother who is also malnourished. In India and Bangladesh, about 30 percent of infants born from 1982 to 1988 had low birth weights (5.5 pounds or less). On the other hand, only 1 percent of infants born in Spain, 6 percent in the Soviet Union, and 7 percent in the U.S. had low birth rates. UNICEF hopes to reduce severe and moderate malnutrition by half and reduce the incidence of low birth rate to less than 10 percent.

Illiteracy

In the United States, the education of children is taken for granted. Worldwide, almost 100 million children of elementary school age are not in any education program. In many countries education is not free, and the children are poor. Nonetheless, a poor economy is not necessarily an indication of poor education. UNICEF plans to provide basic education for all children and ensure that at least 80 percent complete elementary school.

AN INTERNATIONAL COMPARISON

The Center for International Research of the U.S. Bureau of the Census and the National Institute of Child Health and Human Development found, in *Children's Well-Being: An International*

TABLE 10.1

INFANT MORTALITY RATES, SELECTED COUNTRIES, 1990

Rank	Nation	Rate[1]
1	Japan	5
2	Finland	6
2	Sweden	6
4	Canada	7
4	Germany	7
4	Hong Kong	7
4	Netherlands	7
4	Switzerland	7
9	Australia	8
9	Austria	8
9	Belgium	8
9	Denmark	8
9	France	8
9	Ireland	8
9	Norway	8
9	Singapore	8
9	Spain	8
9	United Kingdom	8
19	Italy	9
20	United States	10
20	Greece	10
20	Israel	10
20	New Zealand	10
24	Cuba	11
24	Czechoslovakia	11
26	Portugal	13
27	Bulgaria	14
28	Hungary	15
28	Trinidad & Tobago	15
30	Jamaica	16
30	Poland	16
32	Kuwait	17
33	Costa Rica	18
	U.S., Black	18
34	Chile	20
34	Yugoslavia	20
36	Malaysia	22
36	Mauritius	22
36	Panama	22
36	Uruguay	22
40	South Korea	23
40	Soviet Union	23
42	United Arab Emirates	24
43	North Korea	26
43	Sri Lanka	26
43	Thailand	26
46	Romania	27
47	China	30

[1] Infant deaths per 1,000 live births.

SOURCE: UNICEF, *State of the World's Children, 1992.*
U.S. data are 1989 data from NCHS.

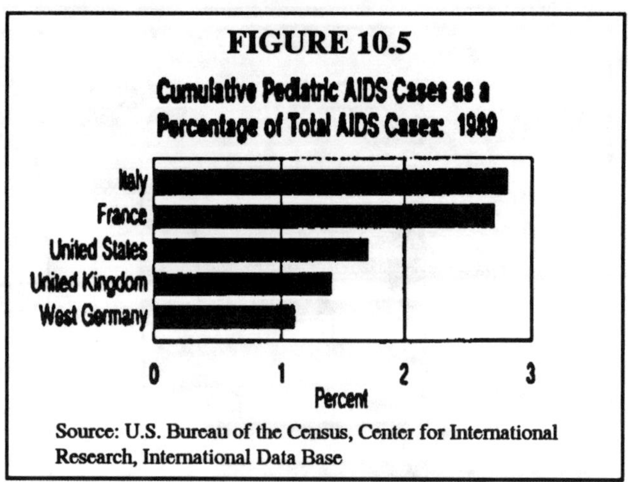

FIGURE 10.5

Cumulative Pediatric AIDS Cases as a Percentage of Total AIDS Cases: 1989

Source: U.S. Bureau of the Census, Center for International Research, International Data Base

Comparison (1990, WDC), that similar economic and political factors do not necessarily produce similar outcomes for children and youth.

Demographic Overview

In 1990, there were 2.8 billion persons from birth to 24 years of age in the world—a number greater than the total world population only 26 years ago. While the number of children per mother has declined, the absolute number has increased because of the growing number of mothers. More young people live in Asia than in all other regions combined. (See Figure 10.1.) Sixty percent of all births were to persons in Asia. Only one out of every nine births took place in North America, Europe, and the Soviet Union combined (Figure 10.2).

Children in Families

Fewer than half of all family households in most developed countries include children. The proportion of family households with children ranges from 25 percent in Germany to 42 percent in Japan. In the U.S., more than one-third (35 percent) of households are families with children. (See Figure 10.3.)

The United States has the highest proportion of single-parent families. Almost one-quarter (23 percent) of family households in the United States are headed by single parents. This is more than all other developed nations in the survey, where percentages ranged from 6 percent in Japan to 17 percent in Sweden. (See Figure 10.4.)

Economic Status

Children in the U.S. are more likely to experience poverty than children in any other industrialized nation. Although Australia has an overall

TABLE 10.2

Percentage distribution of legal abortions, ... iy woman's age, according to country

Measure	≤19				20-24	25-29	30-34	35-39	≥40	Total
	All	≤14	15–17	18–19						
% distribution										
Australia (1988)	19.1	u	u	u	28.1	23.3	16.8	9.4	3.3	100.0
Bulgaria (1987)	7.8	u	u	u	25.2	28.2	21.8	13.1	4.0	100.0
Canada (1987)	22.3	0.8	9.3	12.3	31.7	22.4	13.9	7.4	2.2	100.0
Czechoslovakia (1987)	7.7	0.0	2.4	5.3	23.5	24.3	23.4	15.5	5.5	100.0
Denmark (1988)	14.1	0.2	5.5	8.3	29.1	22.5	16.2	11.8	6.4	100.0
England and Wales° (1987)	24.9	0.6	11.1	13.2	31.5	20.0	12.1	8.1	3.3	100.0
Finland (1987)	16.9	0.2	7.0	11.7	26.6	17.3	14.3	13.3	9.6	100.0
France† (1986)	10.3	0.1	3.8	6.5	23.9	23.8	20.7	15.3	6.0	100.0
German Dem. Rep. (1976)	13.5	0.1	6.4	7.0	20.5	19.2	19.4	19.9	7.5	100.0
German Fed. Rep. (1986)	7.5	0.1	2.5	4.9	24.0	25.5	20.1	15.5	7.4	100.0
Hungary (1987)	11.0	0.1	4.2	6.6	16.7	18.8	24.5	19.8	9.2	100.0
India (FY1986)	5.1	u	u	u	28.0	33.0	23.2	10.2	2.6	100.0
Italy (1987)	7.5	0.1	2.0	5.4	20.5	22.5	21.7	18.3	9.6	100.0
Japan (1987)	5.5	u	u	u	16.3	17.4	23.7	26.4	10.6	100.0
Netherlands° (1985)	13.7	0.3	5.6	7.8	25.4	22.0	19.1	14.0	5.7	100.0
New Zealand (1988)	22.2	0.5	9.6	12.0	29.3	23.7	14.4	8.0	2.4	100.0
Norway (1987)	23.3	u	u	u	30.1	18.2	14.0	9.8	4.6	100.0
Scotland‡ (1987)	28.1	u	u	u	31.9	18.6	11.6	7.2	2.7	100.0
Singapore (1987)	8.6	u	u	u	26.7	27.7	21.2	12.0	3.8	100.0
Sweden (1987)	17.1	0.4	7.1	9.5	26.9	19.3	15.4	13.8	7.5	100.0
Tunisia (1978)	2.5	u	u	u	16.5	25.2	25.3	20.0	10.5	100.0
United States (1985)	26.2	1.1	10.4	14.7	34.5	21.2	11.4	5.4	1.3	100.0

Source: Stanley K. Henshaw and Evelyn Morrow, *Induced Abortion—A World Review, 1990 Supplement,*
The Alan Guttmacher Institute, (NY, 1990)

poverty rate similar to that of the U.S., it has a very high rate among children living with single parents (65 percent compared with 52 percent in the U.S.). In comparison, fewer than 15 percent of Swedish children were living in poverty, regardless of family type.

Health

Infant Mortality

The United States ranks 20th in the world in infant mortality. The U.S. infant mortality rate in 1990 was about 10 deaths before age 1 per 1,000 infants. In comparison, the rates in Japan were 5 per 1,000, Russia, 23 per 1,000, and India, 100 per 1,000 (Table 10.1). The United States, the United Kingdom, and Italy have proportionately more low birth weight babies (placing the babies at higher risk for death) than other Western countries.

Pediatric AIDS

Pediatric AIDS (children under age 13 years) exists in virtually every country that has experienced AIDS cases. In 1989, from 1 to 3 percent of total cumulative reported AIDS cases were pediatric cases in the United States, France, West Germany (Federal Republic of Germany), Italy, and the United Kingdom (Figure 10.5). The majority of pediatric cases resulted from parent-to-child transmission. In countries where the predominant means of transmission is heterosexual contact, such as those in Africa, pediatric AIDS makes up a much larger proportion of total AIDS cases.

Youth Abortions

In 1990, more than six out of ten (62 percent) legal abortions in the U.S. were performed on women between the ages of 15 and 24 years (Table 10.2). This rate is the highest of any country studied and twice the percentage in India, Italy, and Hungary during that time. Scotland, England, and Wales also had high proportions of abortions for young women.

Violent Deaths

The United States led all other nations studied in the percentage of violent deaths to young people. In 1986, more than three-quarters (78 percent) of all deaths to persons ages 15 to 24 years in the

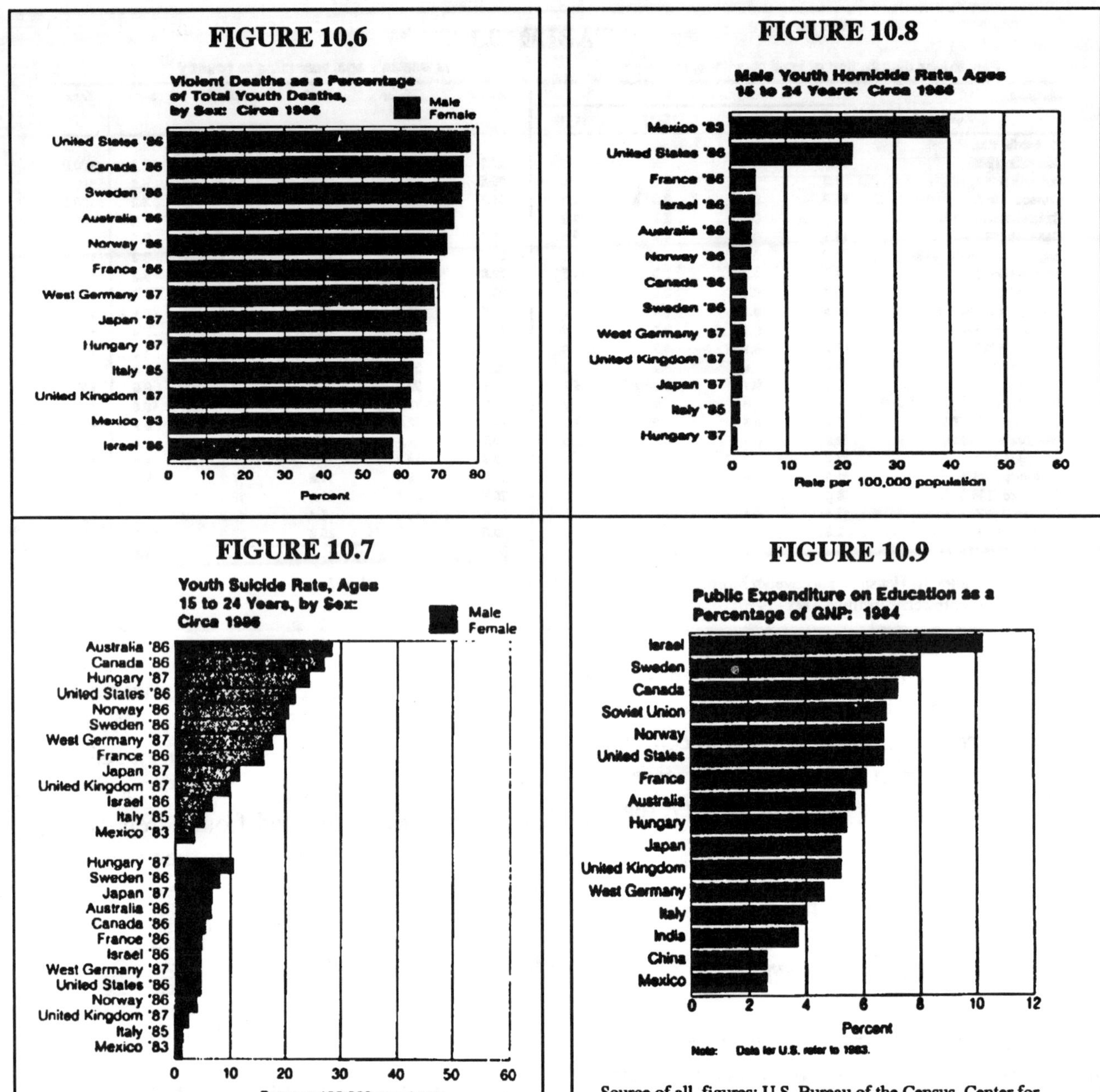

Source of all figures: U.S. Bureau of the Census, Center for International Research, International Data Base

United States were due to accidents, suicides, homicides, or other violence (Figure 10.6).

Male suicides varied substantially. Young male suicides (ages 15 to 24 years) in Australia, Canada, Hungary, Norway, and the United States were double those in Israel, Italy, Mexico, and the United Kingdom in 1986. Rates among young females, were not only much lower, but more consistent from country to country, at about 5 per 100,000 population (Figure 10.7).

Only Mexico had a higher homicide rate among young males than the United States. Male youth in the United States are more than five times as likely to be the victims of homicide than youths in many other developed countries (Figure 10.8). However, the homicide rate for young males in Mexico is twice that for the United States.

Education

The developed countries included in the study spent between 4 and 8 percent of their gross

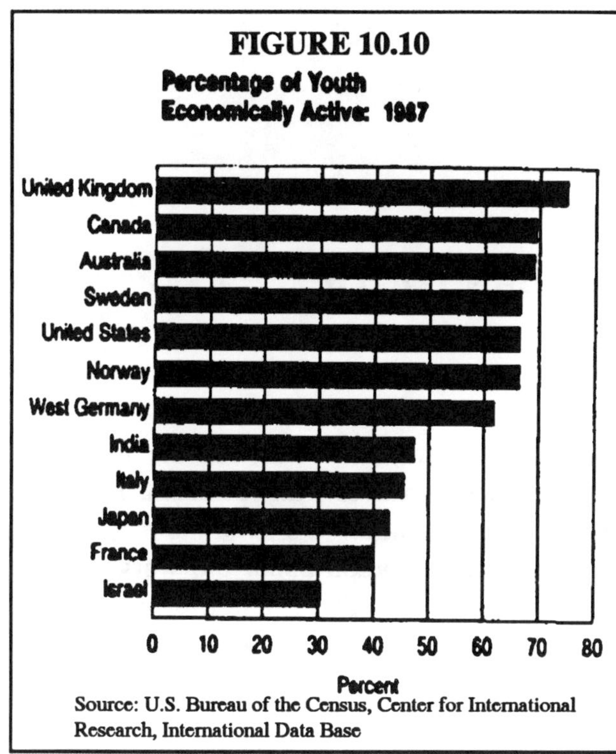

Source: U.S. Bureau of the Census, Center for International Research, International Data Base

school, elementary, secondary, and higher). When viewed as a whole, the U.S. ranks high among the countries studied on education expenditure. However, some researchers observe that if expenditures on higher education are excluded, the U.S. ranking fails significantly.

The United States and other developed nations legislate compulsory education, requiring that all children attend school until a minimum age or grade. Therefore, virtually all young children in developed countries are enrolled in school. However, in developing countries, such as India, young children enrolled in school are a minority (38 percent of those ages 5-14 years), compared with 97 percent in the United States and 100 percent in the United Kingdom and Sweden.

School enrollment among youth ages 15 to 24 years varies by country. While forty-four percent of youth in the United States were enrolled in school, only 30 percent of those in the United Kingdom were in school. These differences are an indication of the proportions of persons who enter and complete college and the labor force participation rates among youth in those countries (Figure 10.10).

national product (GNP) on education (Figure 10.9). The percentage of GNP spent on education by developing nations, with the exception of Israel (11 percent), is lower. The United States and the Soviet Union both spent about 7 percent in 1984. The figures cover all levels of education (pre-

CHAPTER XI

ATTITUDES OF AMERICAN YOUTH

Public attention to the problems of American children, both real and perceived, has grown over the past few years. Drug and alcohol abuse, the high divorce rate, and the ever-increasing number of single-parent households have led to permanent changes in the family structure. The quality of education, the activities of the United States in international affairs, and the continuing movement of women into the workplace have all affected children. The Roper Organization, Inc., under contract to the American Chicle Company, in *The American Chicle Youth Poll: A Landmark Study on the Attitudes of American Youth* (1987, Morris Plains, NJ: Warner-Lambert Company), surveyed the nation's young people (between the ages of 8 and 17) to determine their perceptions of their problems and prospects for the future. The University of Michigan, in its *Monitoring the Future* study, considered the most comprehensive longitudinal survey performed, sampled the attitudes of youths on a variety of isssues since 1979.

THE GENERAL MOOD

Those young people surveyed were generally content with their personal, family, and school lives. While many considered this satisfaction a reflection of youthful innocence and a tendency among the young to deny troubles, others saw it as a positive sign that, while the nation's youth may realize things are wrong, they remain hopeful about their futures. While their responses revealed a very real awareness about the world's problems and a healthy respect for them, they still, for the most part, viewed their own lives with optimism. This is not unlike adult attitudes. While adults may express dismay and frustration about the world's larger problems, such as crime, unless their neighborhood is particularly unsafe, they view it as a problem for someone else.

Overall Satisfaction

The vast majority of American young people like the city or town where they live. Almost 70 percent reported that they liked it "a lot," while another 23 percent liked it "a little." They also expressed overall satisfaction with their lives and

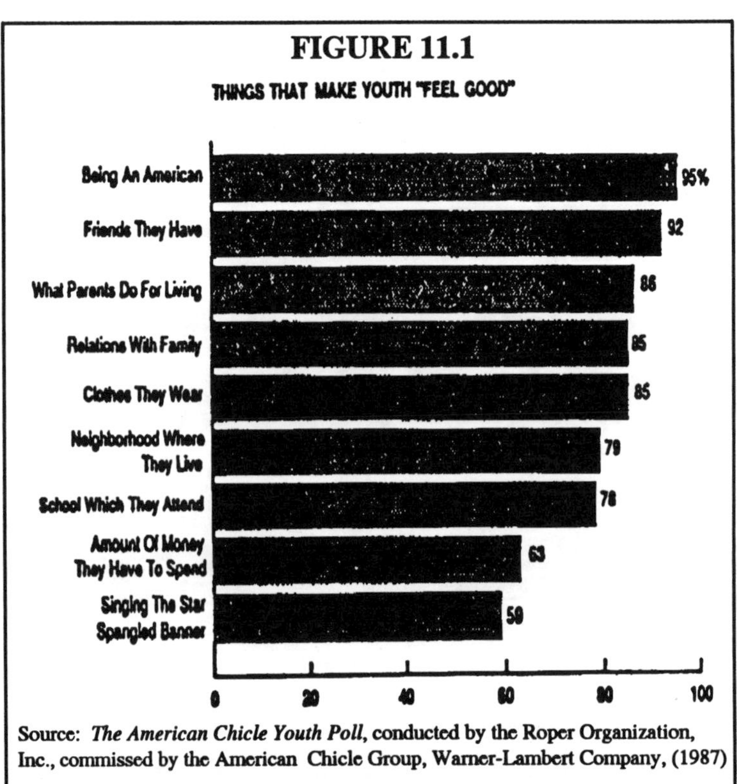

FIGURE 11.1

Source: *The American Chicle Youth Poll*, conducted by the Roper Organization, Inc., commissed by the American Chicle Group, Warner-Lambert Company, (1987)

schools. Ninety percent thought their home life was happy, and 84 percent were happy with the school they attended.

Older teens (15 to 17 years old) and black teens were somewhat less likely to be happy about the town or city where they lived (57 percent of older teens and 60 percent of black teens liked it a lot) and their school (79 percent of older teens and 74 percent of blacks expressed satisfaction compared to 84 percent of the total.) Those from divorced homes were slightly less pleased with their home life than those who were not from divorced homes (83 percent versus 93 percent).

What Makes Them Feel Good?

Almost all (95 percent) of those polled claimed that being an American made them feel good, as did having friends (92 percent) and aspects of their family life, such as what their parents did for a living (86 percent) and how they got along with their parents (85 percent). To no one's surprise, 85 percent felt good about the clothes they wore, but, like most adults, they did not feel as good about the amount of money they had to spend on clothes (63 percent). (See Figure 11.1.)

Problems That Concern Them

More than three-quarters of children and teenagers were very concerned about the kidnapping of young people their age. Females were more concerned than males (84 percent versus 68 percent).

About two-thirds of those polled were concerned about nuclear war and the spread of AIDS. More teenagers than younger children expressed concern about these two issues, perhaps because they had a better understanding of the issues and, no doubt, in the case of AIDS, because they were much more likely to be or to consider becoming sexually active, making the possibility of contracting AIDS a personal reality. The *Monitoring the*

TABLE 11.1

High school seniors reporting that they worry about selected social problems

United States, 1979-91

Question: "Of all the problems facing the nation today, how often do you worry about each of the following?"

(Percent responding "often" or "sometimes")

	Class of 1979 (N=3,308)	Class of 1980 (N=3,286)	Class of 1981 (N=3,656)	Class of 1982 (N=3,616)	Class of 1983 (N=3,339)	Class of 1984 (N=3,294)	Class of 1985 (N=3,286)	Class of 1986 (N=3,073)	Class of 1987 (N=3,370)	Class of 1988 (N=3,326)	Class of 1989 (N=2,849)	Class of 1990 (N=2,595)	Class of 1991 (N=2,595)
Chance of nuclear war	59.4 %	67.4 %	64.3 %	71.6 %	66.6 %	69.4 %	64.5 %	69.1 %	58.3 %	57.3 %	52.4 %	45.1 %	41.5 %
Population growth	43.3	36.1	39.8	34.1	31.5	25.3	25.7	24.1	26.6	27.5	29.6	33.0	30.6
Crime and violence	84.6	81.2	87.8	86.3	85.4	83.9	82.3	79.4	81.9	83.9	86.3	88.8	88.1
Pollution	68.0	62.4	62.0	54.8	53.0	49.1	46.9	44.2	45.2	45.5	55.9	67.2	72.1
Energy shortages	80.9	83.9	75.1	60.3	49.9	40.4	33.7	28.7	28.1	25.1	27.9	32.6	38.2
Race relations	45.0	39.7	47.0	44.0	45.5	43.1	43.4	43.4	44.2	53.3	53.6	57.1	59.4
Hunger and poverty	52.2	52.8	57.2	55.6	59.1	58.3	69.7	65.9	62.2	64.2	64.1	65.9	66.4
Using open land for housing or industry	36.9	34.4	35.2	33.8	31.9	30.0	30.4	26.8	30.5	29.4	30.8	33.9	33.8
Urban decay	22.3	22.8	21.6	21.4	19.5	18.0	17.9	17.0	18.5	19.9	19.8	20.4	21.7
Economic problems	86.0	74.9	73.4	73.7	73.5	66.2	60.4	60.6	55.6	56.2	57.6	56.8	63.9
Drug abuse	66.1	63.3	68.5	70.2	68.7	68.4	69.1	69.2	75.4	78.6	79.5	82.6	79.5

Note: These data are from a series of nationwide surveys of high school seniors conducted by the Survey Research Center of the Institute for Social Research from 1975 through 1991. The survey design is a multistage random sample of high school seniors in public and private schools throughout the continental United States. All percentages reported are based on weighted cases; the N's that are shown in the tables refer to the number of weighted cases.

Response categories were "never," "seldom," "sometimes," and "often." Readers interested in responses to this question for 1975 through 1978 should consult previous editions of SOURCEBOOK.

Source: Lloyd D. Johnston, Jerald G. Bachman, and Patrick M. O'Malley, *Monitoring the Future 1979*, pp. 171, 172; *1981*, pp. 172, 173; *1983*, pp. 174, 175; *1985*, pp. 174, 175 (Ann Arbor, MI: Institute for Social Research, University of Michigan); Jerald G. Bachman, Lloyd D. Johnston, and Patrick M. O'Malley, *Monitoring the Future 1980*, pp. 172, 173; *1982*, pp. 174, 175; *1984*, pp. 174, 175; *1986*, pp. 176, 177 (Ann Arbor, MI: Institute for Social Research, University of Michigan); and data provided by the Monitoring the Future Project, Survey Research Center, Lloyd D. Johnston and Jerald G. Bachman, Principal Investigators. Table adapted by SOURCEBOOK staff. Reprinted by permission.

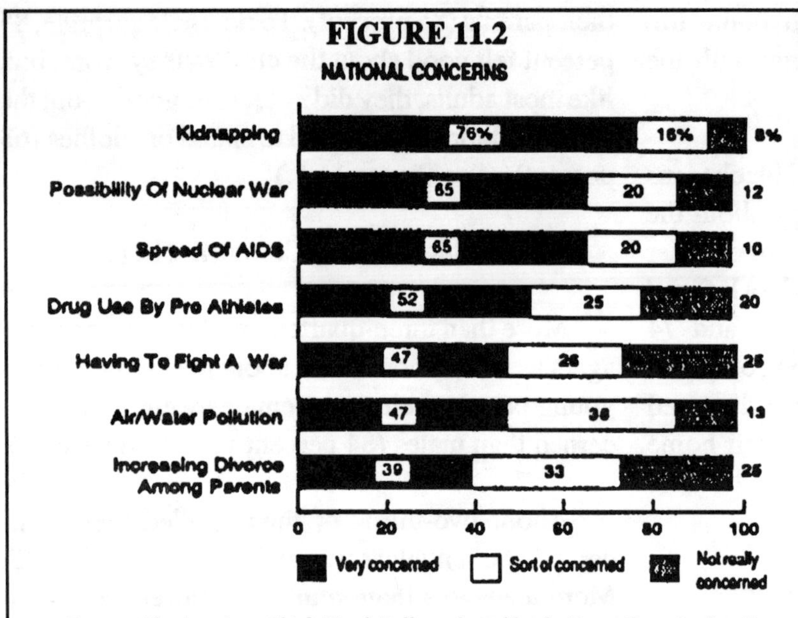

Source: *The American Chicle Youth Poll*, conducted by the Roper Organization, Inc., commissed by the American Chicle Group, Warner-Lambert Company, (1987)

Future study showed slightly less concern about nuclear war (42 percent). (See Table 11.1.)

The Chicle study reported more than half were concerned about drug use among professional athletes, especially the boys, while less than half were concerned about having to fight in a war or the problem of pollution. Fewer than four out of ten were disturbed about the increasing number of divorces among parents. There was very little difference between those whose parents had been divorced and those whose had not. (See Figure 11.2.)

TABLE 11.2

High school seniors reporting that they worry about crime and violence

By sex, race, region, college plans, and illicit drug use, United States, 1979-91

Question: "Of all the problems facing the nation today, how often do you worry about. . .crime and violence?"

(Percent responding "often" or "sometimes")

	Class of 1979 (N=3,308)	Class of 1980 (N=3,286)	Class of 1981 (N=3,656)	Class of 1982 (N=3,616)	Class of 1983 (N=3,339)	Class of 1984 (N=3,294)	Class of 1985 (N=3,286)	Class of 1986 (N=3,073)	Class of 1987 (N=3,370)	Class of 1988 (N=3,326)	Class of 1989 (N=2,849)	Class of 1990 (N=2,595)	Class of 1991 (N=2,595)
Total	84.6 %	81.2 %	87.8 %	86.3 %	85.4 %	83.9 %	82.3 %	79.4 %	81.9 %	83.9 %	86.3 %	88.8 %	88.1 %
Sex													
Male	77.1	73.8	81.7	79.5	78.6	77.5	76.6	70.8	73.7	76.0	80.9	84.8	82.6
Female	91.6	88.5	94.7	92.8	92.4	90.4	88.0	87.4	90.3	91.8	92.2	93.4	93.6
Race													
White	83.8	80.7	87.3	85.1	84.5	83.3	80.9	78.4	80.8	82.8	84.6	88.1	86.6
Black	89.1	83.3	91.0	91.2	91.6	90.4	88.9	81.9	94.2	88.2	91.8	92.7	94.5
Region													
Northeast	84.1	80.5	88.2	86.2	89.0	82.7	80.0	77.0	77.9	81.9	83.0	87.7	86.0
North Central	85.7	83.3	86.9	82.9	79.9	83.6	81.7	78.9	81.6	81.7	83.0	87.0	88.8
South	85.3	81.1	89.3	89.0	86.5	86.0	83.6	82.3	85.3	86.1	89.4	90.4	88.4
West	81.8	79.1	86.6	87.4	87.6	81.9	84.0	78.4	81.3	85.4	88.2	80.4	89.0
College plans													
Yes	86.3	82.4	90.1	87.4	85.9	85.6	83.3	80.9	82.8	85.4	88.0	89.8	89.9
No	82.7	79.5	84.8	84.9	84.4	82.0	81.4	77.2	79.4	80.8	82.8	88.0	83.9
Lifetime illicit drug use													
None	86.6	82.4	90.5	87.9	86.2	87.5	84.5	80.3	83.2	85.8	88.8	90.6	90.7
Marihuana only	83.7	82.0	87.7	84.0	86.2	84.0	80.5	79.2	81.7	83.9	86.6	87.1	85.4
Few pills	87.3	81.1	86.4	88.6	84.3	86.6	81.9	80.0	80.8	83.7	85.2	87.6	86.6
More pills	82.1	79.2	86.4	85.2	84.9	78.4	81.6	77.8	81.2	81.2	81.7	85.7	84.8

. Data are given for those who identify themselves as White or Caucasian and those who identify themselves as Black or Afro-American because these are the two largest racial/ethnic subgroups in the population. Data are not given for the other ethnic categories because these groups comprise less than 3 percent of the sample in any given year (Source, 1982, p. 9). "College plans" distinguishes those seniors who expect to graduate from a 4-year college from those who expect to receive some college training or none. The four drug use categories are based on an index of seriousness of involvement. The "pills" category indicates use of any of a number of drugs including some that usually are not taken in pill form. Respondents indicating the use of one or more of a number of illicit drugs but who had not used any one class of them on three or more occasions and did not use heroin at all fall into the "few pills" category. Respondents indicating such use on three or more occasions and did not use heroin at all fall into the "more pills" category. Respondents reporting heroin use were included in a separate category that is not presented here due to the small number of respondents indicating such use. (Source, 1982, pp. 8, 9, 14.)

Response categories were "never," "seldom," "sometimes," and "often." Readers interested in responses to this question for 1975 through 1978 should consult previous editions of SOURCEBOOK. For survey methodology and definitions of terms, see Appendix 6.

Source: Lloyd D. Johnston, Jerald G. Bachman, and Patrick M. O'Malley, *Monitoring the Future 1979*, pp. 171, 172; *1981*, pp. 172, 173; *1983*, pp. 174, 175; *1985*, p. 174 (Ann Arbor, MI: Institute for Social Research, University of Michigan); Jerald G. Bachman, Lloyd D. Johnston, and Patrick M. O'Malley, *Monitoring the Future 1980*, pp. 172, 173; *1982*, p. 174; *1984*, p. 174; *1986*, p. 176 (Ann Arbor, MI: Institute for Social Research, University of Michigan); and data provided by the Monitoring the Future Project, Survey Research Center, Lloyd D. Johnston and Jerald G. Bachman, Principal Investigators. Table adapted by SOURCEBOOK staff. Reprinted by permission.

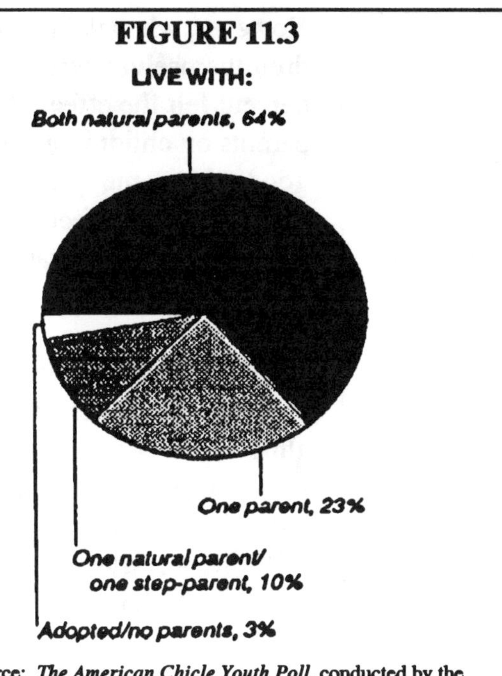

Source: *The American Chicle Youth Poll*, conducted by the Roper Organization, Inc., commissed by the American Chicle Group, Warner-Lambert Company, (1987)

The *Monitoring the Future* survey reported the highest level of concern among high school seniors regarded crime and violence (88 percent). Concern was greatest among blacks and females (Table 11.2). Pollution also worried them (72 percent), as did hunger and poverty (66 percent).

FAMILY LIFE

Home and Family

The decrease in the number of two-parent families is reflected in the finding that fewer than two-thirds of the young people surveyed (64 percent) lived with both natural parents. About one-fourth stayed with only one parent, while 10 percent lived with a natural parent and a step-parent (Figure 11.3). One-quarter had been through a divorce. Those from low-income households were most likely to be living with only one parent (42 percent) and to have been through a divorce (36 percent).

One-third (34 percent) of the black children surveyed lived in a single parent household, compared with 21 percent of the white children. The proportion of black children who had been through a divorce or the death of a parent was about the same as for white children, but black children were more likely to come from homes where the mother had never married.

Working Mothers

Three-quarters of the youth polled had working mothers—about half (46 percent) worked full-time and one-quarter (23 percent) worked part-time. Mothers with only one or two children, black mothers, moth-

TABLE 11.3
WHETHER MOTHER WORKS OUTSIDE THE HOME
(By Demographic Groups)

	Works Full-time	Works Part-time	Doesn't work
Total	46%	25%	28%
Sex			
Male	45	24	27
Female	47	26	25
Age			
8-12 (net)	41	27	28
8-10	40	27	29
11,12	43	28	27
13-17 (net)	50	23	23
13,14	47	25	24
15-17	52	23	23
Race			
White	43	27	27
Black	55	22	17
Socioeconomic status			
Upper/upper middle	47	27	24
Lower middle	48	24	24
Lower	36	22	33
Region			
Northeast	34	37	24
Midwest	49	24	26
South	51	20	27
West	46	22	25
Been through divorce			
Yes	61	19	16
No	41	27	29
Live with:			
Both natural parents	40	28	30
One parent/one step-parent	53	24	23
One parent	50	19	15
Number of siblings			
None or one	53	27	19
Two or three	45	26	26
Four or more	32	23	41

Source: *The American Chicle Youth Poll*, conducted by the Roper Organization, Inc., commissed by the American Chicle Group, Warner-Lambert Company, (1987)

TABLE 11.4

OVERALL EFFECT OF MOTHERS AND FATHERS BOTH WORKING OUTSIDE THE HOME

	Total %	Age		Mother works:		
		8-12 %	13-17 %	Full Time %	Part Time %	Not at All %
Effect on children 12 or under is:						
Good	25	31	19	28	26	19
Bad	39	28	48	35	36	48
No effect	29	31	28	30	33	25
Don't know	7	9	6	7	4	9
Effect on teenagers is:						
Good	26	27	26	29	28	22
Bad	18	20	16	16	20	22
No effect	48	39	53	48	45	47
Don't know	9	14	5	8	8	10

TABLE 11.5

DO YOU PREFER YOUR MOTHER TO HAVE JOB OUTSIDE HOME OR STAY HOME AND CARE FOR FAMILY?

	Total %	Age		Mother works:		
		8-12 %	13-17 %	Full Time %	Part Time %	Not at All %
Prefer Mother to:						
Work Outside the Home	59	50	67	73	71	25
Stay Home	34	43	26	22	24	67

Source of both tables: *The American Chicle Youth Poll*, conducted by the Roper Organization, Inc., commissed by the American Chicle Group, Warner-Lambert Company, (1987)

However, when the younger children themselves were polled, 31 percent felt the effect of working parents on children under 12 was good, the same percentage believed it had no effect at all, and 28 thought the effect was bad. (See Table 11.4.)

Among those whose mothers did not work outside the home, almost half (48 percent) felt the effect on young children was bad, but only 35 percent of those with full-time working mothers and 36 percent of those with part-time working mothers felt the same way. Half of those polled believed that two working parents had no effect on teenagers.

Almost two-thirds of those polled felt that children whose mothers worked outside the home did about as well in school as those students whose mothers were at home; one-fourth felt they did worse. Those whose mothers did not work outside the home were more likely to believe that students with working mothers did worse in school. About half of those polled thought that children with working mothers got into about the same amount of trouble as other children, but those whose mothers did not work felt they got into more trouble.

A majority of teenagers (63 percent) believed that children with working mothers were more independent than those without. However, only 30 percent of those aged 8 to 12 agreed, while 50 percent of the same age group thought there was no difference.

When asked whether they preferred their mothers to work or stay at home, almost six out of 10

ers who headed single-parent households, and Southern mothers were more likely to be working full-time than others. (See Table 11.3.)

A plurality (39 percent) of those polled felt that when both parents worked, the younger children (those 12 and under) were negatively affected. About 30 percent believed it had no effect at all, and 25 percent thought it had a positive effect. Teenagers were more likely than younger children to be opposed to both parents working; 48 percent of teens thought it had a bad effect on young children.

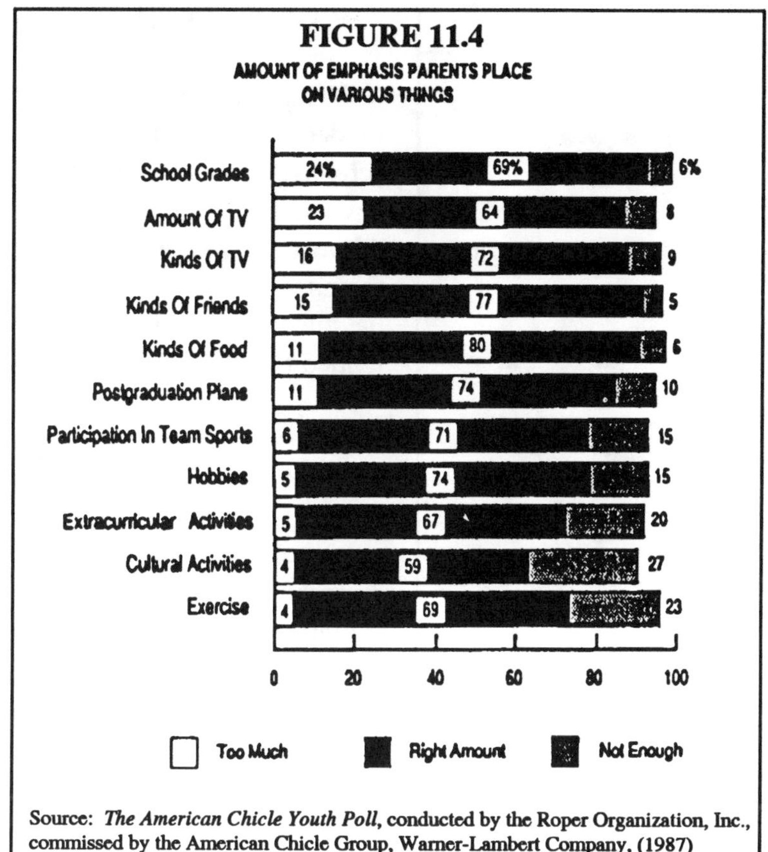

Source: *The American Chicle Youth Poll*, conducted by the Roper Organization, Inc., commissed by the American Chicle Group, Warner-Lambert Company, (1987)

Decision-Making

Only teenagers were questioned about the proper age for making decisions about important issues without relying on their parents' advice. Teens felt that 17 was the median age at which teenagers could decide how late to stay out at night, whether or not to quit school, and whether or not to have sex.

Boys were more likely to have considered an age younger than 17 years as right for deciding how late to stay out, while girls were more likely to think 18 or older was more appropriate. Typically, boys were given later curfews or allowed to make their own curfew decisions more often than girls.

Although 50 percent felt 17 years was the median age at which teens should decide whether or not to quit school, 45 percent thought 18 years or older was the appropriate age. On the question of when to have sex, 38 percent thought 16 years or under; 11 percent thought 17 years; and 42 percent thought 18 years or older.

Thirty percent felt 18 years was the age for deciding whether to drink beer or wine, 25 percent thought it should be 17 years or younger, and 42 percent believed one should be 18 year or older. Almost one-fourth (23 percent) of the teenagers felt 18 years was the median age to decide whether or not to smoke marijuana, with 37 percent choosing an older age. In all these issues, teens from the Northeastern part of the nation tended to support an earlier age.

APPRAISING SCHOOL

Attitudes About School

About three-quarters of those polled claimed that school made them "feel good." Females were

wanted their mothers to work. More teenagers than younger children felt this way (67 percent versus 50 percent). Even stronger differences could be seen between those whose mothers currently worked outside the home and those whose mothers did not. Children with working mothers supported their mothers' working, and children with mothers who stayed at home supported their mothers' staying home. (See Table 11.5.)

Parental Guidance

When questioned about eleven important issues which influenced their lives, American youth seemed to believe that, overall, parents placed the appropriate amount of emphasis on all of them. They did feel, however, that parents placed too much emphasis on grades, the amount and type of television they watched, and, the kinds of friends they had. On the other hand, they felt their parents did not place enough emphasis on cultural activities, exercise, and extra-curricular activities. (See Figure 11.4.)

TABLE 11.6

GRADE POINT AVERAGE OF SELECTED ITEMS
(By Demographic Groups)

	Feeling Safe At School	Teaching Of Basic Skills	Preparing Students for College**	Preparing Students for Working**	Quality of Teachers
Total	3.4	3.4	3.3	3.2	3.1
Sex					
Male	3.4	3.4	3.2	3.2	3.1
Female	3.4	3.5	3.3	3.2	3.2
Age					
8-12 (net)	3.5	3.5	NA	NA	3.4
8-10	3.6	3.6	NA	NA	3.4
11-12	3.3	3.5	NA	NA	3.2
13-17(net)	3.4	3.3	3.3	3.2	3.0
13-14	3.4	3.4	3.2	3.2	3.1
15-17	3.4	3.3	3.3	3.2	2.9
Race					
White	3.5	3.4	3.3	3.1	3.2
Black	3.2	3.5	3.1	3.3	3.0
Socioeconomic status					
Upper/Upper-middle	3.5	3.5	3.3	3.2	3.2
Lower-middle	3.4	3.4	3.2	3.2	3.2
Lower	3.1	3.2	3.2	3.0	2.9
Region					
Northeast	3.3	3.3	3.4	3.1	3.1
Midwest	3.5	3.4	3.2	3.1	3.1
South	3.4	3.5	3.2	3.3	3.2
West	3.5	3.5	3.3	3.2	3.1
Type School Attend					
Public	3.4	3.4	3.2	3.2	3.1
Non-Public	3.7	3.6	3.5	3.2	3.3

NA = Not Asked.
** Asked of teens only.

Source: *The American Chicle Youth Poll*, conducted by the Roper Organization, Inc., commissioned by the American Chicle Group, Warner-Lambert Company, (1987)

Quality of Schools

When assigning letter grades, such as is done in most schools, today's young people gave their schools a solid "B." Almost 30 percent awarded their school an "A." The older the students, the lower the grade tended to be.

When grading specific aspects of their school, certain demographic differences emerged. Younger students and whites tended to feel safer in their schools than older teens and blacks. (See Chapter VIII for attitudes about crime and fear of victimization.) Younger students were more likely to rate teaching of basic skills higher, while whites gave higher grades when rating preparation for college and the quality of teachers. Those attending private schools gave higher evaluations for most of the items. (See Table 11.6.)

slightly more positive than males, and younger children more so than teens. There were two major exceptions. Seventy percent of those from the lowest socioeconomic group felt school made them feel good, while almost 80 percent of those from the higher socioeconomic group thought it did. Only two-thirds of black respondents reported that school made them feel good, while four-fifths of white students did. (Many blacks are likely to be from lower socioeconomic groups.)

More than three-quarters of those polled claimed they liked school, 10 percent disliked it, and 12 percent had mixed emotions. Black students were less likely to feel good about the schools they attended.

Monitoring the Future reported that high school seniors gave an approval rating of only 34 percent to the nation's public schools. They believed that colleges and universities were doing a better job (70 percent). (See Table 11.7.)

College and Career Aspirations

Eighty percent of those surveyed planned to go to college after completing high school. Those whose parents attended college, in private schools, in the highest socioeconomic category, and those nearing college age showed the most interest in college, although interest was consistently high across all groups (Table 11.8). More than two-thirds of American young people knew what they wanted to do when they finished high school. The most popular field was health care (doctors, nurses, other health occupations), which seemed to be particularly appealing to black children, 11 percent of whom hoped to be doctors and 7 percent to be nurses.

Following the health professions, blue collar jobs (18 percent) such as construction, electricians, and beauticians were most frequently mentioned, followed by teaching (7 percent), careers in arts and entertainment (6 percent), and sports (6 percent). Girls were more likely to be interested in health care professions (24 percent) and teaching (13 percent), while among boys, no one field stood out. Sports and athletic careers, especially football (10 percent), seemed to interest the boys, followed by medicine (8 percent), the trades (8 percent), science and engineering (8 percent), and the military (7 percent). (See Table 11.9.)

SOCIAL ISSUES

What Goes On?

More than 80 percent of the teenage students claimed that at least some smoking occurred among their peers, while over half (52 percent) said it happened a lot. More than two-thirds (68 percent) indicated some drinking went on and 30 percent said sexual activity happened a lot. More than half reported some crime (58 percent), drug abuse (58 percent), and marijuana use (55 percent). Two-fifths reported knowledge of at least some teenage pregnancy, and almost one-fourth reported that some cocaine and crack use took place. (See Table 11.10.)

With the exception of crime, girls were more likely than boys to report that these activities happened often. Older teens were more likely to report occurrences of all these things at least some of the

TABLE 11.8

PLANS REGARDING COLLEGE

	Plan to attend college	Do not plan attend college	Don't kno
Total	80%	11%	9%
Sex			
Male	78	12	10
Female	82	10	7
Age			
8-12 (net)	83	7	10
8-10	82	7	11
11,12	83	7	10
13-17 (net)	78	14	7
13,14	83	10	6
15-17	75	17	8
Race			
White	81	10	8
Black	76	16	9
Socioeconomic status			
Upper/upper-middle	87	7	6
Lower middle	76	13	10
Lower	71	17	11
Region			
Northeast	82	11	7
Midwest	81	9	10
South	79	13	8
West	81	10	10
Type of school			
Public	79	12	9
Non-public	89	2	9
Parents attend college			
Neither	68	19	12
One	86	8	6
Both	92	4	4
Attitudes toward school			
Like	84	9	7
Dislike	68	24	9

TABLE 11.9

CAREER ASPIRATIONS OF AMERICAN YOUTH

	Total %	Sex Boys %	Girls %
Medical/health care	16	8	24
Trade/blue collar	8	8	9
Teaching	7	2	13
Arts/entertainment	6	5	6
Sports/athletics	6	10	-
Military	4	7	2
Science/engineering	4	8	1
Design/fashion	3	-	6
Police/fire protection	3	6	-
Computer	3	3	3
Aviation	3	6	-
Business/finance	3	2	4
Law	3	2	4
News/journalism	1	1	2
Architect	1	2	-
Don't Know	31	34	28

Source of both tables: *The American Chicle Youth Poll*, conducted by the Roper Organization, Inc., commissed by the American Chicle Group, Warner-Lambert Company, (1987)

time. Whites were more likely to report smoking and drinking among their peers, and blacks more likely to report crime and teenage pregnancy. Drinking appears to be more common among higher socioeconomic groups, while pregnancy is more prevalent among lower socioeconomic groups.

The *Monitoring the Future* survey reports that, when asked how much people harmed themselves by drug, alcohol, and tobacco use, 1991 high school seniors overwhelmingly state that frequent or daily use of any substance puts one at "great risk," although occasional use was viewed with less concern. Although many students expressed concern, judging from actual drug use statistics, many of the same students are substance users (For information on drug use data, see Chapter V—Health and Safety). (See Table 11.11.) Worry about drug abuse has increased steadily since the study began in 1979 (Table 11.1).

SOCIO-POLITICAL ISSUES AND SCHOOLS

The Criminal Justice System

Monitoring the Future reported that only a quarter of the high school seniors believed that the courts and criminal justice system were "doing a good job." That rating has remained relatively constant since the survey's beginning in 1979. (See Table 11.12.)

TABLE 11.10

WHAT GOES ON AMONG FELLOW STUDENTS
(A Lot/Some Combined, Teenagers Only)

	Smoking	Drinking	Sexual Activity	Marijuana Use	Crime	Drug Abuse	Teen Pregnancy	Use of Cocaine/Crack
Total	81%	68%	67%	55%	58%	58%	43%	23%
Sex								
Male	78	65	65	53	61	55	34	19
Female	86	71	68	57	55	61	52	26
Age								
13 or 14	69	49	51	39	54	44	29	15
15-17	89	80	77	65	61	66	51	28
Race								
White	84	72	68	57	56	59	39	22
Black	72	57	67	55	68	60	66	26
Socioeconomic status								
Upper/upper-middle	83	69	69	55	54	58	36	23
Lower-middle	81	67	67	56	60	59	46	23
Lower	69	59	64	51	62	58	60	18
Region								
Northeast	89	72	67	60	55	63	44	25
Midwest	79	72	69	53	54	52	39	16
South	81	64	68	52	61	57	51	22
West	76	64	63	57	61	64	29	30
Type of school								
Public	84	70	68	57	61	61	46	25
Non-public	57	51	51	33	33	32	14	11

Source: *The American Chicle Youth Poll*, conducted by the Roper Organization, Inc., commissed by the American Chicle Group, Warner-Lambert Company, (1987)

Only 28 percent expressed approval of the performance of the policc and other law enforcement agencies, meaning that most students (72 percent) disapproved of law enforcement agencies' performance. The 1991 rating is lower than at any time since 1979. (See Table 11.13.)

Government

Monitoring the Future showed that 57 percent of high school seniors believed that the then-President Bush and his administration were doing a good job in 1991. Thirty-nine percent approved of the Congress, and 44 percent, the Supreme Court. The military received the highest approval rating (81 percent) since the survey's inception in 1979.

The Corporate World

Slightly more than one-third (36 percent) of high school seniors believed that U.S. corporations were doing a good job. Thirty-one percent approved of labor union performance.

Prayer/Moment of Silence

While 50 percent of students thought public schools should not have organized prayer, a large minority (41 percent) believed schools should. Of those who opposed organized prayer, 33 percent advocated a moment of silence, while 18 percent favored neither. A majority of blacks and a plurality of whites supported organized prayer. Southerners were most likely to prefer organized prayer, Northeasterners, a moment of silence, while Westerners were split three ways.

Busing for Racial Integration

Almost two-thirds (64 percent) of those surveyed favored busing, 23 percent were opposed, 6 percent did not know what busing was, and 7 percent were undecided. No racial and regional differences were found. Busing does not seem to be the divisive issue for young people that it has been for their parents.

Homosexuals and Teaching

About half (49 percent) thought homosexuals should be allowed to teach, while four out of ten (41 percent) believed they should not. A plurality of males felt teaching by homosexuals should not be allowed, but a majority of females felt it should. This could well reflect discomfort among male students in being around homosexuals, while girls feel no sexual threat. A majority of whites thought homosexuals should be allowed to teach, while a plurality of blacks believed they should not. The higher the socioeconomic group, the more likely they were to approve. Those in the Northeast and Midwest were more favorable than those from the South or the West.

TABLE 11.11

High school seniors' perceptions of the harmfulness of drug use, alcohol use, and cigarette smoking

By type of drug and frequency of use, United States, 1979-91

Question: "How much do you think people risk harming themselves (physically or in other ways), if they. . .?"

(Percent saying "great risk[a]")

Type of drug and frequency of use	Class of 1979 (N=3,250)	Class of 1980 (N=3,234)	Class of 1981 (N=3,604)	Class of 1982 (N=3,557)	Class of 1983 (N=3,305)	Class of 1984 (N=3,262)	Class of 1985 (N=3,250)	Class of 1986 (N=3,020)	Class of 1987 (N=3,315)	Class of 1988 (N=3,276)	Class of 1989 (N=2,796)	Class of 1990 (N=2,553)	Class of 1991 (N=2,549)
Try marihuana once or twice	9.4 %	10.0 %	13.0 %	11.5 %	12.7 %	14.7 %	14.8 %	15.1 %	18.4 %	19.0 %	23.6 %	23.1 %	27.1 %
Smoke marihuana occasionally	13.5	14.7	19.1	18.3	20.6	22.6	24.5	25.0	30.4	31.7	36.5	36.9	40.6
Smoke marihuana regularly	42.0	50.4	57.6	60.4	62.8	66.9	70.4	71.3	73.5	77.0	77.5	77.8	78.6
Try LSD once or twice	41.6	43.9	45.5	44.9	44.7	45.4	43.5	42.0	44.9	45.7	46.0	44.7	46.6
Take LSD regularly	82.4	83.0	83.5	83.5	83.2	83.8	82.9	82.6	83.8	84.2	84.3	84.5	84.3
Try PCP once or twice	NA	NA	NA	NA	NA	NA	NA	NA	55.6	58.8	56.6	55.2	51.7
Try cocaine once or twice	31.5	31.3	32.1	32.8	33.0	35.7	34.0	33.5	47.9	51.2	54.9	59.4	59.4
Take cocaine occasionally	NA	NA	NA	NA	NA	NA	NA	54.2	66.8	69.2	71.8	73.9	75.5
Take cocaine regularly	69.5	69.2	71.2	73.0	74.3	78.8	79.0	82.2	88.5	89.2	90.2	91.1	90.4
Try "crack" once or twice	NA	NA	NA	NA	NA	NA	NA	NA	57.0	62.1	62.9	64.3	60.6
Take "crack" occasionally	NA	NA	NA	NA	NA	NA	NA	NA	70.4	73.2	75.3	80.4	76.5
Take "crack" regularly	NA	NA	NA	NA	NA	NA	NA	NA	84.6	84.8	85.6	91.6	90.1
Try cocaine powder once or twice	NA	NA	NA	NA	NA	NA	NA	NA	45.3	51.7	53.8	53.9	53.6
Take cocaine powder occasionally	NA	NA	NA	NA	NA	NA	NA	NA	56.8	61.9	65.8	71.1	69.8
Take cocaine powder regularly	NA	NA	NA	NA	NA	NA	NA	NA	81.4	82.9	83.9	90.2	88.9
Try heroin once or twice	50.4	52.1	52.9	51.1	50.8	49.8	47.3	45.8	53.6	54.0	53.8	55.4	55.2
Take heroin occasionally	70.9	70.9	72.2	69.8	71.8	70.7	69.8	68.2	74.6	73.8	75.5	76.6	74.9
Take heroin regularly	87.5	86.2	87.5	86.0	86.1	87.2	86.0	87.1	88.7	88.8	89.5	90.2	89.6
Try amphetamines once or twice	29.7	29.7	26.4	25.3	24.7	25.4	25.2	25.1	29.1	29.6	32.8	32.2	36.3
Take amphetamines regularly	69.9	69.1	66.1	64.7	64.8	67.1	67.2	67.3	69.4	69.8	71.2	71.2	74.1
Try barbiturates once or twice	30.7	30.9	28.4	27.5	27.0	27.4	26.1	25.4	30.9	29.7	32.2	32.4	35.1
Take barbiturates regularly	71.6	72.2	69.9	67.6	67.7	68.5	68.3	67.2	69.4	69.6	70.5	70.2	70.5
Try one or two drinks of an alcoholic beverage (beer, wine, liquor)	4.1	3.8	4.6	3.5	4.2	4.6	5.0	4.6	6.2	6.0	6.0	8.3	9.1
Take one or two drinks nearly every day	22.6	20.3	21.6	21.6	21.6	23.0	24.4	25.1	26.2	27.3	28.5	31.3	32.7
Take four or five drinks nearly every day	66.2	65.7	64.5	65.5	66.8	68.4	69.8	66.5	69.7	68.5	69.8	70.9	69.5
Have five or more drinks once or twice each weekend	34.9	35.9	36.3	36.0	38.6	41.7	43.0	39.1	41.9	42.6	44.0	47.1	48.6
Smoke one or more packs of cigarettes per day	63.0	63.7	63.3	60.5	61.2	63.8	66.5	66.0	68.6	68.0	67.2	68.2	69.4

Note: These data are from a series of nationwide surveys of high school seniors conducted by the University of Michigan's Institute for Social Research for the National Institute on Drug Abuse from 1975 through 1991. The survey design is a multistage random sample of high school seniors in public and private schools. Depending on the survey year, from 66 to 80 percent of the schools initially invited to participate agreed to do so. Completed questionnaires were obtained from 77 to 84 percent of all sampled students in participating schools each year. All percentages reported are based on weighted cases; the N's that are shown in the tables also refer to the number of weighted cases. "Crack" is a highly potent and addictive form of cocaine. Alcohol and cigarette use are included in selected tables. Readers interested in responses to this question for 1975 through 1978 should consult previous editions of SOURCEBOOK.

[a] Answer alternatives were: (1) no risk, (2) slight risk, (3) moderate risk, (4) great risk, and (5) can't say, drug unfamiliar.

Source: Lloyd D. Johnston, Patrick M. O'Malley, and Jerald G. Bachman, *Smoking, Drinking, and Illicit Drug Use Among American Secondary School Students, College Students, and Young Adults, 1975-1991*, U.S. Department of Health and Human Services, National Institute on Drug Abuse (Washington, DC: USGPO, 1992). Table adapted by SOURCEBOOK staff.

TABLE 11.12

High school seniors reporting positive attitudes toward the performance of the courts and the justice system in general

By sex, race, region, college plans, and illicit drug use, United States, 1979-91

Question: "Now we'd like you to make some ratings of how good or bad a job you feel each of the following organizations is doing for the country as a whole. . ... How good or bad a job is being done for the country as a whole by. . .all the courts and the justice system in general?"

(Percent responding "good" or "very good")

	Class of 1979 (N=3,295)	Class of 1980 (N=3,299)	Class of 1981 (N=3,658)	Class of 1982 (N=3,688)	Class of 1983 (N=3,382)	Class of 1984 (N=3,287)	Class of 1985 (N=3,294)	Class of 1986 (N=3,159)	Class of 1987 (N=3,357)	Class of 1988 (N=3,378)	Class of 1989 (N=2,852)	Class of 1990 (N=2,600)
Total	24.4 %	24.2 %	26.9 %	25.7 %	25.7 %	28.7 %	28.7 %	34.4 %	33.7 %	31.6 %	31.7 %	27.8 %
Sex												
Male	23.7	25.1	27.0	24.3	25.4	29.4	30.0	33.0	36.1	31.7	33.2	30.9
Female	25.3	23.2	26.8	27.1	26.4	28.2	27.2	35.2	31.3	32.1	30.1	24.9
Race												
White	23.9	24.4	27.3	25.7	26.3	29.0	28.8	34.7	33.8	34.0	32.2	27.3
Black	24.5	22.1	25.7	28.0	23.5	25.4	28.9	35.4	30.9	21.6	26.8	26.4
Region												
Northeast	18.6	21.9	25.4	24.7	20.1	26.6	29.2	29.2	32.3	31.2	27.2	22.8
North Central	25.7	24.2	26.7	26.3	28.1	27.6	26.3	34.8	33.3	31.7	33.7	27.2
South	26.2	25.4	25.7	26.0	26.5	26.6	27.2	36.8	34.4	34.1	33.4	31.1
West	26.8	25.5	27.7	25.8	26.9	35.0	31.2	36.3	34.6	27.4	29.9	26.8
College plans												
Yes	25.5	25.0	27.1	25.8	26.7	29.8	28.9	34.2	34.7	32.7	32.3	27.6
No	23.7	23.4	26.1	26.9	25.2	27.2	27.7	34.6	31.8	30.2	31.2	27.8
Lifetime illicit drug use												
None	27.1	25.5	29.1	25.6	25.7	29.3	28.6	33.9	35.0	32.7	31.6	29.9
Marihuana only	24.2	25.6	27.3	23.8	26.6	29.8	31.4	36.4	33.8	31.5	33.2	25.7
Few pills	23.5	21.8	27.6	26.5	25.4	28.5	27.7	36.1	35.8	30.8	28.2	25.4
More pills	21.4	22.6	24.3	25.7	25.8	26.6	26.4	33.1	28.9	29.2	33.6	24.2

Response categories were "very poor," "poor," "fair," "good," "very good," and "no opinion." Readers interested in responses to this question for 1975 through 1978 should consult previous editions of SOURCEBOOK.

Source: Lloyd D. Johnston, Jerald G. Bachman, and Patrick M. O'Malley, *Monitoring the Future 1979*, p. 127; *1981*, p. 128; *1983*, p. 127; *1985*, p. 127 (Ann Arbor, MI: Institute for Social Research, University of Michigan); Jerald G. Bachman, Lloyd D. Johnston, Patrick M. O'Malley, *Monitoring the Future 1980*, p. 128; *1982*, p. 127; *1984*, p. ...; *1986*, p. 130 (Ann Arbor, MI: Institute for Social Research, University of Michigan); data provided by the Monitoring the Future Project, Survey Research Center, Lloyd Johnston and Jerald G. Bachman, Principal Investigators. Table adapted by SOURCEBOOK staff. Reprinted by permission.

TABLE 11.13

High school seniors reporting positive attitudes toward the performance of the police and other law enforcement agencies

By sex, race, region, college plans, and illicit drug use, United States, 1979-91

Question: "Now we'd like you to make some ratings of how good or bad a job you feel each of the following organizations is doing for the country as a whole. . ... How good or bad a job is being done for the country as a whole by. . .the police and other law enforcement agencies?"

(Percent responding "good" or "very good")

	Class of 1979 (N=3,295)	Class of 1980 (N=3,299)	Class of 1981 (N=3,658)	Class of 1982 (N=3,688)	Class of 1983 (N=3,382)	Class of 1984 (N=3,287)	Class of 1985 (N=3,294)	Class of 1986 (N=3,159)	Class of 1987 (N=3,357)	Class of 1988 (N=3,378)	Class of 1989 (N=2,852)	Class of 1990 (N=2,600)	Class of 1991 (N=2,582)
Total	37.6 %	37.2 %	35.0 %	37.2 %	37.4 %	36.9 %	37.3 %	40.5 %	39.5 %	37.4 %	33.6 %	34.3 %	28.0 %
Sex													
Male	37.4	37.8	34.6	37.8	36.9	38.3	38.1	39.9	40.4	37.3	33.5	33.4	29.3
Female	38.2	36.8	35.3	36.6	37.8	35.6	36.5	40.9	38.5	37.5	34.2	35.0	27.2
Race													
White	39.5	39.7	36.9	38.6	38.7	37.6	38.9	42.4	41.9	40.5	35.5	35.4	31.5
Black	28.9	23.1	24.7	30.3	29.8	31.7	29.4	30.3	24.8	22.6	28.3	22.4	11.0
Region													
Northeast	32.5	35.2	32.8	34.5	33.6	32.0	32.7	32.5	37.4	34.0	33.4	28.3	26.3
North Central	38.8	35.7	36.6	36.2	35.9	37.1	36.9	41.4	39.4	38.5	33.8	36.2	35.7
South	35.8	35.6	32.4	37.8	39.0	37.5	36.5	42.7	39.5	38.5	35.2	36.0	22.1
West	46.3	45.7	40.4	42.8	42.7	41.1	44.7	46.2	41.9	37.3	30.7	36.3	30.0
College plans													
Yes	40.4	39.1	35.6	37.5	38.9	38.9	38.6	39.9	40.7	38.7	34.2	34.0	28.5
No	36.1	34.9	34.5	36.8	36.1	34.5	34.9	42.6	38.3	35.4	34.0	33.8	28.7
Lifetime illicit drug use													
None	44.2	42.1	37.5	38.4	42.4	37.3	41.4	43.4	43.0	39.7	35.1	37.7	31.1
Marihuana only	37.7	38.1	36.6	40.6	38.0	37.0	39.3	39.6	39.8	35.1	33.1	33.6	27.0
Few pills	32.7	35.8	39.4	37.4	32.7	38.3	33.8	40.3	38.2	35.9	28.0	31.5	29.4
More pills	31.3	29.8	29.9	30.0	34.4	34.6	30.3	36.9	32.6	35.7	32.8	26.6	17.5

...]. Response categories were "very poor," "poor," "fair," "good," "very good," and "no opinion." Readers interested in responses to this question for 1975 through 1978 should consult previous editions of SOURCEBOOK.

Source: Lloyd D. Johnston, Jerald G. Bachman, and Patrick M. O'Malley, *Monitoring the Future 1979*, p. 127; *1981*, p. 128; *1983*, p. 128; *1985*, p. 128 (Ann Arbor, MI: Institute for Social Research, University of Michigan); Jerald G. Bachman, Lloyd D. Johnston, and Patrick M. O'Malley, *Monitoring the Future 1980*, p. 128; *1982*, p. 128; *1984*, p. 128; *1986*, p. 131 (Ann Arbor, MI: Institute for Social Research, University of Michigan); and data provided by the Monitoring the Future Project, Survey Research Center, Lloyd D. Johnston and Jerald G. Bachman, Principal Investigators. Table adapted by SOURCEBOOK staff. Reprinted by permission.

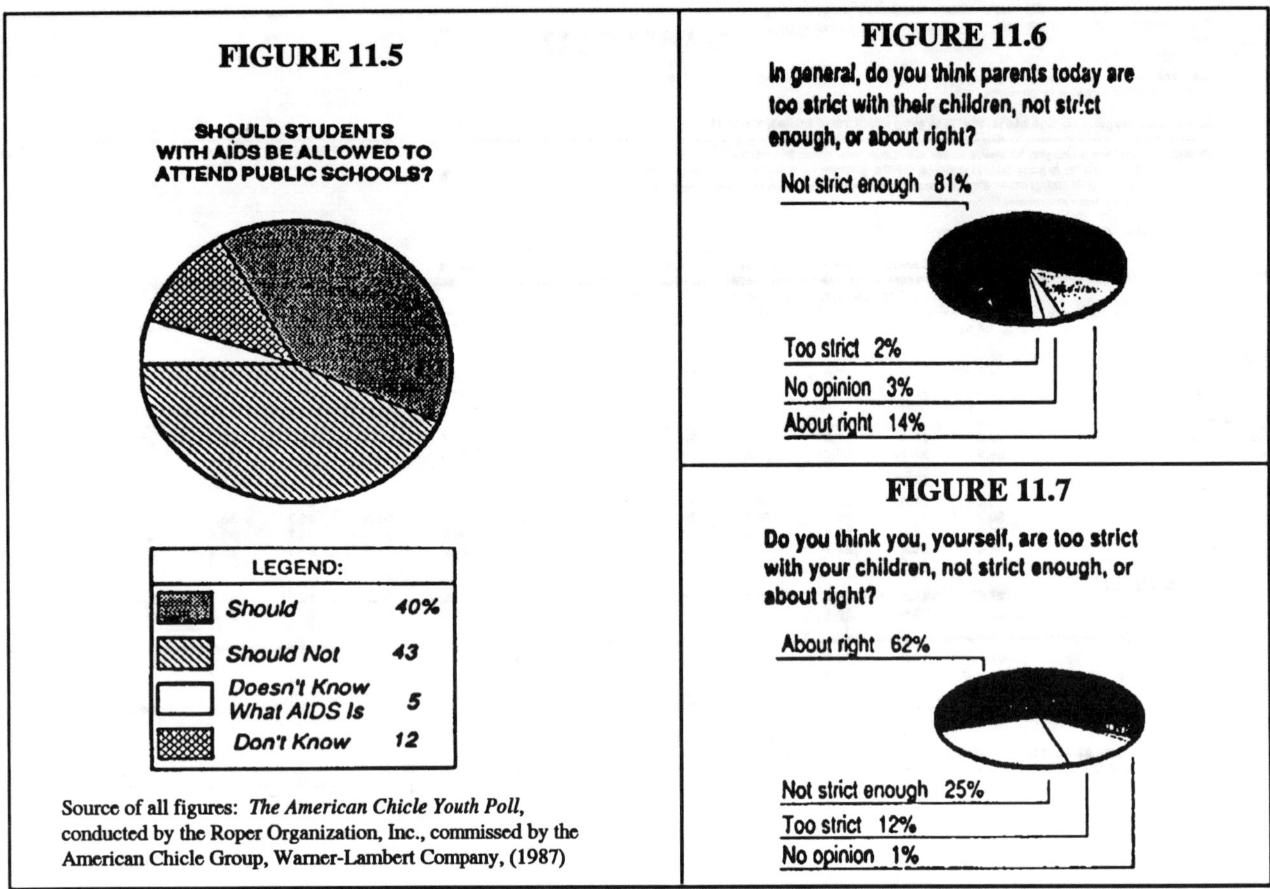

AIDS in School

Forty percent thought children with AIDS should be allowed to attend school, while 43 percent believed they should not be. Males (45 percent) were slightly more likely than females (42 percent) to oppose their attendance. Among the 8 to 12 year-old group, 42 percent favored attendance by children with AIDS, while 38 percent thought they should not be allowed to attend. Teenagers were more evenly divided—46 percent favored their attendance, while 46 percent opposed it. (See Figure 11.5.)

Blacks were more likely to oppose AIDS patients in schools (55 percent), while whites were evenly divided (42 percent felt they should be admitted, and 41 percent indicated they should not).

Those from the Midwest (55 percent) favored allowing student with AIDS to attend school, but they disagreed with those from other regions. A majority of those in the South (51 percent) opposed attendance by students with AIDS, while pluralities in the Northeast (46 percent) and West (44 percent) also felt they should not attend.

ADULT ATTITUDES ABOUT CHILDREN

Standards of Discipline

A 1990 Gallup Poll found that 81 percent of Americans believed today's parents are not strict enough in disciplining children, while only 2 percent thought parents were strict enough (Figure 11.6). However, those who are parents must believe that they are not the ones who lack the necessary discipline with their children, since 62 percent of those polled were satisfied with how strict they were in rearing their children. A quarter did not feel they were strict enough, and only 12 percent considered themselves too strict (Figure 11.7).

Although women are traditionally considered the ones primarily involved with the children, the

TABLE 11.14

Working Mothers

(April 19-22, 1990; Telephone; Survey GO 922008, Q.'s 39 & 40)

(Based on households with working mothers of children at home)

QUESTIONS: All things considered, do you think your child or children would be better off if (your wife/you) were home and didn't work, or is your child or children just as well off even though (your wife/you) work(s)?

If money were not an issue, would you want (your wife) to continue to work or would you want (your wife) to stay home?

	Best for child			Best for mother			
	If wife didn't work	As good when wife works	No opinion	Should work	Should stay home	No opinion	No. of interviews
National	32%	64%	4%	44%	50%	6%	293
Sex							
Male	33	65	2	38	51	11	140
Female	32	63	5	49	49	2	153
Age							
18-29 years	25	70	5	40	54	6	43
30-49 years	34	63	3	45	49	6	230
50 & older	43	54	3	47	49	4	20
Region							
East	36	60	4	46	45	9	75
Midwest	33	65	2	46	48	6	74
South	29	65	6	43	52	5	80
West	33	66	1	39	55	6	63
Race							
White	32	65	3	42	52	6	259
Black	44	48	8	55	39	6	21
Other	21	79	*	65	35	*	12
Education							
College grads.	30	66	4	61	29	10	90
College inc.	23	69	8	35	55	10	67
High school grads.	39	59	2	43	54	3	112
Not H.S. grads.	32	68	*	28	72	*	24
Politics							
Republicans	30	64	6	47	47	6	94
Democrats	36	63	1	39	59	2	79
Independents	34	62	4	48	42	10	109
Income							
$50,000 & over	34	63	3	52	41	7	101
$30,000-49,999	30	67	3	44	51	5	104
$20,000-29,999	34	64	2	33	56	11	44
Under $20,000	38	56	6	39	59	2	38

* Less than one percent

Source: *The Gallup Monthly,* July 1990

poll indicated that many parents claimed the husband was the stricter of the two parents. Fathers said they were stricter than their spouses with the children (48 percent to 34 percent), while wives indicated by a slight margin of 47 percent to 43 percent that their husbands were stricter.

Spanking

Despite recent questions concerning the propriety of physical punishment, a clear majority (65 percent) of all Americans and 62 percent of parents favored spanking. This is a significant decline from 1946, when 74 percent of parents approved. Blacks, Southerners, persons age 60 and older, those whose education stopped at high school, and those without high school education were more likely to approve of spanking children.

Despite the relatively high approval rating, only about half of parents indicated that they had ever spanked their children, and only 28 percent spanked their children once a month or more. Parents with children ages 6 and under were more likely to have spanked a child within the past month.

Working Mothers

When married couples with children and working mothers were asked if they felt children would be better off if the mother stayed at home, or if they were as well off in spite of the mother's working, both spouses, by a two-to-one margin, agreed that their children were as well off with a working mother. However, when families with non-working mothers were polled, 73 percent believed the children would be better off with the mother at home. Overall, half of working parents agreed that they would prefer the mother to stay at home "if money were not an issue." (See Table 11.14)

CHILDREN'S ORGANIZATIONS

Administration for Children, Youth, and
  Families
Health and Human Services Dept.
Children's Bureau
330 C St. SW
Washington, DC 20013
202 245-0618

American Assn. for Marriage and Family
  Therapy
1717 K. St. NW
Washington, DC 20006
202 429-1825

Children's Defense Fund
122 C St. NW
Washington, DC 20001
202 628-8787

Children's Foundation
815 15th St. NW
Washington, DC 20005
202 347-3300

Child Welfare League of America
440 1st St. NW
Washington, DC 20001
202 638-2952

Family Support Administration
Health and Human Services Dept.
370 L'Enfant Promenade SW
Washington, DC 20447
202 252-4518

General Services Administration
Child Care Development and Programs
18th and F Sts. NW
Washington, DC 20405
202 566-1516

National Abortion Rights Action League
1156 15th Street NW
Washington, DC 20005
202 973-3000

National Center for Missing and Exploited
  Children
2101 Wilson Blvd.
Arlington, VA 22201
Toll-free hotline, 800 843-5678

National Child Support Enforcement Assn.
444 N. Capitol St. NW
Washington, DC 20001
202 624-8180

National Collaboration for Youth
1319 F St. NW
Washington, DC 20004
202 347-2080

National Commission on Children
1111 18th Street NW
Washington, DC 20036
212 254-3800

National Council for Black Family and Child
  Development
c/o School of Education
Howard University
Washington, DC 20059
202 636-7343

National Network of Runaway and Youth
  Services
1400 Eye St. NW
Washington, DC 20005
202 682-4114

Phi Delta Kappa
P.O. Box 789
Bloomington, IN 47402
812 339-1156

Urban Institute
2100 M St. NW
Washington, DC 20037
202 833-7200

INDEX